100 Greatest Trips

TRAVEL +LEISURE

100
Greatest
Trips

from the world's
leading travel magazine

2007 EDITION

TRAVEL +LEISURE BOOKS

AMERICAN EXPRESS PUBLISHING CORPORATION
NEW YORK

TRAVEL + LEISURE   100 GREATEST TRIPS   2007 EDITION

Editors Nina Willdorf, Laura Begley, Kathleen Hackett
Creative Director Don Morris
Art Director Philip Welsh
Associate Art Director André Mora
Designer Chloe Weiss
Art Manager Meg Ambrose
Photo Editors James Owens, Paula Trotto
Copy Editors Bob Bowe, Ronni Radner, Shazdeh Omari
Researchers Stephen Clair, Alison Ogden, Mary Staub, Meeghan Truelove
Proofreader Susan Groarke
Design Intern Danielle Hulse

TRAVEL + LEISURE

Editor-in-Chief Nancy Novogrod
Creative Director Nora Sheehan
Executive Editor Jennifer Barr
Managing Editor Michael S. Cain
Research Editor Mario R. Mercado
Associate Managing Editor Jeff Bauman
Copy Chief Jane Halsey
Assistant Editor Elizabeth Woodson
Editorial Assistant Sarah Forrest
Photo Editor Katie Dunn
Production Manager Ayad Sinawi
Editorial Business Associate Andrew G. Forester

AMERICAN EXPRESS PUBLISHING CORPORATION

Senior Vice President, Chief Marketing Officer Mark V. Stanich
Vice President, Books and Products Marshall Corey
Senior Marketing Manager Bruce Spanier
Assistant Marketing Manager Sarah Ross
Corporate Production Manager Stuart Handelman
Senior Operations Manager Phil Black
Business Manager Tom Noonan

Cover design by Don Morris Design
Cover photograph by Patrick Cariou

Page 2: Looking out over the town of Korčula,
an island off the Dalmatian Coast.
Opposite: Amanyara, in the Turks and Caicos.
Page 10: Passage Hotel, in Odessa.

ISBN 1-932624-13-9
ISSN 1933-1231

Published by American Express Publishing Corporation
1120 Avenue of the Americas, New York, New York 10036

Distributed by DK Publishing, Inc.
375 Hudson Street, New York, New York 10014

Manufactured in the United States of America

united states +canada

bermuda+ the caribbean+ the bahamas

mexico+central +south america

western europe

eastern
europe

africa+
the middle east

Above, from left: Sitting dockside on the Dalmatian Coast; Ionic columns in the Oval Plaza at Jerash, Jordan; Silk Road Restaurant, Beijing; tapas at Movida, in Melbourne. Previous pages, from left: A bedroom in Richard Jenrette's Roper House, Charleston, South Carolina; The Reefs Hotel, Bermuda; Panama; Majorca.

asia

australia+ new zealand

introduction BY NANCY NOVOGROD

DESIGNED AS BOTH an inspiration and a companion for the 21st century global traveler, *100 Greatest Trips* delivers the same kind of insider information, authentic experiences, and authority that has ensured *Travel + Leisure* its spot as the world's leading travel magazine. With the help of our extensive international network of writers and correspondents, my editors and I cast a wide net to present options to stimulate and advise our millions of readers, and all the adventurers, luxury seekers, nature lovers, art and culture hounds, and countless other passionate types among them. As remote outposts such as Bhutan, Mongolia, and Patagonia are made more accessible through transportation and digital communication, the quest for reliable information becomes even greater—but in truth, the same can be applied to Paris, London, and New York, where unique travel experiences are increasingly in demand.

100 Greatest Trips is organized geographically by region, with destinations and trip specifics called out in each entry and on each page, to serve as a user-friendly guide for travelers with a particular goal in mind: relaxation or self-improvement or gaining more knowledge about the world. Whether it's visiting the best wine estates in Stellenbosch, South Africa; weekending in the hippest urban outposts in North America; prowling the most exciting new shopping district in Shanghai; or eating the finest *tagliatelle* in Italy, this is a book with roadmaps pointing the way to the delights of travel. The Guide, a directory of essential addresses and listings in each destination, is a final resource section intended to help make the journey a reality.

As every traveler knows, a pleasure trip begins long before the moment of embarkation, unfurling in stages even before all the details are set. The decision-making process, from choosing a destination to locking in an itinerary, can be a shopping spree of the most exhilarating sort—filled with opportunities to transport you to places you have never been or never knew you wanted to go. *100 Greatest Trips* will take you there. +

United States
+ Canada

Looking toward downtown Vancouver from Vanier Park, in Kitsilano.

Matt James and Alison Pray of Standard Baking Co. Opposite: Spinach soup with lobster and currant tomatoes at Francine Bistro in Camden.

down east feasts

A CULINARY DRIVE THROUGH **MAINE**

ARTISANAL BREADS and farmstead cheese, zesty herbs and buttery greens, gold-glowing squash blossoms and sweet corn, wild mushrooms and blueberries, peekytoe crab and plump mussels; up and down Maine's craggy coast, even the humblest kitchens have access to fresh (and some Yankees might say exotic) ingredients once strictly associated with the United States' other coast. What Maine also has, more than ever, is a roster of talented chefs who are changing the face of local cooking. Sure, plenty of restaurants still dish out retro Yankee resort food (maple-glazed salmon, potato-crusted lamb). Now, however, you can find a bold and inventive contemporary cuisine that never places novelty before flavor or gimmickry over essence.

Portland, the state capital, claims to have as many restaurants per capita as San Francisco. For a city of only 64,000, it certainly has more than its share of great ones. Since the 80's, when quirky bistros like Café Always and Alberta's were raising the bar on New England cooking, Portland has been a magnet for aspiring chefs. The city's most inspired cooking can be found at Hugo's, where chef Rob Evans's techniques owe much to the bold inventions of Thomas Keller. (Evans worked at Keller's French Laundry in Napa before moving to Portland and taking over Hugo's in 2000.) He has opened a casual lunch spot called Duckfat right down the street from Hugo's. This is where Evans assembles the city's best sandwiches, including a fall-apart duck-confit *panino* with black-currant chutney and the most decadent fries, twice-cooked in, yes, ▶

duck fat. For dessert, there's a root-beer float made with Italian soda water, sassafras, and two scoops of nearby Smiling Hill Farm's vanilla ice cream.

Over a 10-year run, Fore Street has become Maine's answer to Chez Panisse, with chef Sam Hayward as Alice Waters—champion of local producers, sultan of the greenmarket. Hayward's roasted raft-cultured mussels from nearby Bangs Island is among the most popular of his seafood dishes, but meat and fowl raised in the area figure prominently, too.

Generations have made the pilgrimage farther up the coast to Morse's, a little red farmhouse in North Waldoboro, an area settled by German immigrants adept at both farming and fermenting cabbage. Virgil Morse began selling his "live" sauerkraut in 1918 and continued until 2000, when David Swetnam and Jaquelyn Sawyer took over. Not much has changed. The genial staff scoops out pints into flimsy plastic tubs that inevitably leak. No matter; the final product is tangy and assertive, clean and still crunchy. Not too far away, in Rockland, Melissa Kelly—chef and co-owner of the nominally Italian Primo and a star since her days at the Old Chatham Sheepherding Company

Inn near the Berkshires—turns out dishes that manage to seem light and delicate while employing the robust and assertive flavors, none more so than those that come from her magnificent garden. In nearby Camden, one of the nation's most photogenic seaside resort towns, Brian Hill has transformed the once modest Francine Bistro (when he arrived as a cook in 2002, a single hot plate served as the stove). As the owner, Hill draws a devoted following for his farmer's market–driven menu, rooted less in the sea than in the funky flavors of the earth.

Maine is blessed with a thousand knockout locations for restaurants, but there's a sad lack of restaurateurs here who have the talent to create menus worthy of the view. The exception: the aptly named MC Perkins Cove, set in the uncannily ▶

At the Porthole in Portland. Clockwise from left: Steamed lobster at MC Perkins Cove, in Ogunquit; at the Portland Public Market; chef Sam Hayward serves the freshest local oysters. Opposite: A roadside sign.

T+L Tip

MAINE'S TOP TREATS

From the best crab roll to the freshest smoked salmon to the thickest bowl of clam chowder, here is a list of tasty treats from all across the state:

- Peekytoe crab roll from **Bayview Market & Takeout** (Penobscot)
- Heirloom tomato salad from **Chase's Daily** (Belfast)
- Pick-your-own blueberries from **Sewall's Orchards** (Lincolnville)
- Any dish with foraged mushrooms from **Francine Bistro** (Camden)
- House-grown greens and herbs at **Primo** (Rockland)
- Sauerkraut at **Morse's** (North Waldoboro)
- The lobster roll at **Red's Eats** (Wiscasset)
- **Silvery Moon's** Camembert (Westbrook)
- Gingerbread from **Standard Baking Co.** (Portland)
- Lamb-and-feta flat bread at **555** (Portland)
- Olive-oil *panna cotta* at **Hugo's** (Portland)
- House-made root beer and Belgian *frites* at **Duckfat** (Portland)
- Roasted mussels at **Fore Street** (Portland)
- Smoked salmon from **Browne Trading Co.** (Portland)
- Lobster with Cognac and coral-butter sauce at **White Barn Inn** (Kennebunkport)
- Fried clams and a lobster roll at the **Clam Shack** (Kennebunkport)
- Soup at **Joshua's** (Wells)
- **Barnacle Billy's** classic clam chowder (Ogunquit)
- Deconstructed clam chowder at **MC Perkins Cove** (Ogunquit)

pretty harbor Perkins Cove in the tidy resort of Ogunquit. Chefs Mark Gaier and Clark Frasier, who earned national renown at the rather formal Arrows Restaurant nearby, have gone for the more casual vibe of a seafood shack, and they excel at coastal classics: luscious crab cakes, steamed mussels, and fresh haddock.

Any native Mainer will tell you that lobster doesn't dress up well. There's little a chef can do to improve on the saltwater-steamed preparation—except for Jonathan Cartwright. The chef at Kennebunkport's White Barn Inn has developed a repertoire of inventive lobster riffs that are clever but never cloying. The restaurant is resolutely old-school; the tables are

Fishing boats in Portland.

draped in linen, a pianist in black tie plays during dinner, and the menu spells out the prices ("eighty-nine dollars" for a four-course prix fixe). What's more, jackets are required; if you forget yours, they'll issue you a spare— invariably a navy one with brass buttons. And service is impeccably formal. Cartwright's signature dish: a 1¾-pound lobster removed from its shell and steamed in a reduction of Cognac, cream, butter, and coral (lobster roe), then served atop a nest of white fettuccine with snow peas, carrots, and ginger. The dish is richer than the couple at the next table and ridiculously good. Indeed, you can order lobster for every course and never tire of the flavor.

Sometimes, however, you just need a great lobster roll. For that, head a quarter-mile down the road, and queue up at the Clam Shack, next to the Kennebunkport Bridge. The generously filled sandwich comes with your choice of mayo or drawn butter—or both, which just might prove the tipping point in a coastal Maine culinary tour. ✛

For The Guide, see page 266.

On the lift at Quechee Lakes.

mom 'n' pop mountain

A FAMILY-FRIENDLY SKI AREA IN **VERMONT**

SICK OF SLICK, SUPERSIZE, staggeringly expensive ski areas? Looking for a friendly little place where you can set the kids loose without having to hack into the college fund? Old-fashioned ski resorts are few and far between, which makes Vermont's Quechee (rhymes with *peachy*) Lakes Ski Area all the more appealing. Located just east of Woodstock—home to the elegant inn of the same name and one of Vermont's prettiest towns—in the cozy village of Quechee, the prices are prehistoric, the rope tow's still in operation, and kids have the real run of the place. After a hearty brunch of buttermilk pancakes at the Base Lodge, hit one of the 12 narrow, New England–style beginner and intermediate slopes that crisscross the 100 acres of trails; the terrain is well-suited to those new to skiing and snowboarding. End the day with a starlit ice skating session on the resort's pond or a horse-drawn sleigh ride that will make you feel as if you've schussed your way into a Christmas card.

Sure, you may not find the vertical feet and speedy lifts featured at the far bigger and much better known Killington ski area a half-hour away, but you also do away with end-of-the-world parking lots and mobbed cafeterias. What you get is exactly what drove this country's downhill pioneers to rig up those rope tows in the first place—the simple pleasure of playing in the snow. +

For The Guide, see page 266.

20

UNITED
STATES
+
CANADA

The
Berkshires

Litchfield
Hills, CT

A farmhand working at
Hancock Shaker Village.

restored to perfection

A SHAKER VILLAGE IN **THE BERKSHIRES**

TOURISTS HAVE BEEN COMING to Hancock Shaker Village, in the Massachusetts town of Hancock, since the early 19th century. Among others, Nathaniel Hawthorne, Herman Melville, and Charles Dickens were all interested in the Shaker religious sect. The quality of the group's products, combined with the unusual nature of their worship services—the Shakers of the 1700's shook, jerked, and spoke in tongues, while those who came later performed ritualistic dances and sang songs—have been the main draws. Today, in the Berkshires town, relics of a vastly different time and way of life have been beautifully restored.

The village is a kind of low-tech Disneyland, with hayrides instead of roller coasters and the Round Stone Barn in place of Cinderella's Castle. The houses look like toys laid out on a verdant blanket of lawns, pastures, and medicinal-herb gardens. Of the 56 buildings that once stood here, 20 remain, including the Brick Dwelling House and the Laundry & Machine Shop.

It is the purity of Shaker ingenuity that really makes an impression. In the clapboard Tan House, a windlass operated by a complicated system of pulleys raised heavy loads of animal hides from floor to floor. Water rerouted from a nearby stream powered a turbine that turned a large grinding stone used for sharpening farm implements and woodworking tools. Clearly, time that might otherwise have been spent in pursuit of the pleasures of the flesh was channeled into more practical pastimes. **+**

For The Guide, see page 266.

the bounty of connecticut

SHOPPING IN **LITCHFIELD HILLS**

JUST TWO HOURS outside Manhattan, the white-painted villages of fabled Litchfield Hills have become a destination for savvy shoppers in search of antiques, rare books, and one-of-a-kind products.

The owners of Kent's R. T. Facts, Natalie and Greg Randall, specialize in accent pieces with a power-house presence. The store's front yard is chockablock with iron gazebos, rose trellises, and millstones. The main building holds 1960's cork table lamps and a life-size Newfoundland dog cast in zinc. Just up North

Main Street (Route 7) is Richard Lindsey's airy bookshop, where you'll find a trove of tomes essential to any guest bedroom: memoirs by Alice B. Toklas and the Sitwells, charming cookery books from the 1930's, presidential biographies, travel guides, and gardening books.

At the sunny Dawn Hill Antiques shop in New Preston, the rooms ▶

Owners Natalie and Greg Randall, at R.T. Facts in Kent.

are stocked with refreshingly unrestored 18th- and 19th-century Swedish and French furniture, from the humble farmhouse variety to Neoclassical Gustavian examples fit for a manor house. Epicures can find their dream list of culinary delights—Staub cookware, de Buyer copper pans, all-steel pots by Iittala—at New Preston Kitchen Goods, a slickly renovated 50's pharmacy nearby.

Judy Hornby's namesake 5,000-square-foot emporium in Bantam is filled with art, furniture, and decorative accessories. The goods span centuries: sturdy, 200-year-old armoires from the south of France; a Thonet Art Nouveau love seat; and disco-era mirrors framed in bands of python skin.

Former Sotheby's furniture expert Pete Hathaway has put price tags on the contents of his 1830's house in Salisbury (it used to be an inn) and opened it to the public as Ragamont House Antiques, where the rooms are filled with aristocratic oddments, including dashing oil portraits. Michael Trapp, one of New England's premier antiques dealers and a noted landscape designer and interior decorator, fills his Greek Revival house-shop in West Cornwall with eye-catching funk, from architectural fragments to aristocratically worn tapestries to oddly glamorous seashells.

In Washington Depot, there are more stylish shops. Fresh-faced Finial Home & Garden sells stunning floral arrangements and country furniture and accessories that can be used indoors or out. Next door, Joanna Lombardi's collection of mint-condition vintage clothing at Grape in the Shade is a coup for the clotheshorse: Pucci dresses from the 60's, taffeta gowns fit for Hedy Lamarr, and slingbacks that are pure Gina Lollobrigida. At the Personal Best Monogram Shoppe, the shelves are stacked with just about anything that can be embroidered or engraved. Egyptian-cotton towels and citrus-colored linen guest towels trimmed with grosgrain line a wall; tropical-print totes share space with kicky woven sandals and assorted travel journals. If you appreciate art glass, you shouldn't pass by Adeptus Arts, where a giant stainless steel squid hangs from the beams, and the shelves flaunt Italian Renaissance-style goblets and neo-Murano tumblers. Artisan Timothy Hochstetter makes nearly everything himself on the premises in his pristine studio, using a mixture of color-saturated raw glass from the Czech Republic and New Zealand. ✦

For The Guide, see page 266.

Above, from top: Timothy Hochstetter in his Adeptus Arts glass-blowing studio; Kent's Richard J. Lindsey Bookseller. Below: Linens at Washington Depot's Personal Best. Opposite: Dawn Hill in New Preston.

T+L Tip

BEYOND LEAF WATCHING

As foliage season peaks, the annual Washington Connecticut Antiques Show brings increasingly sophisticated dealers to the area the last week in September. Grab lunch at The Pantry or The Mayflower Inn before or after shopping.

Sean Kelly's gallery in Chelsea.

the new guard

GALLERY HOPPING AROUND
NEW YORK CITY

DESPITE VALIANT challenges in recent years by Berlin, London, and Los Angeles, New York remains the world's arts capital. This is where artists come to compete with their peers, collectors write six-figure checks without breaking into a sweat, and galleries continue to open vast white-walled emporiums that compete with the city's many museums. New York's five boroughs are also big and clamorous enough to encompass grungy, shoestring-budget alternative galleries, where the guy selling you the pieces may be the one making them as well.

In Chelsea alone, there are more than 200 galleries packed into less than one square mile. In the mid-1990's, forward-thinking gallerists such as Matthew Marks and Paula Cooper took residence in this former warehouse district on Manhattan's far West Side, looking for space and light. Since then, each has expanded further, opening satellite venues, also in Chelsea. They have been joined by heavyweights such as the Gagosian Gallery, which shows Richard Serra and Damien Hirst, and Sean Kelly, whose space on West 29th Street marks the northern border of the neighborhood.

With the galleries came condominiums, restaurants, and more galleries, such as Clementine and John Connelly Presents, which ▶

emphasizes emerging artists in the renovated industrial space of the Chelsea Warehouse Terminal Building.

Other art-filled neighborhoods in Manhattan include 57th Street, where the contemporary pieces at Marian Goodman and the Project galleries provide sharply contrasting retail experiences from Niketown and Chanel down the block. On the Lower East Side, storefront spaces emphasizing conceptual work, such as Reena Spaulings and Participant Inc., sit next to bialy stores and 19th-century synagogues, the surviving remnants of the area's Jewish immigrant past.

Across the East River in Brooklyn, Williamsburg has long attracted artists in search of apartments and studios, fleeing the high cost of Manhattan but eager to remain just a subway stop away from the island. As rents rise, many artists are moving farther out in Brooklyn, but Williamsburg's do-it-yourself, small-business-friendly atmosphere perseveres. Pierogi Gallery, started by Joe Amrhein in 1994, is the anchor of the local scene, which swirls around low-slung industrial buildings and tenement-style apartments a few blocks from the river. Upstart galleries with a distinctly noncommercial ethos hold their own here, plying art for art's sake. Just blocks from the L train subway stop and Pierogi are Sarah Bowen Gallery and Jack the Pelican Presents. Outrageous Look, near the Williamsburg Bridge, is a 15-minute walk away via the boutique-lined ▶

A party at P.S.1 Contemporary Art Center, in Long Island City. Opposite, clockwise from top left: Patrick Mimran's billboard in Chelsea; Noguchi Museum, in Queens; Williamsburg's Jack the Pelican Presents; Pierogi Gallery, in Williamsburg.

28

UNITED
STATES
+
CANADA

New York
City

Long Island

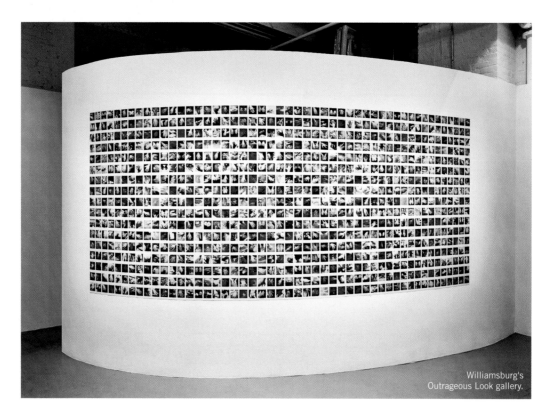

Williamsburg's
Outrageous Look gallery.

Bedford Avenue. Don't expect bucolic landscape painting in Williamsburg galleries, where the only rule for the material on view is that it strives to break rules.

The habit of nonconformity persists across Newtown Creek, the oily waterway dividing Brooklyn and Queens. In Long Island City, a Queens neighborhood just two miles north of Williamsburg, diners and taxi stands share the streets with the world-class galleries. Affiliated with MOMA, the P.S.1 Contemporary Art Center is the oldest contemporary space of its kind in the country. Founded in 1976, it fills a red-brick former schoolhouse, where bathroom stalls are occasionally flanked by noisy videos. Nearby are the nonprofit Dorsky Gallery and the Sculpture Center, the latter of which is housed in a trolley repair shop that was renovated by Maya Lin. Sculpture here can mean anything from an entire giant tree to a glass outhouse. A few miles north, along the East River, is the unruly outdoor lawn of Socrates Sculpture Park. A stunning contrast, catercorner from the park, is the hush of the Noguchi Museum, where white- and black-stone monoliths by Japanese-American sculptor Isamu Noguchi induce that rarest of New York moments—calm contemplation. +

For The Guide, see page 266.

T+L Tip

EATING AND EXPLORING

● **Chelsea** Foot-weary gallery-goers can break for beer or wine at **Tia Pol**, a Spanish tapas bar with creative bites such as fried chickpeas and creamed lima beans. For something more substantial, there's Mario Batali's **Del Posto**, where the opulent interior encourages the happy delusion that lard-butter is an essential food group. Or try the high-end, down-home American fare at **Cookshop**.

● **Williamsburg** Rub elbows with real artists at the charmingly cramped **Diner** or **Marlow & Sons**, which sit next door to each other under the Williamsburg Bridge, or settle in for a leisurely Italian meal at **Aurora.**

● **Long Island City** The bistros **Café Henri**, **Tournesol**, and **Lounge 47** can satisfy cravings for a solid, unfussy lunch, dinner, and late-night snack, respectively.

vintage north fork

NEW VINEYARDS ON **LONG ISLAND**

JUST ACROSS THE PECONIC BAY from the overhyped Hamptons lies Long Island's North Fork, a group of pastoral towns that claim bold new wineries and buzz-worthy restaurants. The former whaling town of Greenport serves as the base for an ideal itinerary. Some of the area's best restaurants cluster on Greenport's Front Street. The wine list at Fifth Season changes weekly to complement the revolving menu, and La Cuvée Wine Bar & Bistro serves 45 local wines by the glass. The top hotel, the Greenporter Hotel, is set to reopen its 5,000-square-foot spa in summer 2007, with what else but wine-inspired treatments? Among the two dozen wineries clustered on the North Fork are The Old Field Vineyard, and Shinn Estate Vineyards, owned by New York City restaurateurs David Page and Barbara Shinn. Drop in for a tour of their 22-acre grounds to taste fruit-forward Merlot and bone-dry rosé. Several wineries, including Castello di Borghese and Palmer Vineyards, host occasional bluegrass concerts in their vineyards in September—right when the grapes are dripping from the vines—and throughout the fall. +

For The Guide, see page 267.

The Old Field, a vineyard on the North Fork.

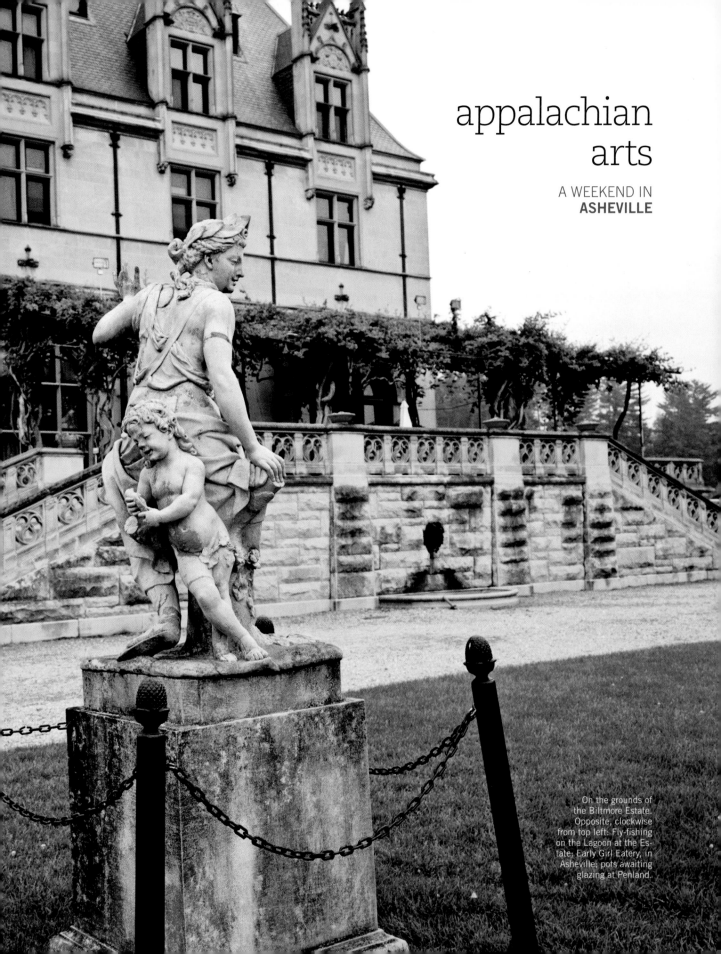

appalachian arts

A WEEKEND IN
ASHEVILLE

On the grounds of the Biltmore Estate. Opposite, clockwise from top left: Fly-fishing on the Lagoon at the Estate; Early Girl Eatery, in Asheville; pots awaiting glazing at Penland.

IF PEOPLE TEND TO THINK of the South as a red-state monolith, then western North Carolina exists to shatter that common misperception. The region is populated with hippie hideaways, monasteries, and idealistic communities of every stripe, and shaped as much by the grandees who summer here every year as by a rich agricultural tradition. Even the top accommodation, the Inn on Biltmore Estate, debunks certain notions of a Southern city. The 111-year-old Vanderbilt-owned château, with its limestone towers and 8,000 acres of rose-and-azalea-filled gardens, seems more fitting of the Loire Valley than of the Blue Ridge Mountains.

Asheville has always been in the vanguard in some way or another. Ever since the hidebound McCarthy era, when Cy Twombly, Robert Rauschenberg, and Josef Albers were splashing paint around at Black Mountain College just east of the city, practitioners and purchasers of art have flocked to the place. Every other downtown block has a gallery to peruse, and those with an interest in pottery, sculpture, and textiles will find plenty to keep them busy. Inside the recently restored Grove Arcade, a Deco mall erected in 1929, you'll find the South's best selection of art—from 19th-century portraits to hand-carved maple rolling pins. Longstreet Antiquarian Maps & Prints, on the town square, holds one of the Southeast's finest collections of antiquarian maps and prints, specializing in panoramic photo-graphs. Southeastern painters are the specialty of Blue Spiral 1, the top gallery in the area. For an optimum crafts perspective, New Morning Gallery has enough pottery, hand-blown stemware, and wrought iron on display to give you *objet* overload. More local work is shown at the intimate Ariel Craft Gallery, a cooperative, and an hour's drive away is Penland School of Crafts, which has a gallery on site. ✛

For The Guide, see page 267.

Charleston residents Harlan Greene and Charlie Smith in their garden, above. Below: Updated low-country cuisine at Slightly North of Broad. Opposite: An 1838 Greek Revival house on Charleston's East Battery.

southern exposure

THE NEW FACE OF **CHARLESTON**

IN THIS HISTORIC CITY, where the past lives on in the present and change has long been an unwelcome stranger, 15 years of growth are culminating in an infusion of youth, wealth, and the culture of the new. While the "too poor to paint, too proud to whitewash" aesthetic is still part of its psyche, a late-80's real-estate boom turned Charleston into one of the most concentrated centers of wealth in the United States. In the downtown area, south of Broad and the commercial district, once-decrepit properties are now as clinically spruced up as Colonial Williamsburg.

The city even has the mandatory late-breaking hip district. On King Street, a string of funky old establishments—What-Cha-Like-Gospel; Reuben's, "the store that puts the change on you," offering the Steve Harvey line of flash wear; and the well-stocked Honest John's Record Shop—serve as a backdrop for such newcomers as the supremely edgy B'zar, a "shop for your lifestyle," with such eclectic items as Kidrobot toys. ESD—Elizabeth Stuart Design—has something cool for everyone among the furniture, handmade jewelry, and regional cookbooks. Moo Roo's scarves, jewelry, and handbags are the creations of local designer Mary Norton. Couture milliner Leigh Magar makes hats that have a devoted cult following. ▶

Charleston

Miami

An antebellum portrait, above, at Charleston's Old Slave Mart Museum. Below: Outside the 1843 Battery Carriage House Inn, once a private house.

On the culinary front, such stalwarts as Charleston Grill, Circa 1886, and Peninsula Grill have yielded to an era of reimagined Southern fare, like the tweaked shrimp and grits at Slightly North of Broad and the ginger-tinged coleslaw at Hominy Grill.

Nevertheless, Charleston's neo-Dixie intelligentsia are forever teetering between the tug of the past and the rush of the present. Harlan Greene, author of *Why We Never Danced the Charleston*, is always ready to mock what he calls the "deliberately Southern" dialectic that has prevailed since *Midnight in the Garden of Good and Evil* was published, while Nichole Green, the curator of the Old Slave Mart Museum (closed for renovations until early 2007), presides over an institution that captures the visceral horror of slavery. At certain moments, it seems as if the entire landscape of Charleston has been dusted in the dogwood blossoms that fall like snow, then sealed in one of those plastic dime-store paperweights: turned one way, the city is a simple proposition of pure beauty; upended, the scenery removed and the past factored into the equation, it means something darker. +

For *The Guide*, see page 267.

T+L Tip

DON'T MISS

Take a tour of private houses with the **Preservation Society of Charleston.** The gardens of the historic plantation **Middleton Place** are a must-see, as is the **Edmondston-Alston House,** one of the first residences built on the High Battery.

south beach and beyond

MIAMI'S HOT SPOTS

THE ELUSIVE CHIMERA that is Miami is made up of very different neighborhoods, a blur of cultures that have frappéd themselves into a new order of contemporary civilization. It's a place that's as fluid—socially speaking—as the water that surrounds it. The city is constantly transforming, and the changes go far beyond the party that has become South Beach.

Downtown, cultural efforts—the Miami Heat's new waterfront stadium, Bayside Marketplace, a new children's museum—are all meant to revitalize nearby Overtown, a collection of shotgun shacks created in 1910 for Bahamian workers. To that end, the city's fathers have even given 24-hour licenses to nightclubs near the high-culture outposts, and now that section of town handily outlasts the ordinary 5 a.m. decadence of South Beach. To the north ▶

Taking the plunge in the Venetian Pool in Coral Gables.

is gritty Liberty City, yet even in this neighborhood
there are glimmers of hope: just past the Dark & Lovely
Beauty Supply Store is the Bahamian Pot restaurant,
where patrons hunker down over pork chop sandwiches.
The Little Haiti district is adjacent, a blur of color out
of a Salvador Dalí painting, with hyperreal faces painted
on the sides of shops. The Haitian meeting spot is on
54th Street: Chef Creole, a take-out joint with oxtail,
salted fish, and the best conch fritters around.

The hyperreal turns to surreal with a drive around
nearby Little Havana, which includes pockets of
Nicaraguans, Hondurans, Panamanians, and just about
every other nationality. The secret society of Santería
initiates, dressed entirely in white and wearing beaded
bracelets, flows through the streets. A stop at Botánica
Nena gives you a chance to stock up on dried fish
heads for deity offerings and horsehair tails for shrine
decorations, among other items. From there, drive past
the Las Palmas Motel, with its neon hearts sign; clat-

Girls' clothing at Genius Jones in Miami
Beach, above. Below left: Architect Elizabeth Plater-Zyberk at the Biltmore Hotel.

tering dominoes at Maximo Gomez
park; and El Rey de las Fritas and
King's Ice Cream, where coconut ice
cream is served in the shell.

In eminently civilized Coral Gables,
south of Miami Beach, Mitchell
Kaplan's Books & Books, housed in
a 1926 Mediterranean-style building, has become the epicenter of the
downtown Gables and local literary
scenes. Kaplan is also co-founder
of the annual Miami Book Fair
International. Originally a Miami
Beach boy, he now lives the family life
in the Gables and South Miami: "For
me, this area is really about places
like the Venetian Pool, which is a
great meeting ground for the community—the kind of thing we've tried
to do at the bookstore." To Elizabeth
Plater-Zyberk, dean of the School
of Architecture at the University of
Miami, the enormous Biltmore Hotel
is the fountainhead of a grand but
pedestrian-friendly city: "In the twen-
ties, George Merrick created beautiful
public spaces here, balancing the civic
and private realms."

Due east, on the other hand, the
island of Key Biscayne is home to an
assortment of white-collar criminals,
exiled dictators, and the rest of what
constitutes regional society; such ▶

Local resident Finlay Matheson at Jimbo's Shrimp on Key Biscayne. Clockwise from top left: The courtyard at the Setai hotel; Adrian Castro, a Cuban poet and Santería priest, in Little Havana; a detail at Vizcaya on Biscayne Bay.

The downtown Miami skyline. Below right: The pool at the Delano Hotel, in South Beach.

perfectly respectable people as Andy Garcia live here, too. A short boat ride away is the terminally real bar Jimbo's Shrimp, whose—over the years—cockeyed cartoon universe has grown to include a psychedelic, non-operational school bus, wild roosters, and bocce ball courts.

In the plush crosstown neighborhood of South Coconut Grove, the circa-1916 Kampong, once a private estate, is now open to the public as the National Tropical Botanical Garden. The architect Lester Pancoast had the good fortune to live in this Garden of Eden during the 1950's and 60's; his wife, Helene, is the granddaughter of botanist David Fairchild, who built the place.

The stretch of Biscayne Boulevard just a few blocks north of downtown Miami is still the haunt of last-chance motels like the Stardust, but the strip has been turning a new trick or two lately. The Upper East Side—a loose concept that includes the Wynwood Arts District and the Design District—has been dressed up with lounges, galleries, gay bookstores, and self-conscious restaurants. Native son Mickey Wolfson, who once lived like the Duke of Miami Beach in his ancestral town (and who turned his art collection into a museum, the Wolfsonian, in South Beach), sums up the state of his hometown perfectly: "No matter what you do, Miami keeps shifting faster and faster. There is no future here—we're all in the future now." +

For The Guide, see page 267.

T+L Tip
STAYING IN SOUTH BEACH

Make no mistake: South Beach still sizzles. Here is where you'll want to stay:

● **Delano** Nothing quite beats the Delano, either for aesthetics or celeb encounters. Where else can you find yourself chatting with Lou Reed by the pool?

● **Setai** An Art Deco landmark from the 1930's; now redesigned to add a bit of an Asian vibe with the best views of the beach.

● **The Raleigh** The hotel where modern South Beach began has been recalibrated for the chic by the Mercer's Andre Balazs.

● **Sagamore Hotel** A stunning all-suite property with an amazing contemporary art collection and cutting-edge furniture. Massimo Vitali's mural, *Pic Nic Allee*, in the lobby, sets just the right note of fun and sun.

● **Shore Club** Designed by British architect David Chipperfield, with Nobu, Ago, and Sky Bar on site—making the hotel a major social scene.

Riding the Wave Swinger at Chicago's Navy Pier, an amusement park in the city.

weekend in the windy city

A KID-FRIENDLY TOUR OF **CHICAGO**

THERE'S SOMETHING ABOUT THE SCALE of Chicago—the country's tallest building, one of the world's busiest airports, the country's largest Ferris wheel—that makes the city a blast for kids. Vast Lake Michigan, with its swimmable water and 29 miles of sandy shoreline, is the city's backyard, and its front yard is the 7,400 acres of public parkland. (No wonder Chicago's motto is *Urbs in Horto*, "City in a Garden.")

There's also something about the weather. People have a running debate about the origins of the city's popular "Windy City" moniker. Journalists say it refers to the long tradition of windbag politicians. On the other hand, as anyone who's walked along Lake Michigan in the winter will tell you, dressing in layers can be a good idea. When it comes to the elements, Chicago is like a big kid: it loves to defy conventional wisdom—such as weather reports. Snowflakes may swirl in May, while a late September heat wave could find residents at the beach.

To give little ones a sense of Chicago's size, first get your bearings. Begin at the neo-Gothic Water Tower on Michigan Avenue, your North Star. Find it, and then look across Michigan Avenue to the Waterworks Visitors Center. It has the city covered—the staff provides maps, tickets to plays and various spectacles, and friendly advice.

With kids in tow, it's always smart to think about your next meal. Walk north to the Original Pancake House, a squat, white-brick building that belongs on a country road, and order the Dutch Baby pancakes. A sure sign that they're delicious: the policemen in the next booth. Once sated, take in a pulse-raising view ▶

Above, from left: At the Notebaert Nature Museum; a view of downtown. Opposite: Sue, the Field Museum's 41-foot-long T. Rex.

of the broad boulevards and grand parks from the Sears Tower Skydeck, where you can see 50 miles on a clear day. The 70-second ride to the world's highest observatory is itself a thrill—especially when those photos of Earth seen from outer space appear on the elevator's 50-inch monitors. Kids will also enjoy the trivia signs (Q: *How many windows are there in this 110-story tower?* A: *16,100*), and before they can get through them all, it will be time to eat again. Walk a few blocks to Greektown for lunch (or dinner). Try Greek Islands, where the highlight is *saganaki*, a flaming cheese dish—and the show the waiters put on when they drop the match and shout "Opa!" For another view from above, board the elevator at the Hancock Observatory (it's the fastest one in North America, at 1,800 feet per minute), and it will get you to the 94th floor in 39 seconds. Don the SoundScope binoculars to zoom in on the city sights and clamor—cheering fans at Wrigley Field, roaring jets at O'Hare. Click a computer button for "Windows on Chicago," and you'll be inside the Bulls' locker room via virtual reality. Or check out the History Wall to trace Chicago's transformation from primeval swamp to modern metropolis.

If you have time to visit only one place, make it the Art Institute of Chicago, where two bronze lions guard the entrance to the museum, a cross between a Greek temple and an Italian palace. The Thorne Miniature Rooms, a showcase for tapestries, late-16th-century chairs, and portraits, is generally a hit with children. Check out Edward Hopper's famed *Nighthawks* and Seurat's giant, Pointillist painting *A Sunday on La Grande Jatte*. Stop at the gift store to purchase *Behind the Lions*, a family-oriented activity book and guide to more than 225,000 works of art spanning 5,000 years. To get the most of Chicago within a single mile, hit the Navy Pier, where jugglers, clowns, and a cappella singers reign. The 150-foot Ferris wheel offers extraordinary views, as does the big screen at the IMAX theater. The Chicago Children's Museum appeals to the under-eight set, especially those willing to build dams. A slightly older crowd can take in a musical at the Chicago Shakespeare Theater. Ready for a respite? Duck into the pier's own sanctuary, the Smith Museum of Stained Glass Windows. After dusk on Wednesday and Saturday, stay for the pier's fireworks display.

Three of the city's great attractions are within a 20-minute walk of one another in Lincoln Park: the Peggy Notebaert Nature Museum; the Lincoln Park Zoo (the oldest in the U.S.); and the Chicago History Museum, where there's everything imaginable for fans of the nation's 16th president. ▶

Beaching it on Lake Michigan, above. Below: The 150-foot-tall Ferris wheel on the Navy Pier.

Along Lake Shore Drive, you can stroll down the pedestrian boulevard to a trio of museums. The Adler Planetarium & Astronomy Museum takes you on a journey through the solar system via nifty armrest controls. At the Field Museum, you'll find the biggest, baddest, most complete tyrannosaurus rex ever displayed. You could easily spend an afternoon among the 8,000-plus creatures at the Shedd Aquarium, but if pressed for time, head straight to the Caribbean Reef exhibit.

A visit to Chicago almost demands you catch a baseball game at ivy-covered Wrigley Field, the second-oldest ballpark in the nation. If the team is on the road, you can take a tour of the field, clubhouse, press box, and dugouts. Singing the blues is another must in the Windy City, and at the Blue Chicago Store you and your brood can do just that. Down in the Basement is a special Saturday-night program for families—no smoking, no alcohol, and no cover for kids under 11. ✛

For *The Guide*, see page 268.

T+L Tip

BEST OF THE WURST

The Chicago hot dog traces its beginnings to two young Austro-Hungarian immigrants who steamed their wienerwursts, topped them with yellow mustard, bright green relish, raw onions, tomato wedges, a pickle spear, and a dash of celery salt, and then served them in warm poppy-seed buns. The classic is served at **Wiener's Circle**, a tiny joint in Lincoln Park with a dozen stools inside and four red picnic tables outside.

The scene at Breitbach's, Iowa's oldest restaurant.

heartland treasure hunt

ANTIQUING IN **IOWA**

IF THE PURPOSE OF TRAVEL is to refresh the soul, then nothing could be more appealing than a state whose landscapes, towns, and residents seem to embody a time before one's birth. Iowa is just such a place: as soothing a state to crisscross as anyone could hope for, and a great place to look for the sort of antiques that reflect a similar ideal—designed simply and built to last, if a bit worn.

The little town of Walnut, about a 1½-hour drive west from Des Moines—a profusion of modest stores crammed with Depression-era glassware, wrought-iron beds, and wooden farmhouse cupboards—has earned the nickname of Iowa's Antique City. The shops' inventories overflow onto the side-walks and consist of just the right ratio of trash (a service-station ▶

sign riddled with bullet holes) to treasure (a painted-wicker porch swing). Among the best of the crop is the Granary Antique Mall, housed in a building that's a wonder of rustic craftsmanship, a cavernous, arklike barn of beams and trusses. The sense of possibility is high here, but who knows what awaits farther down the highway?

The antiques trail will take you north and east past rolling hills and plowed fields, through Boone and to Marshalltown, where the Main Street Antique Mall is good for a few hours of poking around. Head north through Mason City—notable as the site of Buddy Holly's plane crash—and into one or two small antiques stores downtown. Move on to sleepy Spillville to visit a museum devoted to the handiwork of the Bily broth-ers, two woodcarving bachelor farmers who spent their winters building large musical clocks of almost superhuman complexity and detail.

Shopping is a great excuse for stopping in towns that you might not visit other-wise. Such is the case with Decorah and Postville, where the former affords a restful night in the Hotel Winneshiek and the latter a re-minder that it is home to one of America's largest ko-sher meat processors, run by the Jewish sect known as Lubavitchers, many of whom are from New York City. In nearby McGregor, there are more antiques stores than Iowa has rhubarb pies, all with enough interest-ing wares to turn anyone into a confirmed collector of bric-a-brac. In no time, you can return to Walnut, because no time is all it takes to cover Iowa once you say good-bye to the back roads, where you could lose yourself for months on a wayward shopping spree. **+**

For The Guide, see page 268.

At Taylor's Maid-Rite, famous for its simple burgers, in Marshalltown, above. Opposite, clockwise from top left: An Iowa wheat field; treasures spill out onto the front porch of the Granary Antique Mall in Walnut; a sign at the Granary; vintage crockery lines the shelves inside the Granary.

T+L Tip
STOPS FOR SNACKS

With its grain-elevator landscapes and towns that recall a bygone era, Iowa is a blast from the past. The promise of rhubarb pie, Maytag blue cheesecake, and a perfect cornbread pan are reasons enough for a lazy drive. Here are four worthy stops to make along your antiques-filled drive:

David's Milwaukee Diner The restaurant is in the Hotel Pattee, washed in railroad-themed murals, where the Maytag blue cheesecake is rich enough to purge the taste of gravy from your palate. The coffee is the best you'll have in Iowa.

Taylor's Maid-Rite Perhaps the oddest restaurant in the state, this Iowa-born chain of first-generation fast-food franchises has recently begun to expand in the Midwest and Western U.S. Its signature dish, the sublimely uncomplicated Maid-Rite burger, consists of barely seasoned loose ground beef spilled haphazardly onto a white bun, served with pickles, a little bit of onion, and a thin swipe of mustard but no ketchup.

Suzie Q Café This 1940's prefab diner serves up the most delicious curly fries. They're manufactured on the spot using a hand-cranked machine that's clamped to the counter.

Breitbach's It's the state's oldest restaurant, or so people like to say, and the only one to have served "both Jesse James and Brooke Shields." Attached to the walls and dangling from the ceiling are scores of old iron farm tools, wooden chairs, oil lanterns, and other odds and ends for sale. Order some fries and a malt—and you'll also be able to go shopping without leaving the comfort of your table.

midwestern modern

DESIGNS ON ART IN **MINNEAPOLIS**

TARGET GALLERY

QUARTET:
JOHNS. KELLY. MITCHELL. MOTHERWELL

THERE'S NO SHORTAGE of smaller American cities attracting attention these days for cutting-edge art and architecture. But Minneapolis, it's fair to say, is leading the pack.

Celebrity architects have completed a slate of expansions of important local institutions. Most notably, Herzog & de Meuron designed a 130,000-square-foot addition to the Walker Art Center; Cesar Pelli revamped the downtown library; and the Guthrie Theater, which opened in June 2006, is the work of architect Jean Nouvel, a Parisian master of designing buildings saturated in moody, powerful primary hues. His first completed project in the United States—and Minneapolis's latest architectural wonder—is no exception. Nouvel's building for the pioneering Guthrie Theater is sheathed in midnight-blue stainless steel and infused with remarkable light-sensitive colors.

Architecture aficionados have an appropriately modern place to stay: the Graves 601, with 21 hushed

Above, from top: Vanessa Paulson at Chino Latino restaurant; a suite at the Graves 601 Hotel. Opposite: Inside the Walker Art Center.

stories in the middle of downtown, and where the sleek accommodations include a 42-inch plasma TV and a bar of Hermès soap in the bathroom. In the Riverfront District, the ceilings are high, and the use of brick is not ungenerous. To walk the becalmed streets of this district in the slanting sunlight is to enter an Edward Hopper painting. The signage of many of the buildings' former occupants has been left intact; most of them contain the word *flour*. The former factories are being converted into loft apartments, some with views of the beguiling new Mill City Museum, where the towering ruins of its stone walls, left standing after a fire in 1991, contrast beautifully with the aquamarine-glass sheath of the museum. The Lyn-Lake neighborhood—it looks like a college town where no one ever graduates—can't boast a famous architect–designed structure, but it is home to Bill's Imported Foods, a specialty store where you can choose from among 82 kinds of olive oil. A walk around Lake Calhoun leads to the Bakken, a museum devoted to "electricity in life." Downtown, a life-size sculpture of Mary Richards stands amid the skyscrapers. +

For The Guide, see page 268.

Door County,
WI

Marfa, TX

Taking the Green
Bay plunge,
at Peninsula
State Park.

lazy summer days

COOLING OFF IN WISCONSIN'S **DOOR COUNTY**

SCANDINAVIAN SETTLERS were attracted to the wild-flower meadows and endless summer days of Fish Creek, a charming bayside village in Wisconsin's Door County, the pinkie-shaped peninsula that separates Green Bay from the rest of Lake Michigan. Today's drop-ins also get tidy fruit orchards where mouth-puckering cherries grow by the bucketful, markets stocked with artisanal cheddars, and a marina with slips reserved for yachts. Main Street's white clapboard storefronts are enthusiastically sprinkled with Swedish kitsch (count the blue-and-yellow flags and heart-shaped doodads). What's more, the lake is so clean you can skip bath time, and you can also hike, bike, boat, and fish along Door's 250 miles of shore. The 75-mile-long peninsula has five state parks and twice as many lighthouses, not to mention pristine scenery. For landlubbers, the outdoor amphitheater of Fish Creek's Peninsula State Park, the American Folklore

Theatre, offers a crash course in Midwestern humor. In the evenings, take in a round of miniature golf at the delightfully creaky Red Putter in nearby Ephraim, or catch the double feature—and enjoy a foot-long hot dog—at the 1950's Skyway Drive-in Theater, where movies have lit up the screen continuously for more than a half-century. And to remember the whole idyll by? Anything made with tart Montmorency cherries, harvested from mid-July to mid-August at Lautenbach's Orchard Country, will allow you to reminisce about Fish Creek and the tranquility of Door County. +

For The Guide, see page 268.

desert art oasis

GROWING MINIMALISM IN **MARFA**

IT'S IN THE MIDDLE OF NOWHERE: to be exact, on a highland plain in an upper corner of the vast Chihuahuan Desert. To get to Marfa, you have to fly to either El Paso or Midland, Texas, rent a car, and drive for three hours. When Minimalist artist Donald Judd began coming to this desert town in 1973, its destiny changed. With the support of the Dia Foundation, Judd bought up property in and around Marfa, most notably a former army base, which he named the Art Museum of the Pecos and later renamed the Chinati Foundation. Judd displayed pieces of his own work here, along with those of fellow sculptor John Chamberlain and fluorescent-light works by Dan Flavin. Fast-forward more than 30 years, and Marfa has become filled with galleries and a pilgrimage site on the international art landscape—that, and a place full of traditions. Among them is the annual Open House, inaugurated by Judd in 1987 and held every fall, when the town hosts a two-day party that includes art exhibitions, readings, lectures, a street dance, and rock concerts. Though Open House almost doubles the town's population, all events and meals are free. +

For The Guide, see page 268.

Fifteen untitled concrete works,1980-84, by Donald Judd, at the Chinati Foundation in Marfa, Texas.

guadalupe getaway

RIVER SWIMMING IN THE **TEXAS HILL COUNTRY**

NATURE OVERWHELMS most of the Texas Hill Country, where it is possible to experience in solitude the beauty of its hills and canyons, and a swim in one of its clear, cool rivers. The region lies just west of San Antonio and Austin and is a roughly 31,000-square-mile limestone blob, created by the Balcones Escarpment. Beneath its surface is an astonishing system of aquifers, streams, rivers, and caves.

In a landscape that is rocky, rough, and dry, springs burst forth all over the place. The loveliest Hill Country rivers—the Frio, the Medina, the Guadalupe, the Blanco, and the Nueces—are fed by water that is filtered and comes out clear and cool, sometimes cold. On the Frio, you can wade in 68-degree spring-fed water beneath balmy 90-degree air. If you want to go for a more serious swim, head for the South Fork of the Guadalupe, where the river runs deep and stays deep for at least a mile upstream. +

For The Guide, see page 268.

Afloat on the north fork of the Guadalupe River.

51
**UNITED
STATES
+
CANADA**

Texas
Hill Country

Yellowstone

Old Faithful puts on a show in Yellowstone, left.
Above: The fire pit in front of the Big EZ Lodge.

uncrowded montana

A FAMILY TRIP TO MELLOW **YELLOWSTONE**

WITH ITS HOT SPRINGS, mud pots, geysers, and abundant wildlife, Yellowstone is a perfect destination for kids. During the summer, however, RV's are more numerous than bison. But there's a more novel way to appreciate the wilderness without encountering "bear jams"—multiple-car pileups occasioned by the sighting of a far-off sow. Donna and Steve Hicks are among the proprietors of a handful of lodges around the park that provide friendly and comfortable accommodations—and a welcome retreat from the hordes of tourists. The couple shares several thousand acres surrounding the Big EZ Lodge, their mountaintop compound, with guests, most of whom are regulars. Donna, a native Texan and full-time interior decorator, adds to her considerable collection of oil paintings each year. All 13 cavernous guest rooms and adjacent corners of the Big EZ feature her Texas touch. The bronze bears cavorting near the entrance are bigger than any grizzly in Montana. The lone star inlaid in the floor bears a striking resemblance to the one in the capitol rotunda in Austin, Donna's hometown.

After a day spent fishing deep pools along the roaring Gallatin or hiking into Beehive Basin to catch glimpses of moose and bighorn sheep, you can book an hour with the resident massage therapist before tackling one of chef Thomas Blakely's creations. Or you can sit on your terrace and study the moon-dappled crest of the Spanish peaks, a skyline that appears to be yours alone. ✛

For The Guide, see page 268.

utah's big buzz

SALT LAKE CITY, BORN AGAIN

SURE, IT'S A GATEWAY to some of the best skiing
in the country, but Salt Lake City has also become a
destination in its own right, especially the downtown
district. Its current face can be seen in a raft of new
museums, including the Utah Museum of Fine Arts
and the Clark Planetarium. And then there's the new
Moshe Safdie–designed public library, which just
might be the country's most beautiful—a great crescent of light and glass with hanging sculptures and
spectacular rooftop views.

Many of the city's restaurants have breathed life into
industrial buildings; the most award-winning among
them is the sophisticated Metropolitan, in a former
automobile body shop downtown. Nearby, Cup of Joe is
on the ground floor of the old Firestone Tire & Rubber
building, a two-story former warehouse and service
station built in 1925. Farther west on Broadway is the
old depot of the Denver & Rio Grande Railway, Western
Railway, which houses the Utah State Historical
Society. A mile or so north along the tracks is the
former Union Pacific Depot, now a Virgin Megastore. In
between is the Gateway, an elaborate development of
condominiums, restaurants, movie theaters, and shops
strung along pedestrian promenades and alleyways.

In the Avenues district, just northeast of downtown, street life gets a bit cozier; the area known
as the Nines, at 900 East and 900 South, is dotted
with boutiques, an indie coffee shop, a record store,
and a great lunch spot called Guru; the Fifteens,
at 1500 East and 1500 South, is home to the King's
English Bookshop and a trio of top-notch restaurants
(The Paris, Mazza, and Fresco); Sugarhouse, at 1100
East and 2100 South, is a nexus of vintage-clothing
stores, a yoga studio, and a few pubs.

With big-time ski resorts like Alta and Park City only
25 minutes from Salt Lake City, some of the best skiing
in North America is a quick drive away. But it's clearer
than ever that now, deciding what to do in Salt Lake
City is a difficult choice. ✚

For The Guide, see page 269.

The Salt Lake City Public Library,
designed by Moshe Safdie.
Opposite, from top: Squatter's
Pub Brewery, a popular bar;
the Wasatch Mountains; a local
resident at the library.

Chef Dennis Leary at Canteen. Below: The *haute* luncheonette's blancmange. Opposite: San Francisco's Ferry Building's marketplace.

T+L Tip

Don't leave San Francisco without having coffee at **Blue Bottle Coffee Co.,** an artisanal microroaster in the hip Hayes Valley neighborhood. The 10-by-10-foot stand, made from salvaged materials, has a devoted following.

california's culinary capital

A FOOD TOUR OF
SAN FRANCISCO

ASK ANY SAN FRANCISCAN what he loves about his hometown, and he is likely to tick off a handful of food-related passions—eating outside at the Foreign Cinema, late nights at Emmy's Spaghetti Shack, picking up a Mexican hot chocolate from Mijita in the Ferry Building. The building's Farmer Terminal is a landmark so beloved that the legendary *Chronicle* columnist Herb Caen once observed, "The waterfront without the Ferry Tower would be like a birthday cake without a candle." The candle is now beautifully ablaze. A splendidly renovated Ferry Building reopened in 2003, showcasing—what else?— gourmet food. Chef Charles Phan's Slanted Door, relocated from the dog-eared Mission District, contin- ues to turn out his sharp, appetizing Vietnamese cuisine. A large farm table becomes a stage for some of the city's most magical meals at Boulette's Larder.

Elsewhere in town, a fresh slate of first-rate restaurants has sealed San Francisco's reputation as a culinary destination. Wunderkind chef Dennis Leary opened gourmet diner Canteen in the former coffee shop at the Commodore, which was recently resuscitated as a bud- get boutique hotel. Leary was the

prize-winning chef at the famed Rubicon for six years, and he is now the poster boy for San Francisco's food revival. At Quince, Chez Panisse alum Mike Tusk's artistry with house-made pastas makes the challenge of getting a reservation well worth it. The clean white room is a seamless mix of the elegant and the egalitarian that is emblematic of San Francisco itself. And since the menu is so obsessed with freshness, it offers the provenance of every chop and bean. Chefs at A16 pull perfect wood-fired pies, as well as creating simple yet sophisticated Neapolitan dishes. The smart, elegant Michael Mina serves meals in trios, like foie gras, scallops, and tomatoes. And the worldly yet re-laxed Myth is right at home making citrus-glazed salmon and burgers.

San Francisco's reverence for good food can be traced to the original Spanish, Italian, and Chinese settlers, not to mention the city's proximity to some of the world's best agricultural regions. "Restaurants are an expression of good times," explains Leary, of Canteen. One need not look too hard to see just how good the times are in San Francisco today. ✦

For The Guide, see page 269.

Bend, OR

Seattle

Taking a coffee break at Gugina Cafe, in Seattle. Left: At the Patient Angler, in Bend, Oregon.

flying high

OUTDOORS IN **BEND**

WITH SUPERB FLY-FISHING, rafting, skiing, and a slew of rated golf courses, high-desert Bend, three hours from Portland, has graduated from dusty crossroads to bona fide destination for friends of the outdoors. The stately lodge at Sunriver Resort has it all: three sets of links, tennis courts, swimming pools, and a spa. The smaller, quirkier McMenamins Old St. Francis Hotel, right in the town center, is a converted 1936 elementary school with a microbrewery, restaurant, and movie theater.

Landlubbers can tee off among the Ponderosa pines at Widgi Creek, go underground to Boyd Cave, and hit the slopes of Mount Bachelor. Guided fly-fishing outings and white-water rafting on the Deschutes River await the water-bound. Fly-fisherman Peter Bowers, owner of the Patient Angler, swears that what he'll teach you in a 90-minute crash course would take three years to learn on your own; when you're done with your lesson, Bowers sets you up with a rod, reel, and map of the best local holes. ✛

For The Guide, see page 269.

global feast

SEATTLE'S WORLD OF FOOD

BALLARD, A NEIGHBORHOOD once populated by Scandinavian fishermen, has become the city's culinary melting pot, with a score of new restaurants and bars. Fifteen minutes northwest of downtown, most of the restaurants cluster around Northwest Market Street and the small lanes that shoot off this main thoroughfare. Taste the best of Puerto Rico—smashed plantains, deep-fried catfish, coconut flan—at La Isla Seattle. Savor contemporary Tuscan cuisine (truffle bruschetta, homemade pasta in duck ragoût) at Volterra. Striking black-and-white photographs of Mexico at La Carta de Oaxaca set the mood for lamb birria, while exotic takes a new twist at Fu Kun Wu, modeled after a Chinese apothecary. Located at the back of the restaurant Thaiku, Fu Kun Wu is known for its late-night potions like the Yohito—a mojito mixed with the bitter African herb (and reputed aphrodisiac) yohimbe. The Hi-Life churns out regional dishes with a twist: wood oven–roasted oysters, applewood-grilled salmon, and wild-mushroom pizza. For a glass of wine before dinner, stop by Portalis Wine Shop & Wine Bar, which has local artwork lining the brick walls; you can choose from more than 400 wines from around the world. And for an after-dinner drink, tuck into an inventive cocktail at Sambar, an intimate lounge that was once the studio of chef-owner Bruce Naftaly and his wife, Sara. Who needs dessert when you can have the Barbapapa (Hangar One lime vodka, Cointreau, and lime juice, with rhubarb sorbet)? ✛

For The Guide, see page 269.

riding the wave

SURF AND SAND ON **OAHU**'S NORTH SHORE

SINCE THE HALCYON ERA of the 50's, when a handful of madcap California surfers drove from Waikiki to Hawaii's North Shore to stoke themselves silly on their quaint long boards, the world's coolest village has been in the business of myth, churning out visions of paradise. This 26-mile stretch of beach surrounded by hills—called the country on Oahu—has very real surf breaks. In season, from November through April, monstrous waves turn the North Shore into the Everest of surfing, which pretty much means it also becomes a stomping ground for international pop culture.

Ultimately, the North Shore gestalt is about the great surf breaks of Sunset Beach, about eight miles ▶

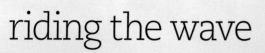

Waiting for the waves at Sunset Beach on the North Shore.

Oahu

Alaska

north of Haleiwa, and the 15,000 or so year-round residents who cling to Kamehameha Highway, forming a community without a real name, town center, or anything to do after 9 p.m. Sunset Beach is a miraculous place, the most organic, pedestrian-friendly, and resolutely democratic town imaginable. But the area proves that every socioeconomic class can play nicely with others; the tone is still very 60's and uncommercialized, with one hotel, one supermarket, and one Starbucks—yet it's the epicenter of surfing on the planet. True watermen here are honored with the reverence accorded to samurai warriors.

The sport of Hawaiian kings, however, has evolved into a multibillion-dollar global phenomenon. The teen icons of the surf world, who can make a quarter-million dollars a year, are compelled by contract to be walking billboards for surf leisure clothes, though

they barely process the 60's notion of selling out. The North Shore may have the capital of Malibu, but somehow it has kept the raw funk of early Venice Beach. In the modern age, money never needs to go to the office anymore, and software designers and financial types might live next door to a garage apartment occupied by some boho character who gets along selling macramé hangings at the flea market.

Heroes and mortals alike confront the limits of paradise day after day on the North Shore. There's an uneasiness that comes with finally reaching the island that dreams are made of and discovering that Valhalla can be as confining as it is freeing. In the end, though, the bohemian heart of the North Shore beats strong—even the smallest aesthetic misstep in the public realm is fought tooth and nail—and it is all the better for it. ✚

For The Guide, see page 269.

North Shore resident and Vans Triple Crown world champion surfer Kelly Slater at Oahu's Quiksilver House during the Rip Curl Pro Pipeline Masters. Above right: Pointing the way to the heart of the North Shore.

T+L Tip

When the surf isn't up, spend your down time enjoying the peacocks, giant lilies from the Amazon, and endangered *Kokia cookei* flowers at the **Waimea Valley Audubon Center** in Haleiwa, run by the National Audubon Society.

tour north

A DRIVE BETWEEN ANCHORAGE AND HOMER, **ALASKA**

IN THE WINTER, Alaska returns to its untamed, natural state. Icy temperatures and mountains of snow make tourists scarce—and it's an unexpectedly appealing time to motor through scenes of unmatched, slightly menacing beauty. Here there are ranks of mountains so thoroughly buried in snow it's as if the whole landscape has been carved from a single piece of ice. See the wind-lashed blue-black ocean and rivers half frozen, steaming in the subarctic chill. The drive from Anchorage to Girdwood, Alaska's adventure-sports capital—and home to the Alyeska Resort, the best hotel in the state—might find you in the teeth of a blizzard. All the better to ski the 1,000 acres of terrain—and to enjoy the view of the Turnagain Arm, a narrow ocean inlet heaped with chunks of ice. A 90-mile drive south over the mountains that form the spine ▶

Tern Lake Junction, on the way to Homer.

Clockwise from top left: A cautionary billboard outside Homer; the lobby at the Alyeska Resort, in Girdwood; baked lobster at the Seven Glaciers, a restaurant accessible by cable-car only, at the summit of Alyeska; Café Cups, in Homer.

of the Kenai Peninsula, a 200-mile-long fin of roadless wilderness, takes you to Seward, where Edwardian buildings—including the Van Gilder Hotel and the Liberty Theater—give the town a faded, old-fashioned gentility. Near the southern end of the Kenai Peninsula, and a 170-mile drive from Seward, lies Homer, which is famous for two things: halibut and hippies. Some call Homer, with its bustling coffeehouse and art-gallery scene, the spiritual and geographical counterweight to Key West. (In summer, tourists pour in by the thousands to fish for Homer's legendary halibut, which can grow to more than 400 pounds.) The Homer Spit, a natural causeway that thrusts 4½ miles out into Kachemak Bay, is lined with docks, marinas, and fish-processing companies—most of which close in the winter, save for a half-dozen charter captains who work year-round.

The return trip to Anchorage—260 miles of travel through America's biggest, wildest state—is pure, cold Alaska, full throttle. ✚

For The Guide, see page 269.

For The Guide, see page 269.

T+L Tip

LOOK, UP IN THE SKY

Don't miss the aurora borealis. The **Alyeska Resort** will alert you when the sky is expected to give its show, usually on clear moonless nights in the winter.

A cluster of wooden treehouses on Blackcomb Mountain, one of Whistler's two main peaks.

canada's stylish slopes

WHISTLER MOUNTAIN AT ITS PEAK

A FORMERLY LOW-KEY, old-fashioned resort, Whistler has transformed itself into North America's "it" ski destination since it won a bid to host the 2010 Olympics a few years back. With an average of 14 feet of snowfall per season, there's always plenty of powder, and the trails don't get skied out, the way they can in Colorado and Utah. And with the most extensive skiable terrain on the continent and more than 32 lifts between the interconnected Whistler and Blackcomb mountains, it's easy to skip lunch in favor of a few extra runs.

That said, Whistler gets serious when dinnertime arrives. The menus here are an extension of Vancouver's celebrated Pacific Rim food culture. Oysters plucked from the Pacific Northwest's icy waters (the Chef's Creeks from Vancouver Island are outstanding),

as well as wild B.C. spot prawns and flying-fish caviar, are just a few of the specialties on offer at area restaurants. Village chefs bring in dairy products and crisp produce from neighboring Pemberton Valley and wines from the Okanagan Valley, British Columbia's emerging Napa. Locals seem to take wine almost as seriously as they do snow conditions. But at the end of the day, with its newly opened Flue bowl and 700 acres of back-country–style terrain, Whistler is—and always will be—about the mountain. ✚

For The Guide, see page 269.

The welcoming committee at Richard Kidd, a fashion atelier in Vancouver's Gastown neighborhood. Opposite, from top: The Four Seasons terrace pool; outside Pleasant Girl on South Main Street.

urban
utopia

VANCOUVER IS IN VOGUE

VIEWED FROM A DISTANCE, the Modernist buildings of Vancouver's West End and downtown rise and swell like formations of aquamarine crystals, spreading out to the peninsula's visible borders, defined by green parks, beige beaches, blue waters, and white mountains. Within lies a colorful array of districts with personalities ranging from posh to punk. Here, Pacific Rim cool merges with British Commonwealth comforts.

Central Vancouver is laid out on an easily navigable grid, with the intersection of Robson and Burrard as its center and the commercial nexus for luxury-goods retailers and chain stores. Lined with boutiques, cafés, and crêperies, Robson stretches for blocks up a gentle hill topped with high-rise apartments and small hotels. Granville, three blocks east of Burrard, is the site of gilded old theaters and a handful of galleries and curiosity shops inconspicuously housed in low-lying buildings. Below Broadway, clothing stores and small jewel-box boutiques like Peridot—which sells luxurious loungewear and furnishings—dot South Granville. Vikram Vij, one of the city's most revered chefs, opened Vij's more than a decade ago. Now an institution, it is beloved not just for its unconventional Indian dishes, but also for its groovy raga-disco soundtrack.

A short cab ride from downtown and the harbor is the Opus Hotel, the central meeting point in Yaletown, ▶

Preparing *izakaya* at Shiru-Bay Chopstick Café,
in the Yaletown neighborhood, left. Above: An
old-fashioned sign, in Vancouver.

a hipster enclave where drinking and people-watching
are part of the show. Nearby Shiru-Bay Chopstick Café
serves *izakaya*, a mix of sushi, kabocha squash, noodle
dishes, and fish charred tableside.

Kitsilano, southwest of downtown, is Vancouver's
answer to the East Village. Some of the city's most
eccentric shops line South Main Street, including
Motherland, where the house brand of sophisticated
punk graphics is for sale. At Pleasant Girl, cutting-edge

frilly clothing and accessories by
Canadian designers fill the racks,
while Eugene Choo is devoted to
young Vancouver labels Dust, Picnic,
and Sunja Link.

The brick buildings, Irish pubs,
music clubs, and port-of-call souvenir shops of Gastown, one of the
oldest neighborhoods of the city,
are located just across the Cambie
Bridge and adjacent to the harbor.
Water Street, its commercial center,
has been reclaimed by upscale
contemporary-furniture stores and
fashion ateliers carrying top-drawer
designer labels such as Balenciaga
and Stella McCartney.

Almost anywhere you go these
days in Vancouver, one unifying
quality merges: it is an uncommonly
versatile place, just large enough
to satisfy the curiosity of even the
most seasoned travelers. **+**

For The Guide, see page 269.

T+L Tip

EXPLORING THREE WAYS

Strolling around Vancouver on foot is just one way to
experience it; seeing the Pacific Coast city from the air,
water, and on two wheels offers a different view.

By Air Grouse Mountain Skyride is the largest aerial tram
in North America.

By Sea Take Aquabus, a short-haul ferry service on
False Creek that stops at the Granville Island Market and
Yaletown, among other popular spots.

By Land Rent a bicycle on Denman Street.

For The Guide, see page 269.

high design up north

MONTREAL REINVENTS ITSELF

YES, THERE ARE PLENTY of quaint clichés like horse-drawn carriages plying Old Montreal's cobblestoned streets, but on the district's quietly cool southern fringe, a slew of hotels, cafés, and boutiques—most a mix of soaring ceilings and polished concrete—have opened. Indeed, Montreal is fast reinventing itself as a design city, and it's places like the Hôtel St.-Paul, with a lobby that centers around an alabaster fireplace, that are leading the way. Guests can choose from four room types including Earth, which adopts a darker palette of browns and tans; and Sky, where natural light enhances the blue-and-white interiors. A stay at Montreal's Hotel Gault exemplifies, too, the ways the city has been redesigning itself to attract a certain breed of urban sophisticate, one who might choose lodging based on the provenance of the furniture.

On the culinary front, design aficionados head to Cluny Artbar as much for its stunning surroundings—featuring huge metal-framed windows, tables made from recycled bowling-alley flooring, and raw-brick walls—as for unassuming dishes like charcuterie sandwiches and white-chocolate bread pudding. **+**

For The Guide, see page 269.

The lobby of the Hôtel St.-Paul.

A lounge area at Jake's, a hotel in Jamaica.

Bermuda +
the Caribbean +
the Bahamas

sleep above the waves

OVERWATER BUNGALOWS IN **BERMUDA**

IT USED TO BE that you had to go to the South Pacific to find a hotel room whose foundation was the bottom of the ocean. But at 9 Beaches, Bermuda's newest resort, 11 of the 84 breezy bungalows on the property sit perched above a narrow, quiet channel between Daniel's Head, a crab-shaped peninsula at the island's westernmost point, and tiny, uninhabited Daniel's Island. The Bermuda resort has many charms—those nine beaches, for one—including incomparable views and a very close proximity to nature. Cabanas are chic and simple, with a sea-blue-and-white décor. At night, rows of tiny pixie lights along the boardwalk point the way to the overwater rooms. Evenings are spent on your terrace, a glass of wine in hand, savoring the silence. You'll almost fall asleep right there, lulled by the quiet rhythm of gentle waves beneath you. Leaving the resort isn't worth the effort: all you really need are those beaches, the view, and that breeze. +

For The Guide, see page 270.

A room at Bermuda's 9 Beaches hotel.

69

BERMUDA +
THE
CARIBBEAN
+ THE
BAHAMAS

Bermuda

Anguilla

Grilled spiny lobster at
CuisinArt Resort & Spa.

pleasure island

ANGUILLA'S TOP RESORTS

AS FAR AS THE CARIBBEAN goes, Anguilla has been
very fortunate. The most serendipitous moment came
in 1980, when the government of the virtually accom-
modation-free island decided to limit development to
discreet, small hotels and upscale resorts. A quarter of
a century later, the 16-mile-long territory known for its
pristine beaches has stuck to this policy (which means
there are no casinos, large cruise ships, or shopping
malls) and now has what is arguably the Caribbean's
highest concentration of luxurious
places to stay. Most of them are on
the western half of the island. (The
eastern portion is more residential.)

Clutching the cliffs above Meads
Bay, the Malliouhana Hotel & Spa
seduces all the right travelers—and
the shelter magazines—with its
enormous Haitian art–filled rooms ▶

70

BERMUDA +
THE
CARIBBEAN
+ THE
BAHAMAS

Anguilla

A room at Cap Juluca on Maundays Bay Beach, above. Below: Shoal Bay East. Opposite: A pool at St. Regis Temenos Villas, Anguilla.

and suites; sexy, jungly terraces and dining areas; and the island's most sophisticated French cuisine. The newest addition to the super-villa set is St. Regis Temenos Villas, Anguilla. Each of its three two-story units resembles a mini resort, wrapping around a spectacular and private infinity pool above a palmy beach. On mile-long Maundays Bay Beach, the Moorish-style Cap Juluca has continued to raise the bar since it opened in 1988. Most of the domed, white-washed buildings are appointed with Moroccan rugs and lanterns; glamorous marble bathrooms have tall glass walls overlooking plant-filled private *solaria*. The resort recently added a fitness center, complete with a yoga and Pilates studio; six spa treatment rooms; and three masseurs from Bali to the staff.

It used to be that serious foodies heading for the Caribbean went to St. Bart's. Anguilla has more than met the challenge posed by its French neighbor and become a culinary destination in its own right; currently, there are more than 100 restaurants, and perhaps the best is Blanchard's, where a palm tree grows through the roof, and teal shutters open to a tropical garden; creamless corn chowder and filet mignon of tuna are just two of the chef's signature dishes. The hydroponic farm at CuisinArt Resort & Spa has allowed chef Daniel Orr, formerly of Guastavino's in New York, to introduce great salads to the menu. Inspired guests are permitted to dig in and even learn to cook in the restaurant's stadium kitchen before feasting on their self-made meals. +

For The Guide, see page 270.

Turks and
Caicos

British Virgin
Islands

hot spot

DISCOVERING THE **TURKS AND CAICOS**

IT'S REMARKABLE, given their proximity to the United States, just how off-the-radar the Turks and Caicos islands are to most Americans. A British crown colony 575 miles off the coast, the archipelago couldn't be easier to reach: it's a short 1½-hour flight from Miami to the capital of Providenciales (a.k.a. Provo), and once there, you'll find superb diving on the world's third-largest coral reef, sportfishing, and magnificent white-sand beaches. The Turks and Caicos comprise some 40 islands and cays, only eight of them inhabited. Launch a boat from the busy marina on Provo, and within minutes you can land on a sand-fringed dot whose only residents are iguanas. Thirty minutes away is the celebrity-studded private-island resort Parrot Cay. The newest resort entry is Amanyara, set along a windswept coastline. Part of the luxury hotel group Amanresorts, the property is the Singapore-based brand's first foray into the West Indies and a decided departure from the typical pastel-hued properties that dot the rest of the Turks and Caicos. Open-sided pavilions made from Indonesian woods, armchairs of teak and rattan, and daybeds upholstered in Jim Thompson silks recall Southeast Asia more than the Caribbean. +

For The Guide, see page 270.

A poolside lounge area at Amanyara.

charting the course

THE **BRITISH VIRGIN ISLANDS** BY BOAT

ENCOMPASSING MORE THAN 50 islands, spread across 1,000 square miles, and home to scores of hotels, villas, resorts, and anchorages, the British Virgin Islands pose a logistical challenge for someone who wants to see more than one place. The ultimate way to traverse the territory is by boat: drifting from one island to the next, sleeping under a million stars. Renting a yacht allows you to follow your own schedule, with no ferries to catch and no rush to check out of a hotel in the morning. An ideal itinerary could start in Trellis Bay in Tortola, home to the island's main airport. After setting sail, moor for the evening in silent, starlit White Bay, off Guana Island. Spend the day exploring Guana's 850-acre nature preserve, one of the largest and most diverse collections of endangered species in the Caribbean. Move on to

Mosquito Island, at the entrance of Virgin Gorda's North Sound. Hike the jungly interior, or snorkel the Baths of Virgin Gorda—giant granite boulders that come together to form watery grottoes. End your voyage by skipping across Sir Francis Drake Channel to Peter Island, an 1,800-acre white sand–ringed retreat bristling with vegetation along most of its mountainous 4½-mile length. It is a fitting conclusion to a trip at sea, as most of the island is gloriously undeveloped— and there's not a car in sight. +

For The Guide, see page 270.

74

BERMUDA +
THE
CARIBBEAN
+ THE
BAHAMAS

St. Bart's

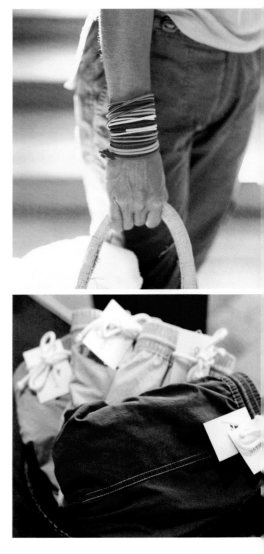

isle of style

SHOPPING IN ST. BART'S

THE FRENCH WEST INDIES has its own maverick dress code, which falls somewhere between Riviera couture and California beach bum. The retail scene boasts luxury brands (there are outposts of Hermès, Cartier, and Chanel), but it is the local boutiques, where the shelves are stocked with limited-edition labels, that really make for the most exciting shopping around.

From the moment you land on the airstrip in St. Jean, you'll notice not only the sparkling water but also a host of stores along the endless beach. The top spot is Mia Zia, Belgian-born Philippe de Nys's Moroccan-inspired shop, filled with a line of merino knit separates. Nys fell in love with the souks of Morocco while traveling there, so he struck a deal with Marrakesh designer Valérie Barkowski to create a vibrant line of clothing for his store. Sporty accessories include silk bungee-cord bracelets, woven straw hats from Senegal, and viscose totes, but the real draw is a terry *djellaba*, which looks as though it came straight from the desert; the baby version is even more adorable.

While you're in St. Jean, make sure to pick up a few baubles at Terra to wear to dinner. Jewelry designer Annelisa Gee, who places rare and semiprecious rough-cut gems in dainty gold settings, has a pedigreed fan club (Marie Chantal of Greece and model Lauren Hutton, to name just a few of her high-profile customers, have snapped up her informal designs). Team one of Gee's single-stranded chokers or cocktail rings with a silk Indonesian pareu or a flirty sundress by Miguelina with a beaded Moyna bag—all for sale, too.

St. Bart's most famous export might be Calypso (outposts of Christiane Celle's boutique, with its colorful clothes and accessories, have sprung up in major cities across the United States). But it's places like Lolita Jaca, in the harbor town of Gustavia, that truly capture the island's stylish sensibility. Owner Jaca Faby has a tightly edited selection of pieces from young, fun European designers. Pick up a shell-encrusted Antik Batik clutch or a demure Lola Parker bikini along with something from Faby's own collection of breezy yet chic pieces. ▶

Above, from top: Bungee-cord bracelets at Mia Zia, in St. Jean; swim trunks at Gustavia's Blue Coast. Below: Beaded slides at Metis, in Gustavia. Opposite: A coverup in the window of Mia Zia.

Sales associate Emanuelle
Bécard at Calypso, in Gustavia.

A few blocks away, hidden in an alley off the harbor, Blue Coast is one of the few stores on St. Bart's to cater exclusively to men. Well-dressed couples grab armloads of the soft linen shorts and shirts by Alfare that line the racks; they're *de rigueur* among St. Bart's fashionable set.

If your rental villa needs a few high-concept knickknacks, drop into home-décor store Syysuna by Free Mousse, also in Gustavia, for its monochromatic imports: creamy linen tablecloths from Latvia, Thai-silk table runners, Laguiole picnic knives and corkscrews, hand-carved Italian salad bowls, and the best hostess gift of all, fuzzy faux leopard–skin nutcrackers. +

For The Guide, see page 270.

For The Guide, see page 270.

T+L Tip

OTHER ISLAND INDULGENCES

Once your shopping appetite is sated, take some time to pamper yourself, enjoy a fabulous meal, and check out the island nightlife.

● Book an appointment for the Molton Brown Templetree treatment at the spa at **Hôtel St.-Barth Isle de France**, which uses sand from the adjacent Baie des Flamands.

● Reserve a table at **Le Gaïac** at the exclusive Hôtel Le Toiny, where the four-course meal of roast lobster, foie gras, and guinea hen is sublime.

● Nights heat up at the tried-and-true tavern **Le Ti St-Barth**, a lounge packed with sexy trendsetters.

● At lunch, the bronzed and beautiful crowd hits **Nikki Beach** in St.-Jean, where tabletop dancing is a traditional activity. Curl up on the canopied beds with a glass of Ti punch, a native concoction of rum, sugar, and lime.

St. Bart's

Jamaica

caribbean flavor

A CULINARY TOUR OF **JAMAICA**

FROM ROADSIDE JERK STANDS to casual hideaways to white-glove resorts, Jamaica has something for everyone. A mile from the Montego Bay Airport, a steadily rising plume of smoke draws travelers to Scotchies, a thatched encampment in a sandy parking lot, where grass umbrellas shade the outdoor dining area, and beer kegs serve as stools. This is the jerk pit dreams are made of: After placing your order at the window, sidestep to a counter that overlooks pork shoulders blackening on

The outdoor terrace at the Rockhouse, in Negril.

78

BERMUDA +
THE
CARIBBEAN
+ THE
BAHAMAS

Jamaica

One of the dozens of roadside fruit stands on the island, above.
Opposite, clockwise from top left: Glenford Walker, a staff member at
Round Hill, in Montego Bay; Round Hill's cottage No. 18, complete with
a bar; a local cactus; the low-key menu at Scotchies.

the smoldering fires. Watch as a cook in blue coveralls transfers it to a takeout container. Ladle on extra marinade, studded orange and green with chopped Scotch-bonnet peppers (whose earthy undertone is the defining feature of jerk). Beef sausages and smoky pork are also top-notch.

The luxury quotient is far higher on the other side of Montego Bay, at Round Hill Hotel & Villas, one of the island's older resorts, which opened in 1953. The jalousied villas in the compound are set on a steep, amphitheaterlike hillside, offering a perfectly composed view of the azure sea: scalloped coves rippling in the distance, framed by floppy banana leaves and latticed arches, tied-back curtains, and clouds. The suites have whitewashed wood walls, tile floors, and bamboo four-poster beds and feature a shared pool as well as a full kitchen. A breakfast table is set on the porch, where diners are presented with ackee, a tropical fruit native to Africa, sautéed with salt cod, onions, and tomatoes to produce the Jamaican national dish, ackee and codfish. It's perfect brunch food.

A drive into Negril, a town with a partying spirit, can feel like a comedown from the beauty of Round Hill—until you get to the Rockhouse. The town's social center is the hotel's restaurant, with an indoor-outdoor terrace cantilevered over the water. The menu updates local cuisine in smart, refreshing ways. A crisp, oniony conch fritter comes with a sweet-and-spicy tomato relish, fried red snapper is battered

with Red Stripe beer, and each table sports its own bottle of Pickapeppa, an aged purée of tamarinds and Scotch-bonnet chiles that is perhaps Jamaica's finest and most overlooked export.

As you travel farther west along the coast, away from the resort centers of Montego Bay and Negril, the texture of the Jamaican roadside becomes more evident. The seaside gives way to a pastoral landscape, a hill country of sugarcane and scallion fields. As the scenery becomes more rural, the roads widen counterintuitively. Take a detour north from Treasure Beach to Middle Quarters, a town famous for fiery pepper shrimp. At the end of a mile-long avenue of bamboo is Howie's, a low shed with a dozen steaming, smoke-blackened steel cauldrons set in a row over burning logs, each balanced on a tripod of rocks and filled with conch, fish, and oxtail. The shrimp is stir-fried with minced Scotch-bonnet peppers, coarse sea salt, black pepper, and vinegar. Spicy, sweet, and addictive, it may just be the most delicious—certainly the messiest—car snack ever. +

For The Guide, see page 270.

For The Guide, see page 270.

T+L Tip

Jamaica's oldest rum distillery, **Appleton Estate**, in St. Elizabeth, offers daily tours that feature an informative introduction to its 21-year-old rum: a mellow, easy, after-dinner drink with vanilla and cocoa notes. If you're lucky, you'll catch a glimpse of Appleton's master blender, Joy Spence.

8o

BERMUDA +
THE
CARIBBEAN
+ THE
BAHAMAS

Harbour
Island,
Bahamas

A traditional clapboard house trimmed in Bahamian blue on
Harbour Island, above. Below: On the island's pink-sand beach.
Opposite: A terrace off one of the suites at the Oceanview Club hotel.

castles in the sand

THE **HARBOUR ISLAND** BEACH SCENE

LEAVE THE HAMPTONS to the crowds. The most beautiful Atlantic Ocean beach easily accessible from the East Coast of the United States is the 3.5-mile-long stretch of reef-protected soft pink sand on the ocean side of Harbour Island in the Bahamas. The water off this wide strand is a glittering shade of turquoise, and the surf is so soft and gentle that little children swim without fear. There are horses to ride, water sports galore, and great food just off the sand at Sip-Sip, on North Beach, and at the justly famous Blue Bar at the Pink Sands Resort, where celebs like Tom Hanks and Julia Roberts get pampered.

But best of all are the hypnotic views to the north, east, and south, and the voyeuristic pleasures of peeking at the beautiful bodies on the beach; and to the west, glimpses of the houses of the rich and famous who have second homes on Harbour Island. Hidden amid the lush tropical vegetation are American WASP's whose lines date back to before the American Revolution.

It's easy enough to reach from New York; if you depart after breakfast, you can be wading in the water by lunchtime, which means Harbour Island is no longer a secret, though you might think so. Because even in high season, you can find yourself alone on that long beach. +

For The Guide, see page 270.

Mexico+ Central +South America

84

MEXICO
+ CENTRAL
+ SOUTH
AMERICA

Riviera
Maya

From left: A thatched-roof bedroom at Ikal del Mar; the ancient ruins at Tulum. Opposite: Relaxing in one of the cottages at Amansala, a yoga retreat in Tulum.

mexico's hottest coast

RESORTS ON THE **RIVIERA MAYA**

NOT SO LONG AGO, the corridor that starts just below Cancún and runs south to the ancient Mayan ruins of Tulum was just a sleepy stretch of Caribbean coastline. Today, a gold-rush giddiness animates the so-called Riviera Maya. A current visitors' map, distributed free at the airport, lists 87 hotels between Cancún airport and Tulum—and the number is still growing. By 2025, officials say, there will be 110,000 hotel rooms along this stretch. Mandarin Oriental is hard at work on a new resort. The owners of Tulum's Amansala, a boho-chic yoga retreat popular with the fashion elite, have turned Pablo Escobar's former estate into Casa Magna, a luxury inn consisting of two villas. And while eco-conscious spots, including Ikal del Mar, a sexy hideaway in the jungle, have been drawing like-minded travelers for years, Mayakoba, a magnificent jungle-and-beach develop-

ment a few minutes south of Puerto Morelos, raises the bar with five eco-resorts, including the Fairmont, the first to open. Built on a system of newly discovered freshwater canals and lagoons, Mayakoba shuttles guests around in silent electric boats, sharing the waters with herons, cormorants, and manatees. In total, Mayakoba will have 1,200 rooms, even though 3,900 are allowed under Mexico's density rules. Meanwhile, an eco-sensitive Greg Norman–designed golf course uses cenotes as water hazards. +

For The Guide, see page 271.

Mexican Independence Day decorations hang above Calle Madero, in Querétaro's Centro Histórico, above. Below: Inside the Tonantzintla church, near Puebla.

the best of colonial mexico

DAY TRIPS TO **PUEBLA** AND **QUERÉTARO**

WITH THE EXCEPTION OF Oaxaca, which is 325 miles southeast of Mexico City, the country's great colonial towns are all a short day trip from the capital. Anyone looking to experience the Old World will discover a vivid architectural history, not to mention good things to eat, in Puebla, 80 miles southeast of Mexico City. Puebla's buildings are sheathed in the area's famous Talavera tiles, the patterns a brilliant synthesis of Islamic, Aztec, and Art Nouveau design. The food here is an equally colorful mosaic, with pre-Hispanic, European, and Asian influences coming together to produce a unique new cuisine. At the restaurant Compañía, the menu, known for *cholupas*, flour tortillas with spiced beef, also incorporates spices ground using a traditional *molcajete* (mortar).

Baroque and Moorish sensibilities, on the other hand, fuse most dramatically in Querétaro, 130 miles north of Mexico City. La Casa de la Marquesa is an 18th-century palace realized in high Mudejar style. The city's spectacular cathedral, Templo de Santa Rosa de Viterbos, also was designed with lavish Mudejar details. Inside, the church is Baroque, with painstakingly elaborate marquetry and extravagant gilding. +

For The Guide, see page 271.

87

MEXICO
+ CENTRAL
+ SOUTH
AMERICA

Puebla and
Querétaro,
Mexico

Mexico City

An anodized aluminum installation at OMR gallery. Left: Sneakers on display at Kulte.

style south of the border

SHOPPING IN **MEXICO CITY**

LONG OVERLOOKED BY THE fashionable elite, Mexico City is now on every style-setter's radar. Locals are reinvigorating the once-sleepy Condesa and Roma neighborhoods, just south of the busy Zona Rosa. Artists stroll the streets, walking dogs and ducking into the shops, galleries, and restaurants that have overtaken European-style town houses and Art Deco storefronts. These neighborhoods feel surprisingly like Europe—though far closer to home and with a much better exchange rate. Design-forward boutiques dot the tree-lined boulevards, upping the cool quotient with their meticulously edited selections. Among the most intriguing is Local, a shop that showcases the avant-garde work of a revolving roster of female fashion and accessories designers. New creations are dropped off weekly, and you can expect to see pieces like sheer polka-dot shirts with built-in 50's-style bras. Around the corner, Carmen Rion sells flowing pants, skirts, and dresses in neutral-toned and pastel-hued cottons and linens, plus a small selection of men's long-sleeved *guayaberas* in white and pink. Fashionistas love Kulte for its sneakers (old-school Nike, Vans, and Adidas as well as Gsus from Holland). The boutique also stocks Savi jeans, funky tees, and watches and bags. Interior-design shops have entered the mix, too. If there's only time to visit one, make it Artefacto, where linens, furniture, and silver jewelry are artfully displayed. Chic by Accident is a favorite of area architects for its antique furniture, as is Galería OMR, a contemporary gallery showcasing the work of both Mexican and international artists. ✚

For The Guide, see page 271.

andean highs

DRIVING **ARGENTINA**'S RUTA 40

LA CUARENTA, the famed stretch of pavement and dirt better known as Argentina's Ruta 40, is one of the longest roads in the Americas. It crosses 18 rivers and 236 bridges, touches 13 lakes and salt flats, and passes by 20 national parks as it follows the spine of the Andes across all manner of ecosystems and incredible topography. Che Guevera traveled down the Ruta on his six-month-long motorcycle journey through Latin America. As the *Motorcycle Diaries* showed, the 3,000-mile stretch between Argentina's northern border and Cabo Vírgenes in the south is among the world's most free-spirited road trips.

Starting in Salta, at the foot of the eastern Andes, a stretch of red dirt leads to Cachí, where the snow-capped Andes tower 22,000 feet above a plain of saguaro cacti; signs warn of crossing llamas. The pavement begins more than 105 miles later, outside San Carlos, where the road is surrounded by some of the highest vineyards on earth. An hour away, across the border into Tucumán province, are the remnants of the indigenous Quilmes civilization; a small museum houses arrowheads and pottery shards. Four hours south is Parque Nacional Talampaya, an undervisited national park sometimes referred to as Argentina's Grand Canyon.

Somewhere around San Juan, in the Mendoza province, the vineyards begin to come fast and furious. The cosmopolitan city of Mendoza, with landscaped parks and wide avenues, is reputed to have more trees than people. It's in the heart of Argentina's thriving wine industry (the country ranks fifth in global production). And at the end of the long drive, it's also the perfect place to indulge in a glass or two of local Malbec. ✛

For The Guide, see page 271.

On the road near Parque Nacional Talampaya, Argentina's Grand Canyon. Inset: An antique car.

going green
ALL THINGS ECO IN **COSTA RICA**

The pool at Hotel Punta Islita, on Costa Rica's Pacific Coast. Opposite: A hanging bridge in the rain forest near Arenal.

FOR THE ECO-TOURIST, Costa Rica is as close to heaven as it gets. It's been that way for a while, or at least since the Hotel Punta Islita arrived on the scene a dozen or so years ago. Built as a traditional Costa Rican cattle and timber hacienda, the ranch occupies a pristine mountain outpost on the country's Pacific Coast. It offers programs to satisfy every kind of traveler: horseback riding and surfing for the sports-minded, bird-watching and river-floating for outdoors lovers, 30 different spa treatments for those seeking rejuvenation, and tours of the village and contemporary art museum for the culturally inclined.

For the epicure, the Creole Cooking School at the Inn at Coyote Mountain teaches visitors to make dishes such as empanadas and tamales, using produce from the inn's gardens.

In Tortuguero, Costa Rica's own mini-Amazon, guests help scientists tag leatherback turtles for the Caribbean Conservation Corporation while living in the research facility's basic (but beachside) accommodations.

Costa Rica's collection of seas, rivers, and jungles provides the ultimate escape for adrenaline junkies. With Costa Rica Expeditions, a multi-sport package will set you up to fly through the tree canopy on a zip-line 98 feet above the forest floor, to raft Class IV rapids on the Pacuare River, and to mountain bike around the Arenal volcano. You can also request a bespoke itinerary, customized to your most heart-racing extreme. +

For The Guide, see page 271.

continental crossroads

THE MANY FACES OF **PANAMA**

PANAMA COULD REALLY be considered three countries: supermodern Panama City; the cool, slow-moving interior; and the surfable, fishable coasts. Panama City is a thriving metropolis, dense with new hotels and sleek office buildings. But the capital is not the only reason for visiting. Just ask Ruben Blades, Panama's official head of tourism. The world's most famous living Panamanian wants his native country to offer cultural, historical, and recreational adventure ecotourism.

A drive out of town to the cloud forest, through Casco Viejo, is a good place to start. On the Azueros Peninsula, near the town of Pedasí on the Pacific Coast, Frenchman Gilles Saint-Gilles, who moved here a decade ago, has built Azueros, a soothing retreat with rooms in neutral beige and brown tones. And in the mountain village of Boquete, the Panamonte, one of the oldest hotels in the country, is set on green, lushly landscaped grounds. Among its many guests have been Teddy Roosevelt, whose administration presided over the American phase of canal construction, as well as the Shah of Iran and Ingrid Bergman—not together.

Perhaps the most spectacular sight in all of Panama, though, is the top of a huge, bulky container ship through the green canopy of the jungle, a bizarre conflation of the man-made and the natural. +

For The Guide, see page 271.

A Ngobe-Buglé indian woman on a coffee plantation outside Panama City. Clockwise from top left: A thatched hut in Pedasí; relaxing at a ranch near Pedasí; a menu at a local restaurant. Opposite: Panama City at night.

Dulceria YELY

CUBIERTA DE CARAMELO....0.25
MANJAR..0.30   DURAZNO.....0.30
VAINILLA...0.30   QUEQUES...0.25
CHOCOLATE.0.30   EMPANADAS.0.25
NUECES......0.30   TRES LECHES.0.50
ZANAHORIA.0.25   FLAN CASERO.0.75
ALMENDRAS.0.30   CAKE
MANZANA....0.25   .15¢
GALLETAS NARANJA

The shores of Fernando de Noronha, an archipelago and national marine park off Brazil's northeastern coast.

95
MEXICO
+ CENTRAL
+ SOUTH
AMERICA

Brazil's
Beaches

secret sands

BRAZIL'S HIDDEN BEACHES

FROM A SAND-SWEPT beach in Ceará state to a one-lane village south of Salvador with five stunning coves, the northern coast of Brazil has countless quiet beaches, where turtles outnumber sunbathers and deserted islands emerge from the sea.

Jericoacoara, Ceará, a four-hour drive west from the northeastern city of Fortaleza, could easily be mistaken for a Saharan desertscape. But the first sight of the blue waters beyond the Pôr do Sol, Jeri's nearly 100-foot-high Sunset Dune, is anything but a mirage. The breeze here can reach gale force, drawing sand boarders and windsurfers.

There are more spinner dolphins and sea turtles than people farther south on Pernambuco's Fernando de Noronha, 340 miles off the coast of Recife. IBAMA (the Brazilian Environmental Protection Agency) limits visitors to this national marine park to an average of 420 a day. The result: its 14 pristine beaches are virtually deserted.

In the 1980's surfers discovered Praia da Pipa, a primitive fishing village one hour south of Natal in Rio Grande Do Norte. Since then, Pipa has gone from bohemian to bourgeois; it's now packed with sunbathers and bars. Head for Baía dos Golfinhos, a dolphin and sea-turtle sanctuary, where an immaculate 1.2-mile sandy stretch backs up against steep cliffs of oxidized clay. +

For The Guide, see page 271.

Above, from left: A vendor at the Manaus fish market; the 1897 Teatro Amazonas, the crown jewel of Eduardo Ribeiro's rain-forest Xanadu. Opposite: Outside Armando's, a bar across from the Teatro Amazonas.

MANAUS IS THE BIGGEST CITY in the world's biggest rain forest. Looking at a map, you realize that it seems bizarrely placed, an uppercase set of letters plunked down on a page of thick green. It is here that two great rivers, the nearly jet-black waters of the Rio Negro from the north and the yellowish flow of the Solimões from the west, come together to form the mighty Amazon. Except that they don't really come together—not exactly. Instead, the two rivers run alongside each other for miles without mixing. When they do, at the Merging of the Waters (high-definition postcards of the scene are available all over town), the sight is captivating enough to justify taking a ferry to experience it for yourself.

The Brazilian city owes its existence, in part, to Eduardo Ribeiro, the governor of the state of Amazonas during the final decades of the 19th century. "I found a village and made it a modern city," he once said. Dreaming of an Oz-like empire in the jungle, Ribeiro presided over the electrification of Manaus's street lamps, built a system of electrically powered trolley cars, and commissioned the celebrated opera house, the Teatro Amazonas. Iron framework from Scotland was steamed up the Amazon; crystal chandeliers came from Italy. The looming cupola (done in the yellow, green, and blue of the Brazilian flag) required 60,000 tiles, ordered from Alsace-Lorraine.

The century-old Manaus fish market, with its soaring tin roof and stained-glass windows, is nothing if not a shrine dedicated to Amazonian biodiversity, a museum of the soon-to-be-eaten, illuminated by strings of hanging 15-watt bulbs. The best time to catch the action is just past dawn. That's when the fishing boats tie up at the Terminal Pesqueiro de Manaus, a quarter-mile-long floating pier that rises and falls with the level of the mighty river.

Now, more than a century after Ribeiro's reign, the free-trade zone has created a second boom in Manaus. The Teatro, the undisputed centerpiece of the city, has been re-stored to its original grandeur. When the show is over, concertgoers walk across the wavy white-and-black stonework tiles of St. Sebastian Square (meant to invoke the Merg-ing of the Waters) to Armando's bar. The eponymous proprietor has been popping the tops off Antarctic beers at his open-air, casual establishment for as long as anyone can remember. And if you're lucky, he might bring you a slab of *pirarucu*, the largest freshwater fish in the world, just off the morning's boat. +

For The Guide, see page 271.

colonial capital

LIMA'S CREATIVE CULTURE

Jewelry designer Ester Ventura, in her shop in Lima's Chorillos neighborhood, left. Below: Icons for sale at Las Pallas. Opposite: San Franciso Church, in downtown Lima.

LIMA IS A COSMOPOLITAN PLACE, a modern capital with skyscrapers and sprawling roadways lined with gigantic shopping malls, cineplexes, and Starbucks, yet amid these current signs of civilization, the essential nature of this historic city remains in place.

The downtown district has the feel of old Lima, with some fine examples of colonial structures still standing. Among them are the San Francisco Church, notable for its catacombs; and the recently restored La Catedral: Baroque, solemn, and imposing, it's a relic of the time when the Spaniards used the might of religious architecture to seduce the natives into becoming Catholic. Next to La Catedral stands the presidential palace, a massive gray edifice that's just as elaborate, bearing silent witness to a history filled with violence and uncertainty.

The city's long tradition of arts and crafts continues to thrive. Peruvian artisans, known for skills passed down from generation to generation, are always experimenting with unusual designs and materials. A trek through the Mercado Indio, in the Miraflores district, a labyrinth of small stalls, offers abundant discoveries of the unique and handmade—handcrafted ribbons, a woven tray inlaid with seeds from the Peruvian jungle, a knit baby blanket. Jewelry designer Claudia Stern crafts exotic necklaces, bracelets, and rings made from velvet-covered wire twisted into strange shapes and dyed an amazing array of colors, which she sells at her namesake shop, in the Barranco district. Another designer, Ester Ventura, makes intriguing gold and silver pieces that incorporate seeds, weavings, seashells, coral, and pre-Colombian fragments.

It's not unusual for old mansions to take on new incarnations as galleries. Las Pallas is the domain of Mari Solari, who for 40 years has dedicated her life to the promotion of Peruvian folk art, traveling to the remotest parts of the country to add to her remarkable stock. Solari's personal collection, on display in the same spot, includes a huge ▶

100

MEXICO
+CENTRAL
+SOUTH
AMERICA

Lima

Santiago

The Dédalo crafts store, in the Barranco district, above. Below: Different flavors of *teja* candy, from candied lemons stuffed with *dulce de leche* to coconut toffee bars, at Helena Chocolatier, in Miraflores.

variety of traditional weavings, magic charms and amulets, and ceremonial drinking vessels. It's all beautifully arranged and guarded by a rare Peruvian hairless dog, whose pedigree dates back to before the time of the Incas.

At Don Pedro de Osma y Pardo's magnificent, recently restored museum in Barranco, you can get a glimpse of a full range of Lima's crafts throughout the mansion; the rich assemblage of more than 5,000 objects includes everything from paintings from the Cuzco school to elaborate silver and furniture. The house itself, built around the turn of the century and once a backdrop for the grand lives of Peru's aristocrats, has large rooms with stained-glass windows and inlaid floors. The Dédalo shop is also in a sprawling mansion in the Barranco neighborhood; each room has one type of craft (toys, jewelry, ceramics) on display. And as you might expect, all of the designers are from the region. To see the exquisite handiwork of pre-Incan cultures, such as Chavin, Paracas, and Mochica, through the Colonial period, visit the Museo de Arte, where a collection of Peruvian art and artifacts is on display.

In Lima, candy-making is considered its own form of art. After a long day of gallery-hopping, wrap things up by indulging in a Peruvian delicacy called *teja*, which consists of filled fruits dipped in sugar. Among the most charming purveyors is Helena Chocolatier, a small confectionery shop in Miraflores, where candied lemons come stuffed with *dulce de leche*. +

For The Guide, see page 271.

chilean chic

MODERN DESIGN IN
SANTIAGO

SANTIAGO IS NO LONGER South America's ugly duckling. The city has recently undergone an $800 million transportation and environmental overhaul. Crumbling architectural treasures are being refurbished, showing Santiago's strong investment in civic improvement.

Young Santiago natives are ▶

Obra Gruesa, by Patrick Steeger, at Galería Animal in Vitacura.

102

MEXICO
+CENTRAL
+SOUTH
AMERICA

Santiago

Beachwear at GAM, a fashion cooperative in Providencia, left. Above: A view of Santiago from Cerro San Cristobal. Opposite: Bar Liguria.

taking it upon themselves to open bright new shops and restaurants. Claudio Soto resurrected a crumbling 19th-century downtown building to open her restaurant Confitería Torres, done up with red-leather booths, French doors, and an oak bar. Fashion veteran Chantal Bernsau fills a large former house with her jewel-toned silk dresses, blouses, and pants, and her New Age "chakra-activating" jewelry made of quartz, fossils, and semiprecious gems. (Her workshop is also in the house.) GAM, which stands for Grupo Anti-Mall, a fashion cooperative for emerging designers, has taken up residence on the first floor of an old mansion in the trendy Providencia neighborhood.

Like its metropolitan counterparts, Santiago has no shortage of cultural establishments. The work of some of Santiago's emerging artists is on display at the contemporary Galería Animal. And Trece is the recently opened remake of what was the city's most important contemporary art gallery in the 1970's.

Santiago nightlife is as vibrant as its neighborhoods.

After-dark revelry takes place everywhere—in basement bars, friendly discos, or groovy lounges. The best place to start—or end—any evening is Bar Liguria, a restaurant by day and a swarming social scene by night. +

For The Guide, see page 271.

For The Guide, see page 271.

T+L Tip

WINE 101

- Any of Chile's 146 wineries make an idyllic day trip from Santiago. **Ruta del Vino de Colchagua** leads the pack.

- For a truly intimate wine experience, **Wine Travel Chile** will arrange private visits to estates in the country.

104
MEXICO
+CENTRAL
+SOUTH
AMERICA

Buenos Aires

paris of the pampas

RECLAIMING NATIONAL PRIDE IN **BUENOS AIRES**

Dancing at Bar Sur. Opposite: Eduardo Catalano's *Floralis Genérica*.

Hernán Marina's sculpture *Coloso* (2004) at MALBA, above. Below: Inside the gilded Lobby Bar at the recently renovated Alvear Palace Hotel, where Evita Perón used to stop for tea in the 1940's.

"WHAT'S NEW, Buenos Aires?" asked the narrator, Che, in the Lloyd Webber and Tim Rice musical *Evita*. Judging by the looks of things now, the answer is simple: what's new is youth, vigor, and a fresh sense of self-awareness that has more to do with a recently discovered national pride than the Europe-yearning of past generations. Buenos Aires is, in fact, a decidedly New World metropolis, a place where a rejuvenated Old World traditionalism meets Beaux Arts architecture. What increasing numbers of *porteños* (the nickname for residents of Buenos Aires) consider *conchero* (cool) is what's created in their own country.

The best of all worlds begins with a morning at MALBA, a museum of contemporary Latin American art. The museum, a $50 million, angular, greige-colored–stone building designed by three young Argentinean architects, houses a collection of pieces by home-grown Impressionists, Cubists, and Abstract Expressionists. Its gift shop sells products by native talent, including furniture designer Amancio Williams and jewelry maker Perfectos Dragones.

After a casual but delicious seafood lunch at Dora, a bustling classic, spend the afternoon shopping in Palermo Soho. Three years ago it was better known as Palermo Viejo, or Old Palermo, a humble working-class neighborhood where modest little houses stood alongside auto-repair shops and mom-and-pop grocery stores. More than 90 shops and restaurants have sprouted up along the shady streets, from hip little cafés like El Taller to fashion boutiques launched by independent Argentinean designers such as Cora

Groppo, Malu, and Carla Ricciardi, as well as furniture shops offering Conran-like essentials or gaucho-inspired wares.

Even the city's hotels and restaurants are in the midst of celebrating Argentinean culture. After a major renovation, the brass trim at the Alvear Palace gleams as brightly as it did when Evita Perón used to stop by for tea in the 1940's. When Fernando Trocca, the executive chef of the see-and-be-seen restaurant Sucre, could no longer afford to import foie gras and French wines, he started using regional ingredients and products.

Buenos Aires comes alive post-midnight. Some of the tango halls, such as Bar Sur, have gone groovy, with DJ's spinning scratchy hip-hop versions of tango ballads originally recorded in the 1920's and 30's. On the other hand, local art makes its own unique mark. Consider Eduardo Catalano's startling *Floralis Genérica*, in the Plaza Naciones Unidas, an 18-ton flowerlike sculpture that opens during the day and closes at night.

Porteños' personal pride is so infectious that international designers have begun to set their sights on the capital city once heralded as the Paris of the Pampas. The gritty port of Puerto Madero Este has been sanitized and gentrified. Its 19th-century warehouses and grain elevators are now flanked by two acknowledged clichés of global cool: a footbridge from Spanish architect Santiago Calatrava and a new hotel-and-condominium complex by French designer Philippe Starck—the stylish Faena Hotel + Universe. +

For The Guide, see page 272.

Puente de la Mujer, the Santiago Calatrava-designed footbridge in the gritty port of Puerto Madero, above. Below: Kicking back at El Taller in the newly chic Palermo Soho district.

Poolside at the
Serena Hotel.
Opposite: The
roulette wheel at
Mantra Casino.

109

MEXICO
+ CENTRAL
+ SOUTH
AMERICA

Punta del
Este

south america's saint-tropez

THE PARTY IN **PUNTA DEL ESTE**

PUNTA DEL ESTE, Uruguay's once-sleepy fishing village, was *the* spot for South America's *beau monde* in the 1950's—think Brazilians with millions. But when the country's economy derailed, so did the conga line of partygoers.

Punta has gotten its glamorous groove back; crowds of bikini-wearing hedonists have returned in full force. La Barra, a bustling, trendy area five minutes by car from downtown, is so popular in summer that it becomes as gridlocked as East Hampton on a Saturday morning. The largest, flashiest entry is the Conrad Punta del Este Resort & Casino, on the river side of the peninsula. A Vegas-style mega-hotel with more than 300 rooms and a casino, the Conrad is one of the few places that shows signs of life in the off-season, between April and December. The hotel also pays big pesos to attract marquee-name Latin entertainers such as Shakira, Ricky Martin, and Luis Miguel, making it an essential stop on the Punta social circuit.

A more sedate place to stay is the Serena, a 32-room boutique property not far from the Conrad. The Serena has possibly the most attentive staff and the best location of any hotel in the area—the view of the marina from the swimming pool is unrivaled. +

For The Guide, see page 272.

Western Europe

The Hotel
Endsleigh,
in Devon,
England.

the country life

THE BUCOLIC INNS OF **DEVON**

A sitting room at the Hotel Endsleigh, above, left. Above, right: An arbored garden path on the grounds of the hotel. Opposite: A bellhop at the entrance to Bovey Castle.

A FEW HOURS' DRIVE WEST of London is Devon and the lonely beauty of that county's most alluring asset, Dartmoor. At 368 square miles, Dartmoor—a national park of stark granite outcroppings—is the largest tract of open terrain in southern England. Nearly half of it is uncorrupted, uninterrupted moorland. The combination of wind-savaged heath, scrawny tors, cairns, stone circles, and menhirs draws people who live to walk, who think nothing of knocking off 10 miles before lunch and another 10 before the evening's first Cosmoquila.

The 65-room Bovey Castle occupies a splendid 350-acre parcel on Dartmoor National Park. The recent object of a $50 million remake, the castle's least expensive room worth considering has lyrical views of the valley. Fifteen minutes from the park, the Hotel Endsleigh has become a modern classic. On 108 acres of lush parkland, the Endsleigh was built in 1812, commissioned by the Duchess of Bedford as a rustic shooting and fishing lodge. Fashioned in the cottage *orné* style—rough oak columns, Gothic gingerbread, shell grotto—the stone manor's cream-hued guest rooms overlook a mossy bend in the trout-laden stream, fires crackle in the paneled library, and mosaic tables from Milan perk up the floral-wallpapered bar. Chef Shay Cooper's tender Dartmoor lamb with herb gnocchi and Devon beef with artichoke *barigoule* and shallot marmalade are fit for a duchess.

Either the Endsleigh or Bovey Castle make an optimal base for plumbing the area, including Chagford, which is the prettiest village in the entire West Country. A cheesemonger, a tearoom, a fruit-and-vegetable stall, a "veterinary surgery," and an amazing department store that masquerades as a mom-and-pop shop line High Street and the square. James Bowden & Son stocks everything from mixing bowls and heirloom-seed packets to hacking jackets and fishing creels. It's all so picturesque—and so storybook England. +

For The Guide, see page 272.

T+L Tip

INSIDER ART

While in the town of Chagford, don't miss a visit to **Wood & Rush,** an artisans' cooperative that showcases jewelry crafted from locally sourced materials.

british accents

A handmade shoe by London designer Georgina Goodman. Opposite, clockwise from top left: Men's shirts from Dunhill; Pringle's signature argyle; handmade suits at Kilgour; Bracher Emden's vibrant storefront.

SAMUEL JOHNSON MIGHT HAVE SAID, "If you are tired of London, you are tired of life." His exact words should have been, "If you are tired of shopping in London, you are tired of shopping." The British fashion capital's retail landscape reflects the town as a whole: sprawling, alternately proper and profane, and freewheeling enough to accommodate the tastes of everyone from Miss Marple to Marianne Faithfull to Kate Moss.

London's world-class style is at its eccentric, individualistic best in such places as Pringle, whose argyle is set to rival Burberry's plaid. Vivienne Westwood is indisputably the high priestess of English couture, and although she now distances herself from her punk roots, she still evinces an affection for renegade classics. The masterly Alexander McQueen is not for the timid either. His dramatic black leathers and artfully shredded pale silks are perfectly at home in his boutique's Sputnik-like space-pod interior. And don't ignore world-famous mad hatter Philip Treacy, who counts among his customers Marilyn Manson, fashion editor Isabella Blow, and the royal family. Pamela Blundell Bespoke, on the other hand, caters to the tailored set, who swoon for her suits in lush fabrics like velvet, silk, and corduroy, many inspired by Helmut Newton's photographs from the 1970's.

Classic menswear has always been a London specialty. David Gale of Dunhill, an elfin man in his fifties, ▶

is the shirt wizard of the city. His sexy, form-hugging designs are beloved by both Mr. and Mrs. Guy Ritchie. Meanwhile, the Tom Ford of Savile Row is Kilgour designer Carlo Brandelli, whose designs—an inimitable blend of English sophistication and Italian brio—attract musician and unabashed clotheshorse Bryan Ferry.

For fabulous footwear, insiders choose the couture, semi-bespoke styles at Georgina Goodman; shoes are made to measure and crafted from a single piece of buttery leather. The heels are fashioned from hardwoods such as olive, elm, walnut, and mahogany, and shoes are padded with hidden cushions.

The variety of handbags available in the city—from Anya Hindmarch's photo-printed bags to Lulu Guinness's *Dial M for Murder* styles to the sophisticated yet unstuffy purses at 150-year-old Tanner Krolle—is endless. Meanwhile, the mood at Bracher Emden is strictly rocker chic, combining Swarovski crystals with brightly hued snakeskins and lacing purses as if they were motorcycle jackets.

To complete your outfit, go to the fashionable Westbourne Grove strip, where talented accessories designers have set up shop. Fiona Knapp, who hails from New Zealand, creates jewelry in a store with mysterious black walls and backlit showcases. Solange Azagury-Partridge's boutique, on the other hand, is a deep vermilion grotto, with velvet-padded walls and a red leather floor. Her droll pieces include a tempting enamel-and-ruby Union Jack ring—the perfect memento to recall your stylish spree. +

For The Guide, see page 272.

Whimsical hat designs at Philip Treacy's namesake shop near Buckingham Palace, above. Below: A bespoke jacket in Pamela Blundell's West End salon, featuring the designer's signature touches—strong shoulders, wide lapels, and a single button on the front.

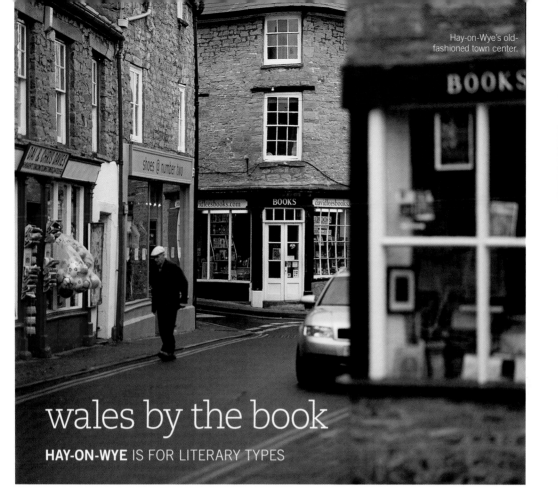

Hay-on-Wye's old-fashioned town center.

wales by the book

HAY-ON-WYE IS FOR LITERARY TYPES

BEFORE RICHARD BOOTH arrived, Hay-on-Wye was a forgotten market town 160 miles from London on the Welsh-English border. Since 1961, however, when the eccentric book dealer founded Hay-on-Wye Booktown, his first store there, the destination has become every reader's fairy-tale fantasy (population: 1,450; bookshops: 30). He later converted the 13th-century Hay Castle into another bookstore that led him to appoint himself "king of the independent kingdom" of Hay-on-Wye. In the courtyard's Honesty Bookshop, customers flip through 1970's volumes on male chauvinism and needlepoint, which are purchased by depositing coins into an "honesty box." Inside another one of his bookstores, Richard Booth's Bookshop, Victorian tiles line the door, and 400,000 volumes fill the shelves.

At B&K Books, beekeepers Karl and Betty Showler carry 500 titles on bees, apiculture, and insects in their house and a garden shed. Nearby, Poetry Bookshop is where owner Chris Prince met his future wife, Melanie, as she perused his selection of first editions, which includes a first-edition (but not-for-sale) William Blake. A gorgeously illustrated first edition of William Morris's *Poems by the Way* was recently sold.

At Mark Westwood Books, a glass-fronted case houses antiquarian and scientific books as well as first editions from the likes of Iris Murdoch and C. S. Lewis. At Murder and Mayhem, paperbacks of Agatha Christie's 1950's "cozy crimes" are best sellers. +

For The Guide, see page 273.

T+L Tip

OTHER BOOK TOWNS

Bibliophiles may find these two destinations worth the drive:

Blaenavon, Wales 40 miles from Hay-on-Wye (population: 6,000; bookshops: 10).

Wigtown, Scotland 300 miles north of Blaenavon (population: 900; bookshops: 19).

dutch design

THE AVANT-GARDE AESTHETIC
OF **AMSTERDAM**

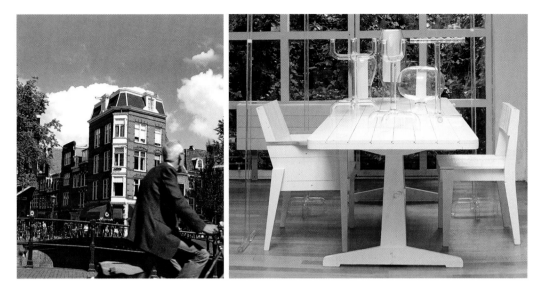

Above, from left: Looking onto Nieuwe Spiegelstraat's antiques row; Frozen Fountain, a contemporary furnishings store. Opposite: Designer shoes and handbags at Shoebaloo, in Pieter Cornelis Hoofstraat.

AMONG THE SHOPPING capitals of Europe, Amsterdam shines in exceptional ways: the people are friendly and speak impeccable English; the stores are charmingly varied (chains have yet to eclipse one-off boutiques); and there's a strong show of merchandise by young and emerging designers with a talent for combining the practical with the whimsical. Perhaps most appealing, you can walk everywhere.

The neighborhood of Nine Little Streets fans out around three of Amsterdam's most lovely canals. The waterways are bordered by rows of stately town houses (their gabled roofs give the area a storybook quality), and the streets are lined with jaunty shops featuring cutting-edge clothing and accessories. Hester Van Eeghen excels at pairing unlikely colors in the handbags at her namesake store; her purple leather rugby bag sports lime piping, while a short-handled calfskin satchel weds milk chocolate to raspberry. Stringy Balenciaga bags and curious coats courtesy of Holland's avant-garde duo Viktor & Rolf are just a few of the irresistible pieces at Van

Ravenstein, which also carries fashion-forward designer Dries Van Noten. Nearby, BLGK sells the resolutely postmodern efforts of a collective of jewelers. At Klamboe Unlimited, the entire stock consists of canopies made from mosquito netting. These have been dyed orange and pink and enhanced with silvery charms, and are meant to hang in stylish bedrooms that have never seen a fly. Trunk is possibly the most eclectic outpost in town, with its mix of beaded Moroccan slippers, Indonesian faux-coral bracelets, Dutch-designed leather bags and wallets, and pink flowerpots, all of which spill into the tiny Rosmarijnsteeg out front. And Amsterdam's famously frisky collective Droog Design is best known for developing arcane but useful products while nurturing young talent. Some of the most popular items for sale include stemware made to resemble bubble wrap and knotted chairs by Marcel Wanders.

An eye for design extends to the look of the shops themselves. On Pieter Cornelis Hoofstraat, a three-block stretch near the Rijksmuseum that is Amsterdam's answer to Madison Avenue, upscale chains line the streets. The exception—and worth a stroll down the *straat*—is Shoebaloo, with a space-age interior straight out of *The Jetsons*. The floor gleams with a greenish glow, and though the undulating shelves yield the usual suspects—Dior heels, Prada boots—there is also occasionally an unexpected, colorful twist, such as a pair of iridescent green Dirk Bikkembergs sneakers. +

For The Guide, see page 273.

europe's most livable city

THE ENDURING APPEAL OF ZURICH

CHIC, SMALL-SCALE, and thoroughly modern, Zurich doesn't blare out its secrets easily. But Switzerland's largest urban center—better known as a banking hub and stopover en route to the mountains—seduces nonetheless. It could be considered a perfect small city. And all perfect small cities require a perfect place to stay. The Baur au Lac is a grand hotel in the truest sense. Legendary Swiss efficiency combines with luxury; you can expect the staff to know your name the moment you check in. The rooms overlook Lake

Track No. 12 at Zurich's Hauptbahnhof, the central train station, above. Opposite: Lake Zurich, seen from the Hotel Baur au Lac.

Zurich, the city center, or the Schanzengraben canal, and are decorated in a range of styles, from Louis XVI to Chippendale. Baur au Lac's location at the foot of the Bahnhofstrasse puts the best of European shopping—Brunos for Italian menswear, Orell Füssli for English-language books on art and architecture, and Confiserie Sprüngli, the Ladurée of Zurich—within easy striking distance. What's more, the lake is just across the road, and the Restaurant Kronenhalle is only a five-minute walk over the bridge.

Anyone who knows Zurich knows the Kronenhalle, in part because it's a culinary classic, in part because it's a scene from another time. The restaurant is divided into a main salon, inhabited by regulars, and a pair of side rooms. Paintings by Marc Chagall and Joan Miró line the walls; the signature dishes, served in double portions, include schnitzel and rösti. The restaurant's bar was designed by Robert Haussmann,

godfather of Swiss Modernism, and is full of smooth tawny wood and bronze lamps created by Diego and Alberto Giacometti.

Evenings in Zurich have an alluring ease about them; it's the kind of place where you can decide to have a night out after you've folded your napkin at 10:30 p.m. At spots like the Odeon and Acapulco, the beautiful people party until the wee hours. And unlike their velvet-rope counterparts in London, Paris, or New York, these bars aren't manned by haughty bouncers. Zurich, after all, is a place that's sure enough of itself to dispense with any attitude. ✛

For The Guide, see page 273.

Germany

Zürs and
Lech, Austria

The Dornröschenschloss
hotel in Sababurg.

a storybook drive

ALONG THE BROTHERS GRIMM'S ROUTE IN **GERMANY**

IF YOU'RE LOOKING FOR CINDERELLA'S CASTLE, it's not far from the Pied Piper's village. No, this isn't Orlando—it's a 375-mile stretch between Frankfurt and Bremen. Two centuries ago, the Brothers Grimm began writing stories about the landmarks along the route, inspired by their fairy-tale–like qualities.

You can create a pilgrimage centered around their work. Start in Steinau an der Strasse at the House of the Brothers Grimm to see the authors' illustrated manuscripts and play electronic games starring Little Red Riding Hood and Snow White. An ideal spot for a deep slumber? Eighty-four miles away, in Sababurg, Sleeping Beauty's ivy-clad castle has become the dreamy Dornröschenschloss hotel. Another place to let down your hair? Rapunzel's 13th-century tower in Trendelburg has also been transformed into the

Hotel Burg Trendelburg, which comes complete with a dungeon. Cinderella's castle in Polle is now a ruin, which is all the better for reenactments of her story. And in the square of Hänsel and Gretel's half-timbered town of Höxter, the stage is set for performances of the siblings' saga from May through September. There's no need to leave a trail of bread crumbs to find your way back to Frankfurt: Get on the autobahn in Verden, and in four hours the whole trip ends happily ever after. ✛

For The Guide, see page 273.

austria's twin peaks

SKIING IN **ZÜRS** AND **LECH**

AUSTRIA'S TINY HAMLETS of Zürs and Lech have just the right mix of rustic style, heavenly powder, and snow bunnies—royal and plebeian. The mountains of Switzerland may be better known and bigger, but the relative modesty of Zürs and Lech, their disdain for hype, and the stodgy and anachronistic ethos of slow growth has turned out to be a boon. ▶

The façade of the Hotel Zürserhof.

Austrian slopes. Right: A room at Hotel Gasthof Post in Lech. Opposite, from top: Coffee hour at the Schneggarei bar in Zürs; slope signage.

In the early decades of the 20th century, the mountain towns were adopted by a snappy international ski set composed of prosperous and well-born Britons, Austrians, Germans, and Americans, who came for the season and climbed the Flexen Pass on foot from the rail station at Langen, their luggage following behind on sleighs. The antic sportiness continued until the arrival of the Nazis.

Beginning in the 1950's, a handful of families transformed Zürs and its sister town, Lech, from farmland into a world-class ski resort. Since then, waves of newcomers have continued to discover it, magnetized by the valley's numerous prime peaks, good powder, 73 miles of interconnected and groomed runs linked by a single-lift system, and 112 miles of off-piste trails. Still, it is a curiously unknown, insider's place, virtually free of the usual cut of British and German good-timers who want two weeks of sport and après-ski. In their stead,

one finds a mix of old European families, blue-chip CEO's, and royalty who have been coming here since skiing became hot in the 50's.

Zürs's pristine beauty, however, is not entirely immune from kitsch and narrative claptrap. In the Austrian Alps, travelers are gently encouraged to partake in the kind of high-altitude rusticity that may have more in common with Disneyland than the Alps. The welter of stag's heads, lederhosen, dirndls, and flower-painted stucco that are so common above a certain altitude are viewed as simple necessities in these towns, which rely on tourism for 100 percent of their income.

T+L Tip

GEAR UP AND GO

Gear Lech's sports emporium **Strolz Sporthouse** has ski and snowboard rentals, fur-lined Prada parkas, and Strolz's famous handcrafted boots, which can be custom-made in 24 hours.

Lessons Private or group lessons can be booked at either the Zürs or Lech ski schools. Both can arrange guided off-piste and heli-skiing outings.

But never mind. Just check in to the Hotel Zürserhof, where guests are presented with a hefty metal room key—one that the proprietor believes is a more human touch than the plastic wafer most hotels now use. Nearly 65 percent of the guests here book the same rooms annually, and the reasons are hardly mysterious—the view is of low slopes mantled with fresh powder. Another place to stay is the 39-room Hotel Gasthof Post, a favorite of the Dutch royals. The 51-room Hotel Almhof Schneider is where Prince Charles often stays. It's a fine example of the prevalent architecture: a peak-roofed ski chalet tastefully supersized.

In an attempt to tweak the area's architectural vernacular, the owners of Lech's Skihütte Schneggarei, a rough-hewn contemporary après-ski spot, prevailed in building a minimalist structure of peeled logs despite heavy opposition. It now attracts a crowd of hipsters to its club nights, where mammoth Vienna sausages and sturdy ales are consumed in quantity while the DJ spins the White Stripes and Missy Elliott in front of a big screen showing the latest snowboarding videos.

A hundred years ago, the area was a patchwork of dairy operations, rustic sheepfolds, and hunting clubs. A few decades later, legendary instructor Hannes Schneider had taken over the area's fledgling ski school and begun promulgating his innovative

stem-christie-rotation technique. Though rendered obsolete by new technology, elements of Schneider's approach persist in the formal elegance that remains a signature Austrian ski style—and a perfect metaphor for the time-stopped atmosphere in this Alpine region. ✛

For The Guide, see page 273.

fresh from the sea

A CULINARY TOUR OF **BRITTANY**

Homard à la Crème, the signature dish at L'Étrave, in Cléden-Cap-Sizun.

IN BRITTANY, the windswept corner of France that juts into the Atlantic toward England, you'll find the country's most ocean-centric cuisine. Prized oysters, *fleur de sel*, and seaweed butter are among the unforgettable ingredients of the twin fishing ports of St.-Malo and Cancale, on Brittany's northeast coast. Much of the oystering is concentrated in Cancale, where native Olivier Roellinger and his wife, Jane, preside over a mini empire of deluxe hotels and food boutiques. Grain de Vanille sells homemade ice cream and pastries, while Épices Roellinger trades in exotic spice blends and essential cooking oils; both serve as suppliers for the Roellinger kitchens at Château Richeux and the more ambitious Relais Gourmand Olivier Roellinger. The Cancale oyster market is presided over by women who shuck oysters to order and set them out on sturdy white plastic plates. The oysters' flavor is unmistakably North Atlantic, with sweet, cucumber-tinged brininess.

In Cléden-Cap-Sizun, on the farthest point of the west coast of the peninsula, the old-fashioned seafood restaurant L'Étrave makes grilled lobster that is legendary. It's nothing more complicated than the freshest specimens split down the middle, sluiced with the heaviest cream, and scorched under a broiler to darken the edges of the meat and the surface of the cream. Served in an oval pan, the lobster is heaven, plain and simple—so heavenly, you'll have to brace yourself for the inevitable return to earth. ✦

For The Guide, see page 273.

france's
seat of
style

CHIC
BOUTIQUES
IN **PARIS**

The Roger Vivier flagship store on Rue du Faubourg-St. Honoré. Opposite: Mona, a boutique on Rue Bonaparte.

AFTER YEARS OF BEING CONSIDERED too traditional, suddenly the City of Light is going modern. Indeed, Paris is proving to be the perfect answer to globalization. Where else could you find popular boutiques specializing in ribbons, walking canes, dollhouse furniture, and taxidermy? The Paris shopping scene changes every day; any one of the 20 arrondissements (really a cluster of little villages) can dramatically metamorphose from one year to the next. For instance, when the Canal St.-Martin area became the new place to live, the 10th was transformed. When renowned art galleries such as Emmanuel Perrotin first moved to Rue Louise-Weiss, the 13th became *la place*. And when the trendsetting store Colette opened on Rue St.-Honoré, the once-sleepy First Arrondissement was turned into the latest "it" destination.

Adapting is essential to life in Paris. As is being in the know. For many, it's where you can dress up in Lanvin or Balenciaga, layer on the chicest accessories with abandon, and don the highest of Christian Louboutin heels. But shopping here means anything but limiting your purchases to high-wattage names. There's a lot of life beyond Saint Laurent and Vuitton in boutiques that stock a well-edited selection of lesser-known but equally bright talents. The best spree involves visiting both types of stores: the classics and the independent newcomers.

The stylish Mona Blonde picks only the crème de la crème of the latest collections for her namesake store Mona. You'll find trousers by ▶

Bottles of Guerlain's Cologne Impériale, above, at the *parfumerie*'s boutique on Avenue des Champs-Élysées. Opposite, clockwise from top left: Bakelite bangles at 20 Sur 20; the Andrée Putman–designed Guerlain boutique; a vitrine at Mona in the Sixth Arrondissement; books on display at Karl Lagerfeld's Librairie 7L.

Chloé, skirts by Lanvin, suits by Alexander McQueen, and shoes by Marc Jacobs. Madame André sells the Gilles Dufour collection plus a mix of inexpensive items, such as perky underwear by I.C. Pearl and colorful bangles from India, displayed in a candy-pink interior. If you're heading to Paris to fill your trousseau, look no further than Fifi Chachnil. Fans of the lingerie designer's 50's-pinup style (push-up bras, marabou trimmings, lacy negligees) include Victoire de Castellane, Christian Dior's fine-jewelry designer. And for last season's designer clothes—both men's and women's—at exceptional prices, follow the lead of savvy Parisians to L'Habilleur. It's easy to spend what you save on your own clothes at Calesta Kidstore, the boutique Inès de la Fressange calls the Colette for kids. The sparse concept shop sells the trendiest European children's accessories and clothes, including jeans by France's Finger in the Nose and some of the chicest children's clothing by England's Caramel Baby & Child.

Every well-dressed Parisian knows that accessories—right down to perfume—can make or break an outfit. To find the season's status-symbol shoe, go to Roger Vivier, where you can easily pass an afternoon in the pampering atmosphere of his airy boutique. The shop 20 Sur 20 is every stylish local's closely held secret. Bakelite charm necklaces jingling with cherries, along with other costume jewelry dating from the 40's to the 60's, can be found at serious bargain prices. One of the rare gems for which the Left Bank is famous is Adelline, where Adeline

Roussel creates understated and infinitely wearable necklaces, bracelets, and dangling earrings out of unpolished gold, set with opaque ruby, smoky topaz, and lemon quartz from Brazil. Find lavish estate pieces—necklaces made of enamel pansies, intricate diamond rings, chunky gold bracelets—at Lydia Courteille, then peruse the hard-to-resist jewel-colored wallets, belts, watch straps, and organizers in ostrich, crocodile, and shagreen at Atelier du Bracelet Parisien. Having artisans on hand means quick turnaround of bespoke orders for out-of-towners. Everything is handcrafted and remains in pristine condition, even after years of use. The flagship Guerlain boutique on the Champs-Élysées has been superbly refurbished by style arbiter Andrée Putman. Take the gold mosaicked stairs, designed by architect Maxime D'Angeac, to the first floor for unfettered access to the house's more than 70 scents. If that doesn't satisfy, there's Editions de Parfums, renowned for putting sultriness back into scent. ▶

Owner and superstar perfumer Frédéric Malle's recently opened space—not to mention his seductive new fragrance Carnal Flower—lives up to that expectation. Finally, check out the sunglasses at the celebrated E. B. Meyrowitz Opticiens. They carry the best of both worlds: all the fabulous designer frames, plus their own exclusive line. Try them all, and channel your inner Jackie O.

Just as indulging in the fashion scene is essential to understanding Paris, so is grazing in the rarefied atmosphere of the antiques stores and bookshops. Antiquarian Pierre Passebon, the curator of Galerie du Passage, has impeccable taste and stocks the best 20th-century French furniture, made by the likes of Jean Royere and Emilio Terry, as well as works by contemporary artists such as Wendy Artin. The tomes at fashion designer Karl Lagerfeld's Librairie 7L are mostly photographic and are laid out like jewels on browser-friendly tables. Lagerfeld devours books at a daily rate and glibly describes the selection as "artistic Left Bank." But it's much more cosmopolitan than that. Recommended titles, many unavailable outside the country, include Raphaelle Saint-Pierre's *Villas 50 en France*, and *Paris* by the 30's photographer Moi Ver.

The retail scene in Paris may change often, but there are constants: always say *Bonjour* when you enter a shop, and hold the door when exiting the Métro. +

For The Guide, see page 273.

Boho Paris

A NIGHT OUT IN MONTMARTRE

The neighborhood of Les Abbesses in Montmartre is an artists' hangout. For one, singer Keren Ann (above) lives there. It's also a good starting point for a night out in Paris. Here is an ideal itinerary:

6:45 p.m. La Mascotte This unassuming brasserie with old wall tiles and a Bordeaux-themed clock is a good bet for belon oysters and a glass of chilled Macon. It looks like a scene out of Jean-Pierre Jeunet's *Amélie*, which was filmed nearby.

7:30 p.m. L'Oeil du Silence Look for hard-to-find DVD's and books in the high-ceilinged book and music shop with an eclectic mix of stock.

9:00 p.m. Café Burq Sit at the intimate bar with a glass of champagne at this true neighborhood spot (above) lit with sherbet-colored wall sconces. Menu highlights: roasted Camembert, chicken liver with mango and asparagus, rump steak with shallots and soy sauce.

9:45 p.m. Pigalle Down the hill from Les Abbesses on the bustling Boulevard de Clichy, this quartier is where you'll find the famed Moulin Rouge. It is also the home of the other Montmartre music halls, like Théâtre Le Trianon, with its red velvet seats and slanted stage.

10:15 p.m. Aux Noctambules Nights often end at this kitschy cabaret-style bar, where the drink specialty is a Vodka Pomme Frozen, made in a slush machine. The house act is an old-timer named Pierre Carré, who sings French classics while playing a keyboard or accordion.

The candy-pink storefront of Madame André.

The façade of the Hôtel Negresco.
Left: Sunseekers along the
Promenade des Anglais.

riviera reinvention

THE TWO SIDES OF **NICE**

NOT LONG AGO, IT WASN'T EASY being Nice. Travelers shunned France's fifth city as isolated and passé, electing not to spend their Riviera holidays in a listless community of shuffling retirees whose last wish before dying was a perfect hazelnut tan. Far from languishing beyond some imagined sell-by date, the city is being reinvented by an inspired citizenry of artists, chefs, designers, and hoteliers who are making Nice the destination for restless, heat-seeking Europeans. Even Parisians have changed their song—Nice has become their favorite weekend bolt-hole.

The grandeur of Nice has returned with the relaunched Palais de la Méditerranée, an Art Deco landmark built in 1930's. Shuttered in 1978, it is now a casino and luxury hotel that sits not a little imperiously on the Promenade des Anglais. It is also home to Le Padouk, a *restaurant gastronomique,* an alfresco zone with colossal windows that afford views of the Mediterranean. Down the street, the glass-domed Negresco, which opened at the height of the Belle Époque, is a good, old-fashioned hotel where owner Jeanne Augier and her poodle lunch every day.

The young face of Nice is more fun-loving. The Hi hotel, designed ▶

by Philippe Starck protégée Matali Crasset, has all of the playfulness of Starck's interiors, and then some. Crasset also created the Happy Bar, a very tonic, very graphic space inspired by the ribbed interior of a ship's hull. The Hôtel Beau Rivage is more in the Christian Liaigre mode: little color, lots of abrupt angles, dark-chocolate wood. The attraction for the buff couples in Pucci crushers and Burberry T-shirts is the hotel's beach club—the only one in town with a whiff of St.-Tropez.

There's not a Nice shopkeeper who hasn't been influenced by Jacqueline Morabito, the visionary decorator-designer with a namesake gallery and embroidery atelier in nearby La Colle sur Loup. Morabito made her name selling an idea of rusticity—poetic, theatrical, and somehow sincere despite its essential fauxness—to the bourgeoisie. Her store is filled with chunky furniture, ceramic-pearl necklaces, and wax candlestick holders. In a corner of her gallery next door, Morabito's Petite Épicerie stocks vintage tea towels, excellent olive oil, and a range of baskets.

A triple shot of Nice nightlife begins with a performance at the Opéra de Nice. The 1885 opera house is adorned with frescoes of Apollo so lyrical you'll leave the theater humming them. Next up: dinner at Le Grand Balcon, decorated by Jacques (Hôtel Costes) Garcia as the tufted salon of a lesser Rothschild. And finally, have a nightcap at the Café de Turin, which is falling apart, and the waiters aren't just gruff, they're mean—but it's still fabulous.

No matter your age, the way to do this city is to mix it up. ✦

For The Guide, see page 274.

Above: Le Padouk, the restaurant at the recently relaunched Palais de la Méditerranée, a Deco fixture dating from the 1930's.
Below: Strolling through the city's historic Place Centrale.
Opposite: The view from a balcony at the Negresco.

sets and the city
A CINEMATIC PILGRIMAGE TO **ROME**

Outside Cinecittà studios.
Opposite: Rino Barillari,
whom Fellini called the
first paparazzo.

THERE IS THE CITY of Rome. And then there is the city of Rome as it appears in movies. Federico Fellini called Rome "the most wonderful movie set in the world." It is in his pictures that Rome is most conspicuous, self-conscious, and beautiful. Indeed, when you're there, Fellini's movies seem more like life and less surreal.

Any Fellini-inspired pilgrimage to Rome would ideally begin with a visit to the Fellini Museum at Cinecittà film studios—if only it were that easy. Getting into the museum, which is not open to the public and is overseen by a man named Mannoni, a.k.a. The Widow, because of his singular devotion to his former boss, requires patience and perseverance. Protecting the Fellini flame is The Widow's one and only job, and it's up to him who is allowed to visit. The Fellini Museum includes a replica of the director's office, exactly as it existed at the time of his death in 1993. It's like one of those ancient castles that gets transported stone-by-stone from the European countryside to someone's backyard in Connecticut—except, in this instance, it got moved from one room on the lot to another. If you're lucky, you also get to see a faithful reconstruction of Fellini's work space. There is a huge desk, above which hangs a giant montage of faces, all in black-and-white, a crossword puzzle of headshots, some gorgeous and young, others disfigured, elegant, happy, somber—the whole pantheon of human expression filtered through a selective eye always looking for the extreme, the vulnerable, the needy, the exhibitionist, the unusual. A huge pea-green couch sits behind a low glass-topped table covered with neatly arranged magazines, whose covers all feature Fellini. Giant leopard-skin pillows rest at both ends. On the walls are storyboard drawings and photographs of starlets, with little thought bubbles scribbled above their heads.

Cinecittà's fortunes have waxed and waned, and in the late 90's it was privatized. Now it has a new management team and new momentum. It was where Scorsese shot *Gangs of New York*, Wes Anderson shot *The Life Aquatic*, and George Clooney shot *Ocean's Twelve*. Rome does not appear in these movies as a specific location, but it still comes through in other, more subtle ways. +

For The Guide, see page 274.

Celluloid Rome

From trendy Trastevere to the Trevi Fountain, Fellini's city is for film lovers. Jump on a scooter and see Rome, real and imagined.

Café de Paris Scene of the original *dolce vita*, later captured in the film; just beware of the paparazzi.

Caffè della Pace A favored perch of artists and literati.

Cesarina Specialties from Emilia-Romagna, at Fellini's old haunt.

Colosseum Without it, the swords-and-sandals epic movies—from *Ben-Hur* to *Gladiator*—might never have existed.

Harry's Bar Legendary piano bar where Frank Sinatra sang and film luminaries gathered.

Mouth of Truth Pinocchio's nemesis, and the portico where princess Hepburn tested the dissembling Peck in *Roman Holiday*.

Pantheon Setting for many a golden-age film.

Pino's Barbershop A baptism awaits at Fellini's former barber. Pino dunks his patrons into the sink face-forward before cutting their hair.

Scooters for Rent See the city by Vespa, as in *Roman Holiday*.

Spanish Steps Stunning city views above, high-end shopping below.

Trevi Fountain American girls used it to find husbands in *Three Coins in the Fountain*; Anita Ekberg preferred it as a tub.

Trastevere Director Wes Anderson's neighborhood of choice is lined with hip boutiques and bars.

The window display at Branchini Calzoleria, a boutique known for hand-stitched dress shoes. Opposite: A bird's-eye view of Piazza Maggiore, at the center of the city.

italy's best-kept secret

GETTING TO KNOW **BOLOGNA**

UNLIKE FLORENCE, ITS NEIGHBOR to the south, Bologna was a well-kept secret until 2000, when it was selected as a European Capital of Culture and tourism became a priority. World-class shopping followed. Considered Bologna's first concept store, L'Inde Le Palais draws the avant-garde crowd with periodic art exhibitions and a hip café across the alley that serves 35 varieties of wine. The impossibly cool staff sells everything from rare CD's to Valentino and Missoni couture gowns. Nearby, Spazio Minghetti is Italy's only Fendi furniture store open to the public. The Baroque, gold-laminated entryway and a garden with 19th-century statuettes offer a fitting contrast to the 16,000 square feet of contemporary pony-hair-covered sofas and antelope-skin rugs. In the center of town, designer Giovanna Guglielmi features her two clothing labels at 37 San Felice: the Working Overtime line plays with bias-cut pleats and ruffles, while vintage-inspired Tadashi features wrap skirts made from wool sweaters. Set on a wide avenue that attracts residents ▶

From left: Lasagne at Ristorante Diana; the café at L'Inde Le Palais.

for a nightly stroll, the packed Cappelleria Trentini more closely resembles a double-decker closet than a store, but the friendly assistants ensure a pleasant browsing experience with items from up-and-coming designers, including Bolognese-English duo Fiorentini + Baker's 40's-style leather sandals, and Flu's Ear white cotton dresses. The classics, however, still remain: La Perla, Les Copains, and Furla all got their start here. And the highest concentration of luxury boutiques, including dress-shoe maker Branchini Calzoleria, is in the area dubbed the quadrilateral, bordered by Via Rizzoli, Via Castiglione, Via Farini, and Via D'Azeglio.

A visit to Bologna would be incomplete without partaking in another form of conspicuous consumption here: eating. Bologna is the mother of many culinary staples—tortellini is practically an official city symbol. Legend has it a local baker modeled the shape after the belly button of the woman with whom he was having an affair. One of the best places to find the city's signature dish, *pasta in brodo* (broth), is the elegant Pappagallo, where autographed portraits of artists, actors, and diplomats testify to its affluent clientele. For an authentic Italian family-style meal, visit the pocket-sized Trattoria ai Butteri, south of the historic center. The 13 tables fill up fast with patrons craving Italian comfort food, like oversized portions of spinach-and-ricotta tortellacci and thick-cut *fiorentine* steaks.

Residents top off a day of indulgence at Gelatauro, which is run by three brothers who make organic gelato with oranges from their grove in Calabria. The ice cream shop has become internationally famous—so much so that it has attracted one of the local luminaries, Umberto Eco. ✦

For The Guide, see page 274.

For The Guide, see page 274.

T+L Tip

SWEET ON SWEETS

Looking for a decadent souvenir or a good way to end a meal? Treat yourself to some Cognac-filled chocolates at **Roccati**. Famous for the *gianduja* chocolate their ancestors made for the Princes of Savoy, the husband-and-wife team running the confectionary puts on a show for passersby in the shop's open-air laboratory, located right next door to their **La Sorbetteria Castiglione**, a one-of-a-kind *gelateria* where the sorbet flavors are named after family members.

master class

LEARNING TO DRAW AND PAINT IN **FLORENCE**

IT IS SAID THAT ONE-THIRD of the world's most important works of art are located in Florence. Indeed, for a few short centuries, the city produced some of the most talented painters in history—from Masaccio to Michelangelo. It's never too late, however, to take up a brush—or ▶

Student drawings at Charles H. Cecil Studios in Florence.

polish up on your drawing skills—and join the ranks of the latest Renaissance masters.

In Florence's Oltrarno district, where for centuries the art of the region has been made and mended in neighborhood workshops and bottegas, Charles H. Cecil Studios—the oldest operating atelier in the city—has been in continuous use as a drawing studio since the late 18th century. In fact, it's one of the last schools of fine art in the world that teaches pupils how to draw and paint like the Renaissance greats. Cecil, a tall man with strong chiseled features and longish hair, looks like everyone's idea of a master painter. Gravely exuberant, he welcomes students with a whirlwind tour of the atelier—the cast room; the sculpture room; the *gipsoteca*, a silo-like space that soars 90 feet high; and the drawing studio, where the first-year life class is held—all the while expounding on the importance of upholding the tradition of naturalistic figure painting. Cecil, who studied at Yale and apprenticed with two American painters, opened the school in 1983.

The atelier method discourages big enrollment numbers, which accounts for the fact that there are 35 or fewer students in the whole school and just 14 in the life-drawing class. Some attend short-term, to do a year's foundation course for art college or university; others are committed to becoming painters. The training is rigorous and intensive, but not without a wealth of enthusiasm on Cecil's part. On his designated two days for teaching, the gravely exuberant master stalks the room—kept steamy as a sauna for the life model's comfort—using his charisma to breathe fire into amateur souls. Despite this, a hushed concentration pervades the room. Cecil typically stands back, strokes his jaw, and proffers critiques that carry an authority invested in him by Michelangelo. Studio time is balanced by hours spent simply looking at art, an endeavor in which Cecil is glad to help. His strategy is based on opening hours: museums in the morning, churches in the afternoon. There are face-to-face encounters with works such as Leonardo da Vinci's *Annunciation*, Uccello's *Battle of San Romano I*, and Botticelli's magical *Primavera*. The

From top: Mixing blue pigment for paint; a bird's-eye view of Florence; a student in Charles H. Cecil's life-drawing studio. Opposite: A model sits for a painting class.

number of possible self-administered field trips is infinite. Each day after class, there's a chance to unlock the secrets of the masters; Cecil's instruction forces you to open your eyes regarding line and form. A visit to Santa Maria del Carmine's Brancacci Chapel, to see Masaccio's groundbreaking use of light and shade in the folds of a beggar's cloak, or a trip to Museo di San Marco, to detect the pencil work behind Fra Angelico's pious frescoes, are just a few examples of self-guided opportunities to apply your newfound knowledge. Thursday is lecture night at the atelier, with Cecil presiding over a large audience from Florence's English-speaking community. Afterward, everyone stands around drinking wine from paper cups and talking earnestly about tradition—just as artists have been doing for centuries. +

For The Guide, see page 274.

T+L Tip

EUROPEAN DRAWING SCHOOLS

Florence Academy of Art The school offers an all-year drawing program, and in July, month-long courses are taught in English.

Lavender Hill Studios Co-run by a Charles H. Cecil Studios alum, this London studio features informal sketching and atelier sessions plus drawing and painting classes.

Sarum Studio Nicholas Beer, also a Cecil alum, teaches two-week classes in the sight-size method in Wiltshire, England.

The bar at Arola, in
Barcelona's Hotel Arts.
Opposite: A view of Frank
Gehry's *Pez* sculpture
near Paseo Marítimo.

new catalan cuisine

A TASTING TOUR OF **BARCELONA**

WHEN IT COMES TO the sport of divining the next great food trend, all bets are off in experimental Spain, where traditional notions of dining are being pushed to the limit. Is there life after liquid-nitrogen caipirinhas and calcium-chloride ravioli? Barcelona's hotel restaurants might hold the answer. Though it's home to El Bulli Taller, the lab where Ferran Adrià develops his innovative (and wild) dishes, Barcelona never truly bought into alchemical cooking. This is a city as practical as it is playful, and restaurateurs here understand the need to reconcile progress with profit. So recently, when some of

the country's most visionary chefs opened informal places, they had to reexamine their cooking in order to please crowds and give those avant-garde critics something to chew on. As a result, chefs concocted a fresh urban style.

When Rosa María Esteva, the legendary *dueña* of the Tragaluz restaurant group, teamed up with the creative Roca brothers chef–sommelier–dessert whiz trio, they created Moo, the design-centric restaurant at Esteva's Hotel Omm. Famous for desserts that replicate the fragrances of well-known perfumes, the Rocas are now channeling their obsession with scents into revolutionizing wine and food pairings. After sniffing out the citrus, vanilla, and saffron notes in your Château Doisy Daëne Sauternes, marvel at the uncanny precision with which they are mimicked in a dessert of orange cream, saffron flan, honey *gelée*, brioche cubes, and apricot sorbet. ►

With its banquettes, *Jetsons*-like chairs, and small plates, Arola seems to recall a dozen other sceney hotel restaurants from Hong Kong to Hawaii, where the DJ outshines the chef. Then you actually taste El Bulli–trained Sergi Arola's food. His whimsical interpretations of tapas include dishes like faux *jamón* (tuna carpaccio drizzled with *jamón ibérico*–infused oil), wood-smoked sardines with seaweed *romesco*, and partridge *gelée* accented with pickled wild mushrooms. The reinvented *patatas bravas* (twice-cooked potato "cylinders" hollowed out to hold spicy tomato sauce and garlicky aioli) deserve a place in history.

Barcelonans are turning out in full force at Restaurant Gaig. Set in its mod room at Hotel Cram, the kitchen sends out retro dishes like airy salt-cod cakes, cubes of rare salt-cooked salmon atop velvety zucchini cream, and brittle-skinned suckling pig. Modern doesn't necessarily mean cutting-edge at Caelis, the dining room at the Hotel Palace, where Taillevent- and Ducasse-trained chef Romain Fornell exercises restraint in dishes like vibrant, light-as-air asparagus custard, and lamb that is cooked *sous vide* until it is soft enough to eat with a spoon. If formal dining is more your style, make sure to visit the expensive Drolma, at the Hotel Majestic. A specialist in grand, traditional dishes—*lièvre à la royale*, whole roasted *jarret de veau*—Drolma's Fermí Puig is among Spain's greatest

Clockwise from top left: Two of the three Roca brothers at Moo; Arola's smoked sardines; Chef Carles Gaig at his namesake restaurant; Moo's beet mousse with mandarin orange purée.

chefs. In a salon that seems plucked from an old master painting, Puig pampers Barcelonan businessmen and politicos with seasonal menus that might include langoustines with artichokes, potatoes, and a surprise hint of caramel; or *ventresca* (buttery tuna belly) enlivened with caviar and a palate-cleansing Chantilly.

For the best indication of where post-Adrià cooking is moving, head to Cinc Sentits, helmed by chef Jordi Artal, a Canadian with Catalan origins. Locals, tourists, and even those grouchy Madrid restaurant critics adore the place, and not just for the modestly stylish look and the gracious multilingual service, courtesy of Artal's charming sister and mother. +

For The Guide, see page 274.

T+L Tip

FOOD DETOURS

Come Saturday, Barcelonans leave town to eat at Catalonia's most famous restaurants. Here are three that are worth a trip:

● A scenic 45-minute train ride from the city, the Michelin-three-starred **Sant Pau**, in the seaside village of Sant Pol de Mar, is home to the modern Catalan food of chef Carme Ruscalleda.

● Santi Santamaría (Ferran Adrià's Michelin-three-starred archrival) redid his **Can Fabes** in Sant Celoni, 50 minutes from Barcelona, with an interior as contemporary as the cuisine is traditional.

● Santamaría also opened the less formal restaurant nook, **Espai Coch**, here, too. Use the money you save on dinner to book one of the five sleek guest rooms above the restaurant.

Shadow Amid Rings of Air, 2003, by Mexican artist Gabriel Orozco, at the Palacio de Cristal in Madrid's Parque del Buen Retiro. Opposite, clockwise from top left: The new wing of the Museo Thyssen-Bornemisza; its exterior; *Brushstroke,* 1996, by Roy Lichtenstein, in Reina Sofía's plaza.

art reigns in spain

THREE MUST-SEE MUSEUMS IN **MADRID**

IN 2005, WHEN QUEEN SOFÍA OF SPAIN inaugurated the spectacular $100 million, 290,000-square-foot expansion of her namesake museum, the Reina Sofía, in Madrid, she threw open the doors to a whole new era in the Spanish capital. With the massive expansions of its three biggest museums—Museo Nacional Centro de Arte Reina Sofía, Museo Thyssen-Bornemisza, and the eminent Prado—Madrid now has housing suitable for its peerless collections of masterworks by El Greco, Raphael, Velásquez, Rubens, Goya, Picasso, and Miró.

The Reina Sofía lures modern-art lovers not only with its shows, but also with the Jean Nouvel–designed complex itself, an assemblage of glass, steel, and fiberglass-composite structures that house galleries, a library, auditoriums, a restaurant, and an interior plaza. A five-floor addition to the Museo Thyssen-Bornemisza holds more than 200 works on loan from the Baroness Carmen Thyssen-Bornemisza collection, including canvases by non-Iberians like Hopper, O'Keeffe, and Kandinsky. Pritzker Prize–winning architect Rafael Moneo's new Prado, upon completion in spring 2007, will have double the floor space—it can now accommodate the museum's once-stored collection of 19th-century Spanish canvases—and will include a vast un-derground wing linking the museum's landmark building to several other structures. Not surprisingly, the Spanish government has thrown itself into promoting Madrid's Big Three, dubbing the culturally dense zone along the grand boulevard Paseo del Prado the Paseo del Arte ("Art Walk"). +

For The Guide, see page 275.

The pool at La Residencia,
with the town of Deya beyond.

artist colony

MAJORCA'S SERENE SIDE

WITH ITS SEMITROPICAL CLIMATE, Majorca, the largest of the Balearic Islands, has been drawing creative types ever since George Sand wrote the dyspeptic *Winter in Majorca*, about her 1839 sojourn with Frédéric Chopin. "Majorca is the painter's El Dorado," she noted. In 1871, Archduke Ludwig Salvator abandoned the Austro-Hungarian Empire and lingered here for years, working to preserve ancient olive trees and create walking paths in the mountains. He was embraced by the locals, who appreciated his reverence for their remote world. Sixty years later, Robert Graves, the English poet and novelist, settled in Deya, just inland from the northwest coast. "I found everything I wanted as a writer: sun, sea, mountains, spring-water, shady trees, no politics, and a few civilized luxuries such as electric light," Graves wrote about his adopted home. Since then, many artists have come to see Majorca as a similarly hospitable place to settle.

Accessible by quick flight from most of Europe into a modern airport, Majorca attracts more than eight million travelers a year; one out of every four people on Majorca is a foreigner. Still, it's surprisingly possible to find calm in a couple of places around the island: the mountainous northeastern area near Cap de Ferrutx; the towns of Pollença, in the north; and Soller, near the west coast.

Designer Sebastián Pons lives in Alquería Blanca, a tranquil village in the southeast, 15 minutes from the sea. "Everyone from the Greeks to the Romans to movie stars has come through or lived here," says Pons, whose father is a retired farmer on the island. "On Majorca, you live with people who influence you in all kinds of ways." José Carlos Llop, a prizewinning Majorcan-born author, lives in an undisturbed fishing village near Valldemossa on the east coast of the island. Another native son, renowned artist Miquel Barceló, has been working on a ceramic relief that will cover the expanse of the Cathedral of Palma. It tells the story of creation as Barceló sees it—that the world was born on his island. ✚

For The Guide, see page 275.

From top: The Formentor Peninsula; Artist Miquel Barceló poses in his Majorcan studio; in the garden at fashion designer Sebastián Pon's estate on the southeast side of the island.

modern revival

THE SECOND COMING OF **VALENCIA**

VALENCIA HAS ALWAYS been known for its oranges and paella, but these days Spain's third-largest city is more likely recognized for its stylish makeover. Once-neglected districts have become hipster hangouts; innovative restaurants and boutiques have sprouted; and the Valenciano skyline is embellished with the sprawling Ciutat de les Arts I de les Ciències, Santiago Calatrava's swooping collection of white, organically contoured museums and theaters.

Upmarket designer hotels, especially, signal Valencia's change in fortunes. The tranquil Hospes Palau de la Mar, two remodeled 19th-century buildings, balance contemporary steel and glass touches with ornate original details; and the modernist Hotel Neptuno, on the Platja de Malvarrosa, evokes Miami.

A host of innovative chefs are raising Valencia's gastronomic standing, too. Intrepid gourmands venture into the less-polished Grao neighborhood to seek out Ca'Sento, the intimate family-run haute temple now headed by Ferran Adrià disciple Raúl Aleixandre. Just off the Plaça Reina, hip Valencianos and tourists alike drink *vinos tintos* at the inviting Burdeos in Love. +

For The Guide, see page 275.

Dining at Valencia's Burdeos in Love, left.

Valencia

Alentejo,
Portugal

A vineyard in Alentejo, left. Above: Rounds of *queijo artesanal* on display at the Saturday market in Estremoz, a good starting point for a wine expedition.

uncorking the old world

A TOUR OF **ALENTEJO**

IT'S ONLY AN HOUR'S DRIVE east from Lisbon to the mountainous Alentejo region, but that's far enough to transport you to a Portugal of another time: one of oxcarts, sleepy medieval villages, and, along the Rota dos Vinhos (or Wine Route), centuries-old vineyards. Lately, however, many of these wineries—with the help of vintners from Australia, France, and the Napa Valley—have begun updating their methods, introducing grape varieties similar to those that revolutionized dormant vineyards in Tuscany and southwestern France. The result: some of the most exciting new wines in Europe.

Herdade do Esporão, in the center of Reguengos de Monsaraz, is one of the region's best-known wineries. Its Esporão Reserva is a complex blend of native and Cabernet Sauvignon grapes, drinkable as is but with a tannic structure clearly intended for Bordeaux-like mellowing with age; sip some at the winery's airy restaurant, where regional specialties such as salt cod and chickpea stew are on the menu. The glamorous Quinta do Carmo dates back to the 17th century and is currently owned by the Rothschilds of Château

Lafite. Each grapevine here looks as well tended as a bonsai. The robust reserve is made with 75 percent local grapes, with Cabernet and Syrah accounting for as much as 40 percent. This is a big wine that will stand up to hearty Alentejan food like fried pork with clams—or a juicy American steak.

Of course, some of the area's wineries have kept things deliberately old school. At the picturesque and quirky Herdade do Mouchão, owners Ian and Emily Richardson operate as if electricity and winemaking advances were never invented (grapes here are either hand-crushed or trod on). Once you taste the Mouchão Tinto, you'll realize there's something to be said for resisting modernity. ✛

For The Guide, see page 275.

The dining room at Restaurante Eleven in Lisbon. Opposite: In the lobby of the Four Seasons Hotel Ritz Lisbon.

portugal's star turn

LISBON AFTER DARK

THERE'S A SPIRIT OF CELEBRATION in the air today. Foodies, design buffs, and aficionados of boutique hotels flock to the sun-drenched city, which Francisco Capelo, a prominent 50-something donor to the Museu do Design, which is currently undergoing renovation, characterizes as "Santa Monica surrounded by 800 years of art."

Since 2001, about one-third of Lisbon's buildings have been renovated. Faux-hawked hipsters still party in the streets of the Bairro Alto neighborhood, but now they share graffiti-etched corners with boutiques from independent fashion designers and, most notably, the airy Bairro Alto Hotel, a 55-room jewel in a renovated 18th-century building. It's been more than two decades since promoter Manuel Reis opened Frágil, his first dance club in Lisbon. The Bairro Alto venue sealed the city's reputation as a town that can get down. A shopping focal point in the neighborhood is the boutique Alves/Gonçalves—Portuguese society's designer team of choice—who fashions chic, ready-to-wear suits and gowns and sells them

from their Chiado outpost. This is also where the city's artistic elite go to eat top-notch Portuguese soul food; Pap'Açorda is a casual minimalist mainstay. Around the marble-walled room are vases with pale pink peonies under a ceiling of Murano glass.

A similar rebirth is happening in Lisbon's other precincts, too. The once-abandoned San Apolonia docks now house megaclub Lux, its chic sister restaurant Bica do Sapato (co-owned by John Malkovich), mid-century Modernist furniture boutique Lojadatalaia, and Deli Delux, a gourmet-food emporium.

Worldwide attention hasn't stripped the city of its traditional flavor. In fact, *lisboetas* are embracing their hometown's customs like ▶

A Lisbon hipster, above. Right: At Bica do Sapato. Opposite, from top: Pear cake at Pastelaria-Padaria São Roque; the nightclub Lux.

never before, even those that are a bit redolent of Salazar's dictatorship. A case in point is *fado*; the mournful national music of love and loss was actively promoted by the dictator. And while locals still turn their noses up at *fado* clubs, which they consider touristy, invite one to join you at a place like Sr. Vinho, a low-ceilinged boîte in the quiet Lapa neighborhood, and you'll see your friend silently mouthing the words as the shawl-draped *fadista* wails along to the acoustic guitar. Another instance of the appreciation for the ambiguous beauty of a checkered past is the enduring social centrality of Four Seasons Hotel Ritz Lisbon, a stunning example of high Modernist glamour originally commissioned by Salazar in the 50's. It is a capacious, gilt-edged sanctuary with museum-

quality sculptures and tapestries on every wall. In 2003, an appropriately luxurious spa and pool were added to the storied hotel.

Lisbon's warm embrace of the past, however, reaches further back than the mid 20th century. Portuguese architect Miguel Cancio Martins, the designer of Paris's Buddha Bar and New York's Man Ray, is making over a late-18th-century mansion on the grand, tree-lined Avenida da Liberdade for Lisbon's Hoteis Heritage group. The city's oldest neighborhood, the windy, steep Alfama, which dates back to the eighth century, is where you'll find smart boutique hotels created from castles. The three-year-old yellow-washed Solar do Castelo is a former 18th-century maisonette inside the walls of a Moorish castle; the elite, eccentric Palácio Belmonte, is an 11-room, antiques-filled oasis fashioned from a 15th-century house.

Not that shiny new venues are getting overlooked. Droves of Lisboáns make weekend-afternoon pilgrimages to the Parque das Nações, which was recently built on what used to be a dingy industrial wasteland northeast of the city. Now it's a large garden

adjoined by striking examples of contemporary architecture, especially Alvaro Siza's spaceship-style sports arena and exhibition hall, Pavilhão de Portugal, and Peter Chermayeff's Oceanário, the second-largest aquarium in the world. Another addition to the city is Eleven, a sleek restaurant with an ambitious contemporary Mediterranean menu by chef Joachim Koerper that became an instant hot spot when it opened in the Amália Rodrigues garden of Parque Eduardo VII. Its steep prices have caused a bit of an uproar, but the clientele is solidly Portuguese. Eleven's one Michelin star was the city's first.

Still, this is no spit-shined capital like Copenhagen. In Lisbon, you might attend a dance party in an old mansion in a rather tumbledown state, where peeling, formerly grand frescoes are more sensuous than sad. But ramshackle doesn't stop even sixty-somethings from showing up. Nobody seems to mind the last packs of chatty photographers, DJ's, graphic designers, and rowdy teenagers spilling out of the dozens of dimly lit techno-music bars around town at 2 a.m. on any given weekend. They'll be gone in the morning, when stray cats and old ladies gladly resume their daytime dominion of the place. +

For The Guide, see page 275.

untouched isles

A LONG QUIET DRIVE THROUGH THE **AZORES**

WITH THEIR VELVETY PASTURES and calm, subtropical breezes, the tranquil islands of the Azores are among the last places in Europe where the quaintness isn't manufactured. Indeed, this autonomous region of Portugal has been off the map for non-European travelers until recently, when an increase in direct flights from the United States and a mini-hotel boom placed it squarely on the radar.

The best way to take it all in is to drive. São Miguel, the largest island, is easily the most cosmopolitan place between Montauk and Gibraltar, though this is not immediately apparent. New hotels recast local tradition, such as Convento de São Francisco, where a 16th-century former nunnery has been fabulously refurbished. A two-hour drive along the rugged southern shore reveals Nordeste, a town where romantics thrill to the craggy, empty coastline from the lookout points at Ponta da Madrugada. On the northern side of the island, visit the Gorreana Tea estate, Europe's only green-tea plantation, then race up the narrow straightaway west of nearby Ponta Delgada to Sete Cidades, the fabled twin azure crater lakes.

Terceira, the sunniest of all the islands, also has the most action. The colorfully tiled waterfront town of Angra do Heroísmo attracts an international yachting crowd. Those who don't overnight on the water stay at the Quinta das Mercês, a converted 18th-century farmhouse with plush beds and an infinity pool; or the Pousada at Forte de São Sebastião, a stylishly updated 16th-century fortress. A detour through the middle of Terceira brings you to Terra Brava, a dense green landscape of broken hills created by violent lava eruptions. Along the north shore, more than 10,000 vantage points offer stunning water views on the way to Ponta da Furna, a jagged cove with black-lava formations frozen in the surf. +

For The Guide, see page 275.

A view of the countryside.
Opposite, from left: Local
residents; an entrance
to the botanical garden
on Terceira island.

Mykonos windmills. Right: Salmon and sea-bass sashimi with truffles at Matsuhisa Mykonos in the Belvedere. Opposite: An afternoon party at Super Paradise Beach on Mykonos.

greece's party central

SUN AND FUN ON **MYKONOS**

ON MYKONOS, THE OCEAN air is the only trace of a chill vibe. The cosmopolitan Cycladic island has a history of wild nightlife that dates back to the disco era. Though it's often represented on postcards by sun-bleached churches (there's a minimalist aspect to its white-on-white architecture, as if Calvin Klein had designed the entire island), jet-setters who descended in the late 60's have less pristine memories. Then considered an unpretentious alternative to St.-Tropez, Mykonos was the "it" place for Studio 54 habitués who barhopped in flip-flops. Some ambitious locals are giving Mykonos the makeover it deserves.

Nowhere is this more evident than at the Belvedere. The Greek island's Schrageresque boutique hotel has a Delano-worthy pool scene, a luxurious in-house spa, and Matsuhisa Mykonos, an outdoor outpost of the restaurant Nobu. "Before the big hotels came, it was all about eccentricity: gay, straight—everyone had a good time," says Tasos Ioannidis, who, along with his brother Nikolas, manages the Belvedere.

Mykonos's party scene takes place at all hours, and some of the wildest dancing is done on the beaches—especially the bikini-optional ones. Not only does Mykonos claim a famously clothing-optional strand

called Paradise (home to the moonlit raves of Cavo Paradiso, a cliff-top club where famous DJ's spin), but it also one-ups the nirvana concept with Super Paradise, a onetime gay beach that's now the site of some of the island's most enthusiastic and impromptu daily dance parties. +

For The Guide, see page 275.

T+L Tip

SIDE TRIP TO SANTORINI

When you're in the Cyclades, it's worth taking a 2½-hour high-speed ferry from Mykonos to the photogenic island of **Santorini**. The iconic isle is best known for white-washed buildings, craggy cliffs, and stunning sunsets. The **Katikies Hotel,** in the northern town of Oia, has some of the best views from its traditional cave houses.

Eastern Europe

The view north from the colonnade of St. Isaac's Cathedral, across the Neva River, in St. Petersburg, Russia.

croatia's côte d'azur

ALONG THE **DALMATIAN COAST**

AMONG A CERTAIN SET, the coast and islands of southern Croatia are the premier destination in the Mediterranean. They glimmer on the periphery enough to attract the trendiest of visitors, yet hang enough off the radar to elicit blank stares among the rest.

Europeans have long favored Croatia's resorts as a low-key alternative to Greece, Italy, and Spain. For good reason: this is the most stunning coastline in Europe—a mix of limpid bays, craggy bluffs, hidden

coves and beaches, vineyards, olive groves, and forests of cypress and pine. Remarkably well-preserved ancient towns hold vivid examples of Greek, Roman, Venetian, and Slavic architecture. The sailing and yachting scene rivals any other destination, with hundreds of ports and dozens of marinas and countless natural inlets scattered across a thousand islands. Dalmatian cuisine—consisting of superb fish, shrimp, octopus, and oysters, along with increasingly recognized wines—has much in common with Italian cooking, and borrows heavily from it: here, risotto becomes *rizot*, and prosciutto becomes the delectable *pršut*. But Dalmatian food is earthier and rougher than Italian, blending hints of Hungarian, Turkish, and Slavic. It's also exceptionally affordable.

There's a town or island along the coast to suit every style: the two-faced Dubrovnik, with its push-cart vendors proffering handmade olive soaps alongside Benetton and Diesel boutiques, thickly forested Korčula's pine-fringed promenade and pebbly beaches, glamorous St.-Bart's-on-the-Adriatic Hvar, sporty Brač, and insular Vis.

Dubrovnik, Dalmatia's most famous city on the mainland, is touted as an unspoiled gem. While it's not yet as overrun as, say, Prague or Positano (the two unlikely places that Dubrovnik most resembles), it's well within the crosshairs of mass tourism. The summer crowds tend to gather on the main streets of the Old Town, but if you walk up any lane into ▶

Sunning on Zlatni Rat (Golden Cape) in Brač, Croatia's most famous beach, above. Below: The harbor in Korčula Town, on Korčula Island. Opposite: Korčula Town by night, overlooking the harbor.

the higher parts of town, you'll be alone in breathing in the jasmine and lemon-tree scented air and taking in the view across the city's orange roofs to the vividly blue Adriatic beyond.

The sharp scent of pine resin mingles with salt air on Korčula, a three-hour ferry ride from Dubrovnik and one of the Adriatic's most verdant islands. It's known for top-notch wines and for being one of several alleged birthplaces of Marco Polo. Korčula's main attraction, mean-while, is the town by the same name, a snow-globe version of Dubrovnik, with a compact historic quarter encased within stone walls. The place looks to be carved from a single piece of stone—like an Adriatic Petra on a decidedly smaller scale, with squat fluted windows and minuscule doorways rimmed with green shutters. One can alternate stints at the sun-drenched beach with cooling strolls down the old quarter's narrow, winding lanes. After biking out through the vineyards on nearby Lumbarda, where the island's famous Grk wine is made, head to Vela Przina beach, a sandy strand on Korčula's southern peninsula, for a bracing and beautiful swim. ✚

For The Guide, see page 276.

The rocky Dubrovnik shore.

poland's cool central

THE NIGHT IS YOUNG IN **KRAKÓW**

WHILE HISTORY—in the form of Baroque churches and 15th-century reliefs—attaches itself to nearly every street in Kraków, the city, since the arrival of capitalism in 1989, has also become a place to let loose. Kraków's ancient streets are being infused with vital new energy, as ancestral palaces are converted into ▶

A regular at Bar Propaganda in Kraków.

A sculpture on display in Kraków, left. Above: Kraków's main square, Rynek Główny. Opposite: A sculptural birdcage at the Bunkier Sztuki Café.

hotels and a vibrant crop of cafés and art galleries opens up, recalling the transformation of Prague in the early 1990's. Much of the vigor is concentrated in the nightlife scene, with its countless bars, dance halls, and music clubs filled with youthful international travelers.

At 10 acres, Rynek Główny is the largest medieval square in Europe. The buzz of activity in Kraków radiates out from Rynek Główny for a few blocks in each direction to areas just outside the Old City—most notably the newly fashionable, bohemian district of Kazimierz. The appropriately named Dym (Polish for "smoke") is the rendezvous spot for the aristocratic set, a place to stop in at any hour for a drink or three before moving on to another bar or for a walk across the square. A former courtyard garage, Dym is decorated with found bentwood

chairs and round wooden 1930's tables; the walls are painted an appropriately smoky blue-gray. A few blocks down from Dym, on Florianska, a busy pedestrian street lined with bars and sneaker shops, is Pauza, a bar that is a favorite with late-night regulars. Carefully hidden one floor above the street, this dimly lit spot, dotted with low-slung sofas, is the ultimate chill-out lounge. A wall opposite the long bar is plastered with 8-by-10 head shots of the regulars. Nearby, at Bar Propaganda, the busts of Lenin and posters of handsomely muscled workers supply a tongue-in-cheek nostalgic mood that attracts artists and resident hipsters. Down Florianska and across the square is Prozak, a noisy disco and bar half a flight below street level, where most of the men wear sports jackets and some of the women look dressed for the hunt.

And then there's the café scene. Guidebooks list more than 300 places to raise a glass or sip a coffee in the Old City alone. Among the most popular coffee houses for the art, literary, and music crowd are the Bunkier Sztuki ("Art Bunker") Café in Kraków's museum of contemporary art and Café Brankowa on the grand square, the ultimate spot for people-watching. +

For The Guide, see page 276.

For The Guide, see page 276.

white christmas

CELEBRATING IN
ST. PETERSBURG

SOME COUNTRIES live off collective memory—rough-hewn stone monuments, mournful anthems, goats ritually slaughtered in honor of some lunar god—but in Russia the national pastime is forgetting. It is not, however, commonplace to forget the winter holidays. According to a law passed recently by the country's parliament, Russians now enjoy a 10-day respite (January 1 through January 10) from their jobs, centered around the Russian Orthodox Christmas: the holiday season to end all holiday seasons.

If you don't believe that St. Petersburg is the most beautiful city in the world during Christmas, wake up in Room 403 of the Grand Hotel Europe and look out your window. Directly ahead you'll find the vast snowed-in lemon wedge of the neoclassical Mikhailovsky Palace. To the left, the flamboyant gold and tutti-frutti domes of Church of the Savior on Blood. Built as a nationalist rebuke to this elegant and slavishly European city, the church will bring to mind the famous onion domes of St. Basil's in Moscow (no wonder St. Petersburg's Europhile architectural snobs wanted to dynamite it). To the right, the golden spire of the Engineers' Castle, a quirky apricot fortress-like château, erected on the orders of the rightly paranoid Czar Paul, who was strangled with his own sash a mere 40 days after moving in. And, finally, in the ▶

The pedestrian
Lion's Bridge over the
Griboedov Canal.

distance across the Neva River, the festively lit Soviet-era television tower.

No matter how much *gorilka*—a Ukrainian firewater often blended with honey and pepper—one puts away the previous night, in the wintertime it is important to wake up, drink some coffee, and get your galoshes on by 8:30, just before the sun is about to rise. Marvel at the four winged lions on the pedestrian Lion's Bridge, then stroll across the Neva River to fashionable Petrogradskaya and the St. Petersburg Mosque—reminiscent of the fabled mosques of the Silk Road city of Samarkand. Down Kronverksky Prospekt stands the mansion of the prima ballerina Matilda Kshesinskaya, lover of ill-fated Nicholas II, the last czar of Russia. Inside one can find the Museum of Russian Political History, a collection of artifacts tracing Russia's experiments with monarchism, Communism, capitalism, and any other *ism* to come along.

Theme restaurant *Zov Ilyicha* (Lenin's Mating Call) brings the whole Soviet era into perspective by interspersing Communist party speeches with western pornography on a series of flat-screen televisions. If you're a budding grad student looking for a post-structuralist dissertation, look no further. Despite all of the distractions, the food, surprisingly, is excellent. The *zakuski* include a delicate salmon in vodka, slippery marinated

mushrooms, and a comforting plate of homey boiled potatoes. Entrées, like the bear-meat *pelmeni* (Russian ravioli)—are imbued with a vague hint of winters comfortably spent in a lair. The new elite, however, prefer to dine at modernist Moscow, where waiters in perfectly distressed jeans and T-shirts toss around $20 plates of foie gras and veal kidneys.

Though kitsch and minimalism are locked in a daily struggle throughout St. Petersburg, Christmas here is still a remarkably low-key affair. On Christmas Eve, an austere meal of honey-soaked wheat kasha is served. Midnight mass takes place in the city's main functioning church, the Kazan Cathedral, an elegant early-19th-century version of St. Peter's in Rome. Inside, the proceedings are suffused with a lavender glow, overpowering incense, and flickering amber candles. ✚

For The Guide, see page 276.

T+L Tip

ST. PETERSBURG STOPS

Devoting time to see the azure tiles and twin fluted minarets of the St. Petersburg Mosque and attending holiday midnight mass at the Kazan Cathedral, the city's main functioning church, are musts, but so, too, are the following attractions:

Chesme Church The raspberry and white candy box is an outrageous example of the neo-Gothic in Russia, made all the more precious by its location between an unremarkable hotel and a particularly gray Soviet block. The eye reels at the church's mad collection of seemingly sugar-coated spires and crenellations; here is a building more pastry than edifice.

Moskovskaya Ploshchad A model of Soviet "gigantomania," the enormous Stalin-era square is centered around a statue of Lenin with his coat sexily unfurling in the wind (some locals have dubbed him the Latin Lenin).

Nevsky Prospekt A combination of New York's Fifth Avenue, Chicago's Michigan Avenue, and L.A.'s Sunset Strip, and home to the Grand Palace mall, built with enough marble to redo the Parthenon.

Mikhailovsky Palace at The Russian Museum This city-block-size structure houses the permanent exhibition of the museum, tracing the entire history of Russian art from the 10th to 20th centuries.

Dacha A hip club near Nevsky Prospekt. Picture the most crowded, of-the-moment joint in Williamsburg, Brooklyn, and multiply the density by 10. Kraftwerk blares from the sound system, "No more Putin!" graffiti covers the bathroom walls, and foosball is played in the back

A waitress at the Soviet-themed restaurant Lenin's Mating Call, above. Below: Inside Moscow, a trendy restaurant where minimalism rules. Opposite: Lighting candles at St. Petersburg's Chesme Church on the Russian Orthodox Christmas day.

ukrainian tradition

THE PLEASURES OF **ODESSA**

Odessa's St. Panteleimon Church. Opposite, from top: A display at the Odessa Literary Museum; at the Pushkin monument.

FOR ANYONE WHO HAS TRAVELED elsewhere in the former Soviet Union, Odessa feels like a sunstruck Mediterranean version of Russia, where strolling couples promenade with Neapolitan insouciance along the seaside walks, jackets draped over their shoulders.

In the 19th century, Russian aristocrats built summer villas here, designed not as places to live so much as stage sets for the all-night balls in which the counts and countesses delighted. Many of the old palaces are crumbling, but a few have been at least partially restored as museums and private art galleries. Thanks to a less thoughtful recent construction project, the bronze likeness of the Duc de Richelieu, the region's first governor, in exile from France, now gazes at the Hotel Odessa, a glass-and-steel building that hulks between the famous Potemkin steps and the harbor—a reminder that the influx of foreigners, and foreign capital, has begun afresh. Nevertheless, the city's essence remains captured in the architectural ensemble of St. Elias Cathedral and St. Panteleimon Church, as well as the antique Assumption Monastery.

Odessa has a long legacy of attracting artists. Tchaikovsky came to Odessa to conduct at the Academic Opera and Ballet Theater. Liszt played piano recitals here, and Gogol staged a comedy. Chekhov wrote his letters from the Londonskaya Hotel—a vast Romanesque pile—and Pushkin lived in the city for several years in the 1820's, writing poems and taking in performances of Rossini. Odessa is a different place now, but the many beautiful façades remain the same. ✚

For The Guide, see page 276.

the big chill

LAPLAND'S GULF OF BOTHNIA

THIS POLAR STRETCH of northern Finland is not just Santa's stomping ground. From December through April, a former Arctic icebreaker operates four-hour excursions from Kemi, Finland, into the glacial Gulf of Bothnia. Passengers tour the colossal ship, hike across pack ice, and wear watertight suits for one of the world's chilliest dips—in 31-degree waters. On clear nights throughout the year, visitors can catch a glimpse of the striking yellow, green, and red of the aurora borealis. Top off the adventure with a cool stay at Kemi's unusual Mammut Snow Hotel, which is located within the walls of the world's biggest snow castle, open from January to April—or until the rooms start melting.+

For *The Guide, see* page 276.

A cool swim in the Gulf of Bothnia.

finnish line

DRIVING FROM **FINLAND** TO RUSSIA ON THE KING'S ROAD

WHEN SWEDISH KINGS PLUNDERED eastward into Russia, and Russian czars plundered back, they followed what's now known as King's Road. The same stretch runs from eastern Finland, over the border into Russia, through St. Petersburg, and on to Moscow. The unofficial road has been cobbled together from history and hearsay. It sometimes follows highways but more often runs along byways, winding through pine and white-birch forests, past country manors and stone churches. Start in Turku, home of Finland's National Cathedral and its oldest medieval castle, both of which date to the 13th century; stop in Helsinki for a steam; look out for numerous freshly restored, often yellow, palaces on the banks of the Neva River; and arrive finally at the golden spires and brick walls of the Kremlin and the fittingly majestic Hotel National. ✛

For The Guide, see page 276.

King's Road, near the Finland-Russia border.

The Galata Bridge, above. Inside the Grand Bazaar, left. Opposite: Istanbul's 17th-century Blue Mosque, in Sultanahmet.

eastern empire

EXOTIC MEETS MODERN IN **ISTANBUL**

ISTANBUL HAS ALWAYS BEEN marked by contrasts— east and west, secular and sacred. Now, as it attempts to bridge the gulf between Europe and the Muslim world, the city's split personality is more intriguing than ever.

Old empires, as the saying goes, cast long shadows, and few things rival the sensation one has in the ancient part of Istanbul of immersion in continuous history, of time compressed and consciousness intensified. In fact, a visit to the city's fabled Grand Bazaar is one of the best ways to take pleasure in flowing into the overlapping realities of the place. The great welter of fabulous colors, thick aromas, and dinning commerce are set in a labyrinth of 4,000 stalls, which could easily command any number of return trips. Buried among the fake red Capri coral, machine-milled Anatolian carpets, and ubiquitous bone-inlaid boxes, there are fantastic treasures to be found.

One could spend a week exploring the mosques of Mimar Sinan; wandering through the subterranean world of the Basilica Cistern, with its mossy vaults and thicket of ancient columns; and admiring the treasures of the Topkapi Palace, and so much else. Two, or even three, visits would be barely enough for the Archaeological Museum, which houses the contents of Hadrian's villa.

By staying in the Sultanahmet (the Old City), where 21-year-old Sultan Mehmet captured Constantinople on May 29, 1453, you can choose among lodgings that afford spectacular views of the Blue Mosque, Istanbul's 17th-century architectural masterpiece, the sublime Hagia Sophia, and the absurd purple sunsets that frame hills pin-cushioned with sky-pricking minarets. The options ▶

T+L Tip

THE ISTANBUL FOOD SCENE

In a city being touted as Europe's new capital of cool, there are many restaurants that live up to the hype.

Balikçi Sabahattin Frequented by the local power elite, this spot is a favorite for its mezes and fish.

Hamdi Restaurant The typical kebab restaurant has a tremendous variety of mezes and great views of the city.

Mabeyin This sultan-worthy setting for spicy Gaziantep cuisine is fitted into a 19th-century wooden villa that once belonged to a pasha. Claim a table under a pine tree in the garden.

Nisantasi Brasserie Stylish street-level restaurant for people-watching at the Beymen department store in the posh residential quarter of Nisantasi.

Reina A kind of mall of open-air restaurants and lounges, set on the Bosporus. This is where the beau monde goes to see and be seen.

360 Istanbul The concrete-and-glass space atop a 19th-century apartment building has sweeping views of Istanbul, from the Bosporus to the Sea of Marmara. The globetrotting menu takes its influences from Spain, Lebanon, China, and Turkey.

range from a simple, clean room in a mansion to the Four Seasons Hotel Istanbul.

But the city's historic wonders are only part of the story. New museums, shops, and restaurants make it easier than ever for visitors to explore the contemporary side of Istanbul, where the population has grown from 900,000 to 10 million in just over 50 years. The Istanbul Modern, an airy space on the Bosporus, houses collections of Turkish and international sculpture, painting, and new media. The fine, privately funded Pera Museum, set in an opulently converted 19th-century mansion, on a ridge overlooking the Golden Horn, is another example of modern Istanbul.

At the end of the day, stillness takes over finally, broken by the cawing of gulls around the domes of the great mosque and a brief crackling microphone sound as a muezzin prepares to intone the last of the day's prayers. Recited by observant Muslims, the Yatsi invokes God's blessings and concludes a cycle of daily devotion that will begin again just before dawn. ✚

For The Guide, see page 276.

The Interior of the Suleymanie
Mosque. Opposite, from top: The crowd
at 360 Istanbul; Nisantasi Brasserie.

contemporary czech

BRNO'S MODERN ARCHITECTURE

BRNO IS THE Czech Republic's second-largest city, a modest Chicago to Prague's increasingly flashy New York. Between the wars, it embraced the design ideals of the Bauhaus and adopted an architectural style that became known as Brno Functionalism. The 1,000-plus clean-lined Modernist buildings around town are as big a draw as the cafés in its medieval square.

Finding the houses, schools, churches, and stores represented by the 44 dots on the "Modern Architecture in Brno" map can fill up days. The Vila Tugendhat, one of Ludwig Mies van der Rohe's first important works, is built into the side of a hill overlooking town. The building's main floor has an open plan similar to his Barcelona pavilion, with massive windows, curving walls, and an iridescent onyx room-divider.

While the Vila Tugendhat is quite grand, Nový Dům is what Brno Functionalism was really all about: simple, practical architecture for ordinary people. These three-story row houses feature details such as balconies that are so rudimentary they might have been fashioned from Play-Doh.

For those craving something more monumental, Pavilion A, the result of the 1928 architectural competition won by Prague architect Josef Kalous, embodies both a Modernist passion for structure and a Gothic sense of awe, with its giant wishbone-shaped concrete ribs supporting a glass (now Plexiglas) ceiling. Quiet, understated Brno is slowly beginning to trade up: the naïve optimism of Modernism's past for the unvarnished opportunism of the present. **+**

For The Guide, see page 276.

Inside Ludwig Mies van der Rohe's 1930 Vila Tugendhat, above. Below: Pavilion A, constructed for the 1928 Exhibition of Contemporary Culture in Czechoslovakia. Opposite: One of the Nový Dům row houses, built in 1928 to commemorate the republic's 10th anniversary.

the new switzerland

A DRIVE THROUGH SLOVENIA

SLOVENIA HAS ALL the romantic attributes you'd expect to find on a trip to Switzerland—cobblestone streets, sky-blue lakes, snowcapped mountains, historic grand hotels—plus a cosmopolitan capital (Ljubljana) and an up-and-coming wine region. A five-day drive from Ljubljana in the center, then southwest to the coast and north on the Italian border to the Julian Alps, is the perfect way to see—and taste—the best of the country.

After a night in Slovenia's first design hotel, Hotel Mons, just outside of Ljubljana, take Highway A1 past green fields, cows, and an occasional barn that give way to rocky cliffs and heathered hills on entering Portorož. The town is Slovenia's version of Atlantic City but is also known for its sea cures: saltwater, mud, and mineral baths. The local Istrian loam is rich in microalgae and plankton and is said to be able to heal ailments from rheumatic disease to skin rashes. Whatever the benefits, don't miss a chance to try what's called a *fango* pack treatment—being slathered in warm mud and wound in a cocoon of plastic wrap.

The region's towns are close enough that you can walk from one to the next; at dusk, stroll to the nearby ancient Piran, filled with 13th-century architecture, for a simple meal of fish, shrimp risotto, and sautéed spinach. The next morning, before heading out for Lipica, visit the Lipizzan stud farm. Before World War I, when Slovenia was part of the Austro-Hungarian empire, the horses bred in Lipica were used by Austria's Spanish Riding school. During half-hour dress performances, the best-trained stallions prance around to techno-ballet Muzak, including a disco version of *Flight of the Bumblebee*. The studs weave past each other, meet in the center of the

Clockwise from top left: Ljubljana's Tromostovje (Triple Bridge); Gostišče Pri Lojzetu's chocolate mousse with wild strawberries and cream; Aleš Kristancic, the eighth-generation vintner at Movia; a Lipizzan stud farm, in Lipica. Opposite: Gostišče Pri Lojzetu, outside Ajdovšcina.

field, and then spiral out diagonally, doing a sideways skip.

The drive north from Lipica takes you through wineries, farms, and blink-and-you-miss-them villages of the limestone-rich Kras region. Gostišče Pri Lojzetu, a hilltop restaurant outside Ajdovšcina, has views of the surrounding hills. The freshly baked bread, addictive horseradish sauce, goose prosciutto with shaved white truffles (gathered from a local forest), and asparagus risotto with nettles provide fuel for the next day's adventures.

Overlooking Brda hills and Italy's Friuli-Venezia Giulia region, Movia is Slovenia's oldest privately run winery. As well as being an oenophile's heaven, it provides a necessary respite before the hairpin ascent through the Julian Alps. Your reward is Lake Bohinj, Lake Bled's wilder and less touristy sibling. Because it's located in Triglav National Park, Bohinj is protected from development. For the last leg and a nice endnote, head to the town of Bled, take a gondola to the little Baroque church, and soak in the view of the surrounding snowcapped peaks. ✦

For The Guide, see page 276.

Exploring Africa's Namib Desert.

Africa+
the Middle East

moroccan made

ESSAOUIRA'S
EMERGING ART SCENE

189

AFRICA
+ THE
MIDDLE
EAST

Essaouira,
Morocco

IN THE EARLY 1950's, Orson Welles descended upon the windswept Moroccan seaside town of Essaouira to shoot his film *Othello*. In the 1960's, the town became a hippie haven; Jimi Hendrix hung out, supposedly writing "Castles Made of Sand" after having seen the ruined sultan's palace just south of the city. But when the flower-power era waned, so did Essaouira's cultural heyday.

Once again an artistic center, Essaouira is back in the limelight. While a recent civic overhaul certainly ignited this renaissance, it is the resident artists and international boosters who have helped turn the town around.

A slew of galleries highlight what has become known as the Essaouira school of painting. Galerie Frédéric Damgaard is one of the town's cultural landmarks, and in European art circles it is known as the home of the Essaouira movement. Danish art dealer Frédéric Damgaard opened the gallery on the ground floor of a stone mansion in 1988, after having fallen in love with both Essaouira and the work of the self-taught local artists. His spacious gallery is full of eclectic regional pieces, featuring anything from the primal monsters depicted in the dot paintings of the brothers Hamou and Youssef Aït Tazarin, to the folkloric signs and symbols exploding on the canvases of Fatima Ettalbi.

A block from Galerie Damgaard, down a narrow cul-de-sac, is the Espace Othello, which features the work of a stable of young Moroccans, including the acclaimed Mohamed Zouzaf, who paints on animal skins. And up along the passageway known as La Skala, local artist ▶

The bar at Chalet de la Plage, Essaouira's legendary restaurant on the beach, above. Below: On Avenue de l'Istiqlal. Opposite: Detail of a painting by Azeddine Sanana at Galerie Frédéric Damgaard.

The courtyard of the Riad Gyvo hotel. Right: A painting by Mustafa El Hadar, at Essaouira's Galerie Damgaard.

Ahmed Harrouz runs the city's most unusual gallery, Atelier Le Bastion-Ouest, a narrow multilevel affair housed within a turret of the ancient ramparts.

Strictly speaking, Riad Gyvo, a five-apartment guesthouse in the medina, is not a gallery. The hotel is owned by Guy Bellinkx and Ivo Grammet, two expatriate Belgians who discovered the town in the late 1970's, when they frequently traveled through southern Morocco and Mauritania in a camper van, searching for Berber and Judaic art. Finding Essaouira to be an ideal base for

their wanderings—and for Bellinkx's windsurfing passion—they rented an apartment here in the 1980's in a building they wound up buying. "We didn't think of turning it into a guesthouse at the time," Bellinkx says. "But right after we bought it, a series of storms damaged the property so badly that we had to restore everything. So we made apartments for our friends and family." Since its official opening in 1998, Riad Gyvo has hosted everyone—from windsurfers to VIP's in the Moroccan government and the international art world—in its museumlike spaces, where contemporary paintings hang alongside traditional Berber artifacts. Like many others, Bellinkx and Grammet are attracted to the area's art, energy, beauty, and the artistic community, which can be found gathering on any given afternoon at Chalet de la Plage, a seafood restaurant on the beach. +

For The Guide, see page 277.

T+L Tip

THE WINDY CITY BEAT

Essaouira's renaissance also extends to its music scene. Check out these festivals:

Gnaoua & World Music Festival The annual concert, held in June, attracts some 30,000 fans, who dance and sway as mystical Gnaoua musicians (descended from African slaves) play hypnotic, enchanting tunes.

Festival of the Atlantic Andalusias Hear a range of musical styles, from Sephardic love songs to Arabic violin suites to flamenco rock and Mexican folk music. You can also take a seminar on Andalusian music. The festival is held every September.

kasbah chic

THE REVIVAL OF **TANGIER**

A FEW YEARS AGO, Morocco's progressive new king, 43-year-old Mohamed VI, became taken with the idea of returning the northern part of the country to its past cultural heights. Tangier was a long way from its glam days in the 1960's, when expat literati—including William Burroughs, Allen Ginsberg, Jack Kerouac, Jean Genet, Tennessee Williams, and Paul Bowles—lined the tables of the Café de Paris. Today, a return trip to the café shows just how successful the king's plan has been: business types with fat dossiers rush by while clusters of locals scrutinize architectural plans and workers restore the Beaux Arts façades of neighboring buildings. Streets and boulevards have been widened and are edged with trees. Down along the beach, swim clubs and discotheques are being rebuilt.

Over in the walled medina and up in the Kasbah quarter, a mini-*riad* revolution is under way. Where there were once cheap pensions and backpacker hostels, there are now a growing number of traditional Moroccan residences that have been turned into sleek boutique hotels. One of the top places to stay is Dar Nour, which has two skinny houses with three terraces, sublime ocean views, and seven rustic guest rooms. Equally alluring is Dar Sultan, a wittily furnished six-room hotel with a delicious blue penthouse. Nearby, romantic Dar Zuina (Arabic for "pretty house") is set in rolling hills outside the seaside town of Asilah and decorated with rough ▶

The view from Dar Sultan's roof, in Tangier.

Photograph of a young Paul Bowles at the Tangier American Legation Museum, left. Above: A room at Dar Sultan. Opposite: An outdoor lounge at Dar Zuina.

Berber furnishings and antiques. Meanwhile, the beachfront Rif hotel, a mid-century–modern landmark, has reopened after 12 years behind shutters.

The restaurant scene is also thriving. Despite its unprepossessing setting in a mini-mall, Relais de Paris has been wildly successful. On any given night, many of Tangier's major movers and shakers—government ministers, hoteliers, artists, and architects—can be found dining here. Villa Joséphine's hydrangea-filled veranda, overlooking Malcolm Forbes's former palace, is the place to have lunch. And at Riad Tanja, in a restored medina mansion next door to the American Legation Museum, new Moroccan cuisine (mini fish tagines, mille-feuille desserts with caramelized fruits) is served in sleek salons with *tadelakt* (polished plaster) walls.

The city now hosts several annual festivals, including the Tanjazz (a series of jazz concerts in May), which welcomes more than 100 international jazz artists and groups; Les Nuits de la Méditerranée (three weeks of world music in June and July); the Mediterranean Short-Length Film Festival of Tangiers (a film festival held every September); and a literary week in February called Le Salon du Livre. And against all odds, Tangier is once again back in style. +

For The Guide, see page 277.

T+L Tip

GOOD READS

***The Dream at the End of the World: Paul Bowles and the Literary Renegades in Tangier* by Michelle Green** Richly detailed account of Paul and Jane Bowles's life in Tangier.

***The Sacred Night* by Tahar Ben Jelloun** An enchanting tale by Tangier's most acclaimed novelist.

***The Sheltering Sky* by Paul Bowles** The expatriate's definitive North African classic.

195

AFRICA
+ THE
MIDDLE
EAST

Bamako,
Mali

mali's music capital

THE **BAMAKO** BEAT

THERE IS NOTHING TO SUGGEST at first glance that Bamako, the capital of Mali, is a musical hot spot. The West African city's anarchic collection of neighborhoods sprawls from the banks of the Niger River in Mali, filled with single-story dwellings and women cooking in their courtyards on charcoal braziers. The place feels like one big village, with music everywhere.

Walk through the labyrinthine central market, which takes up most of downtown, and the haunting melodies and intricate rhythms of Wassoulou, Malinké, and a host of other indigenous styles mingle with the sound of bartering. On the streets, you might happen upon a percussion band giving a spontaneous performance. Numerous clubs hop till 3 a.m. most days of the week, resembling the juke joints in the American South of the 20's. None of this should be surprising, given Mali's 600-year-old musical tradition. And in the last 15 years, artists like singer Salif Keita and singer-guitarist Ali Farka Touré have shot to international fame, making Mali the center of West African music and Bamako one of the premier places on the planet to hear it live.

It's not unusual to stumble into one of the ramshackle bars or nightclubs only to find that internationally known *kora* master Toumani Diabaté has stopped in to play his 21-string harp. If you'd rather not leave it to luck, stop into Mali Cassette, a store in Quinzanbougou that carries a weekly broadsheet of who's playing where. The schedule isn't always reliable—Diabaté might be booked at one place and pop up at another—but you can stock up on music from the shop's enormous collection from the likes of Habib Koite, a singer from western Mali; Djelimady Tounkara, one of the country's best guitarists; and Boubacar Traoré, a singer, guitarist, and songwriter. Or on a lucky day, you might just meet a prominent local musician. After all, in this city's musical hothouse, anything is possible. **+**

For The Guide, see page 277.

Above from left: *Kora* player Toumani Diabaté; Boubacar Traoré, an icon of the Bamako music world. Opposite: Guitarist Djelimady Tounkara.

Tanzania

Namibia

Zebras, spotted on a safari in Tanzania.

animal kingdom

A FAMILY-FRIENDLY **TANZANIA** SAFARI

HOW DO YOU TAKE A TRIP of a lifetime with kids in tow when said children are far more interested in Space Mountain than in ancient ruins, powdery beaches, or good food? When a zoo will no longer do, pack them up to go see the real thing—on an African safari. The thrill of hearing 1,000 buffalo thundering by or seeing a cheetah hotly pursuing a gazelle is enough to impress even the most blasé of the adolescent-and-under crowd.

With 25 years of experience in Tanzania (known for its stable government, good hotels, and the highest density of wildlife on the continent), Thomson Safaris knows what works for families: carefully paced trips, stays at campsites as well as lodges with pools, plenty of game viewing, and guides who are master kid wranglers. Before the trip, your children can exchange letters with Tanzanian pen pals, and later they can meet their mates during a school visit.

A typical day starts with a Land Rover ride to spot black rhinos, elephants, leopards, and lions. In the afternoon, you might stop at a Masai village, and in the evening, snack on freshly toasted cashews around a campfire. Children should be at least six years old to appreciate the sometimes-arduous journey. But rest assured, teens have been known to drop their beastly attitudes after hearing elephants trumpeting just outside the tents. **+**

For The Guide, see page 277.

zen africa

LUXURY SAFARIS IN **NAMIBIA**

WITH AN EMPTY desertscape on one end and a rugged, fogbound Skeleton Coast on the other, Namibia is for adventure junkies who crave a different kick.

This is also a country that works, and in recent years a clutch of stylish lodges have opened up. A good spot to begin your introduction to Namibia's safaris is Wolwedans Dunes Lodge, a series of nine platformed chalets in the NamibRand Nature Reserve. The lodge is one giant step up from the rough-and-ready tents at the Wolwedans Dune Camp nearby. But like at the camp, guests are in constant contact with the magnificent surroundings; each villa has canvas walls that can be rolled up and down for maximum exposure to, or protection from, the sun, sand, and wind. The result is rustic yet polished, like Namibia itself.

Getting to Sossusvlei Wilderness Camp, a three-hour drive north of Wolwedans, is another metaphor for traveling to Namibia. The splashy resort is in the middle of nowhere, at the end of a rocky track that's difficult for even the toughest SUV to negotiate. On arrival, however, not only is the 360-degree sweep of scenery impressive, but so, too, is the fresh-faced spirit of the enterprise. Chalets are decorated in an utterly up-to-the-minute blend of colonial and tribal ▶

Ballooning aerial of NamibRand Nature Reserve in Namibia.

Above the Namib Desert. Clockwise from below: Himba tribesperson; a plant at the NamibRand Nature Reserve; an ostrich. Opposite: A Himba woman strolls through the desert.

199

**AFRICA
+ THE
MIDDLE
EAST**

Namibia

furnishings, and each has its own little cliffside plunge pool along with an infinite concertina-window view of the graveled lunar landscape and the legendary Sossusvlei dunes. From the chalet, brief walkabouts bring sightings of Namibia's "small five"—ant lion, leopard tortoise, rhino beetle, buffalo beetle, and elephant shrew. The Namib-Naukluft Park, a 16-mile drive from the lodge, is the site of one of the country's main attractions, Sossusvlei, a desiccated river basin where travelers can climb the tallest sand dunes in the world, some reaching 1,000 feet.

From there, take a flight over the 45-mile-wide dune belts to the other extreme of the country's harsh beauty. While staying at the six-room luxury Skeleton Coast Camp, it becomes clear how this 300-mile stretch of foreboding coast along the icy Atlantic got its name. The area is full of menacing shipwrecks, broken ribs of wooden boats, and decaying skeletons of seals and whales. But it's by no means all doom: there are bright flocks of flamingos descending from the mist, colonies of seals barking up a storm, and herds of giraffes grazing on the shrubbery—all of it evidence that even in a place as seemingly desolate as Namibia, the life force runs strong. ✛

For The Guide, see page 277.

T+L Tip

BEST NAMIBIA SITE

The final stretch of the Namib Desert lures travelers with its vast open spaces and herds of wild horses. Don't miss a trip to **Nemesis,** a rock formation outside the town of Aus, set between Namibia's fabled sand dunes to the west and Fish River Canyon to the east. It juts more than 300 feet into the sky, giving trekkers views of one of the most spectacular landscapes on earth.

200

AFRICA
+ THE
MIDDLE
EAST

Mozambique

an undiscovered
oasis

THE BEACH RESORTS OF **MOZAMBIQUE**

The entrance to Pemba
Beach Resort Hotel.
Opposite: The
untrammeled shore at
Pemba in Mozambique.

EVEN FROM 2,000 feet, flying beneath low-lying clouds, the silvery flash of dolphins and sailfish corkscrewing through the transparent ocean is visible. Stretching to the horizon is a ribbon of palm- and mangrove-studded atolls rimmed by halos of ivory sand—and little else. There are no high-rise hotels, no cruise ships, just the odd *dhow*, sails billowing in the wind. Maybe one day the 32 coral islands comprising the Quirimba archipelago will rival the Maldives, but for now they remain blissfully off the map. Few Mozambicans, let alone foreign travelers, have swum in the pristine waters, stayed at the handful of luxe resorts, or reeled in some of the best game fish in the world. Even in Pemba, the mainland gateway to the Quirimbas, where a frontier-town energy pervades, the Pemba Beach Resort Hotel offers a spot of serenity. The luxurious hotel

rises from the western edge of Wimbe Beach, its adobe arches and sweeping lawns reminiscent of an Arabian palace. In the terra-cotta-tiled lobby, birds sing in palm trees planted in urns.

Indeed, few Matemo Island natives have ever set foot on the mainland. The drive to the Matemo Island Resort passes through seaside villages of thatched mud huts shaded by swaying palms. Beautiful Quimvani women standing along the roadside stare, their faces masked in white paste from the *mussiro* plant, which is used to moisturize their skin. The shoreline is patrolled by bare-chested men wielding miniature bows and arrows, hunting fish. Unlike in other African resorts, where a faux-tribal scene is served up to Westerners, there is nothing ersatz about this village or its people. A first glimpse of the resort is breathtaking; the crescent-shaped beach, framed through the sweeping Moorish arch of the entrance, appears so radiant it hurts the eyes. The resort's man-made elements are equally stunning, all Afro-Arab opulence: Zanzibari daybeds, piled high with colorful Moroccan cushions, and stained-glass lanterns line the walls.

Decidedly less flashy is the nine-room Quilálea Island Resort, set on one of the most ecologically blessed

203

AFRICA
+ THE
MIDDLE
EAST

Mozambique

A fisherman's shack on Mozambique's Matemo Island. Opposite, from left: A bedroom at Quilálea Island Resort; inside Pemba Beach Resort Hotel.

islands of the Quirimba, where the delicately preserved ecology is the draw. Less than a half-mile wide, the island is too small for an airstrip—or much of anything—and the resort is its only tenant. In 2002, the Mozambican government declared Quilálea and neighboring Sencar Island marine sanctuaries—which isn't to say they're off-limits for exploring. You can take deep-sea-diving excursions over the protected reef: manta rays, hawksbill turtles, and humpback whales populate the waters here, as well as the exceedingly rare dugong, a near-extinct mammal with humanlike breasts, from which the ancient myth of the mermaid likely derives. Beyond the sanctuary are storied fishing grounds.

Coastal Mozambique is to big-game fishing what Kenya once was to big-game hunting—except instead of a mounted-head trophy, you'll have to settle for a photo. Most of the catches are tag-and-release. Even so, fishing in these waters is pure exhilaration. The southern current passes through this part of the Indian Ocean, and just east of the archipelago, the sea floor drops precipitously—a happy confluence of conditions that translates into a wealth of marine life, including kingfish, dorado, queenfish, yellowfin tuna, and sailfish.

Aside from fishing, snorkeling, and diving, Quilálea offers little to distract you, which is the point. The island's name comes from the Swahili *lala*, meaning "sleep," and as you nap on the beach, it's easy to forget that the outside world exists. +

For The Guide, see page 277.

T+L Tip

WATER EXCURSIONS

The deep channel and long reef east of the Quirimbas makes for some of the world's top game fishing—the catch includes marlin, sailfish, and barracuda. Book through your resort or **World Charters** in Pemba.

If you want to go diving or snorkeling, you'll find PADI-licensed instructors at every resort, but for the best trips at bargain prices, visit **Pemba Dive** on Wimbe Beach.

modern vintages
SOUTH AFRICA'S WINE COUNTRY

A bathroom in a suite at La Résidence in Franschhoek. Opposite, from left: La Couronne in Franschhoek; a detail of grapes at Waterford Winery in Stellenbosch.

205

AFRICA
+ THE
MIDDLE
EAST

South Africa

IN SOUTH AFRICA'S WINELANDS region, which begins minutes outside Cape Town, the landscape is like something out of a fairy tale: craggy mountain ranges fringed in clouds rise dramatically from green, green valleys; gargantuan 300-year-old camphor trees and gardens dense with hydrangeas and roses envelop elegant farmhouses, all gleaming white stucco and gables and thatched roofs; sloping hillsides and wide fields that stretch to the edge of the mountains are planted with row upon row of vines, citrus trees, and lavender. *The Lord of the Rings* may have been filmed in New Zealand, but Tolkien was born in South Africa, and it is this land that many believe inspired his vision of Middle-earth.

The area also has some of the country's best food and wine. Perhaps no place sums up its pleasures better than the picture-postcard village of Franschhoek. Several B&B's line the town's single street, but for true pampering, book a room at La Résidence, the most stylish hotel in town. The five suites are eclectically furnished, from ebonized Victorian divans to painted Balinese cabinets. (The property is set to close in early 2007 and reopen in a 10-room villa.) For travelers who care more about awe-inspiring topography than high style or easy access to town, there is yet another option in Franschhoek: La Couronne. Nearby, Le Quartier Français is a hotel that's a mini village within the village, with four whitewashed buildings trimmed in lacy wrought iron and wide porches surrounded by rose gardens, all set around an oval pool that functions as a kind of town square. The 17-room luxury inn with a screening room, a restaurant, a shop, and a spa, is surrounded by rolling vineyards.

One of the best reasons to stay here is that you're assured a table at Le Quartier Français's restaurant, which has racked up dozens of awards. For the past decade it's been rated one of the country's top 25 restaurants. You'll understand the accolades once you taste the creative yet restrained cuisine, such as *brandade* of salmon trout with seafood bisque and preserved lime, baby greens topped with truffle hollandaise, and a crème brûlée that defies description.

All the restaurants serve local bottles, but it's still worth touring the wineries. The wines—and the extremely knowledgeable and friendly employees—are only part of the appeal. The estates in South ▶

T+L Tip

MUST READ
Published annually, *The John Platter South African Wine Guide* offers complete listings of the country's producers. You can purchase it at any airport or bookstore in South Africa, or order it at www.cybercellar.co.za.

206

AFRICA
+ THE
MIDDLE
EAST

South Africa

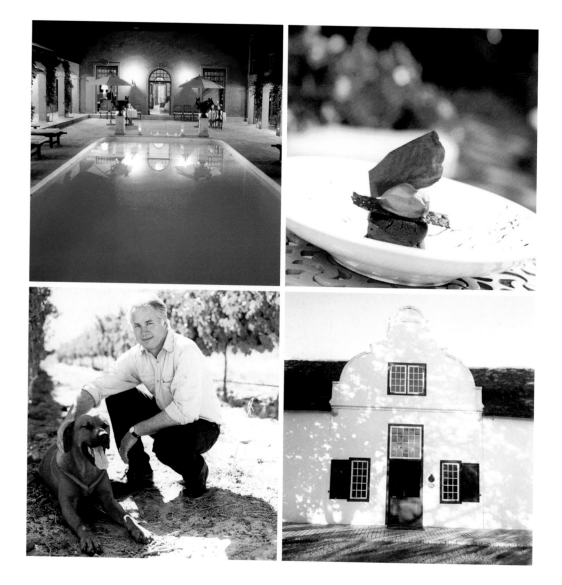

Africa tend to be architecturally interesting, too. Stellenbosch's Dornier Wines, run by Swiss artist Christopher Dornier, for example, would be notable for its resolutely modern design even if vintner Ian Naudé's releases weren't so exceptional. Six-year-old Waterford is one of the region's most extravagant wineries, a Tuscan-style building with an allée of clementine trees. Vintner Kevin Arnold still has room to grow, but he's well on his way to making Waterford a classic. At Le Riche Wines, Étienne Le Riche creates beautifully structured Cabernet Sauvignons on this cult-favorite Stellenbosch estate,

while Laibach makes a fantastic Pinotage and the supple Friedrich Laibach Cabernet-Merlot blend. Just outside of Paarl, the young Avondale has a cathedral-like tasting room and excellent releases, among them an unusual sweet Muscat Rouge with a fresh jasmine nose. Near Paarl, at Roggeland Country House, a 17th-century, family-run hotel, the dishes use fresh local produce, and evening wine tastings take place on the lawn.

While larger farms are located in Stellenbosch and Paarl, Franschhoek has more than 30 niche vineyards, many open for walk-in tastings. Cabrière Estate is one of the best known; try their award-winning white, a citrusy Chardonnay Pinot Noir. Nearby Stony Brook is also not to be missed. At 35 acres, the farm is small, but its spicy Pinotage and plummy Merlot pack a big punch. +

For The Guide, see page 277.

Waterford Winery's entrance.
Opposite, clockwise from top left: The
pool at South Africa's La Résidence;
dessert of purple fig gratin with walnuts
at La Colombe Restaurant in Constantia-
Utsig; Roggeland Country House in
Diemersfontein; wine maker Kevin Arnold
with his dog Shiraz at Waterford Winery.

ancient adventure

IRAN'S INTRICATE BEAUTY

MOST AMERICANS ONLY KNOW Iran through the news headlines. And on that front, it can seem like a forbidden, even intimidating, country. But visitors who can get past the convoluted politics will discover a rich and lively history that lives on in the ruined palaces of Persepolis, in the gardens of Esfahan, and in the bazaars of Tehran.

Iran's capital is utterly urban, and it's worth more than just a stopover, if only to visit the Tehran Bazaar, on the south side. Billions of rials pass through the humble stalls, representing a third of all commercial and retail trade in Iran. (The conservative *bazari* hold great political power and were a driving force behind the Islamic revolution.) The Saturday scene buzzes: mule carts dodge speeding wheelbarrows, a chai vendor trudges past, carrying two buckets roped to a stick, one containing a samovar, the other full of cups and sugar cubes. (Iranians like to hold a cube between their teeth while sipping tea.) At the rear is the famous carpet showroom, where a fine cloud of dust is kicked up by the clap of unfurling rugs. Most patterns are traditional and stunningly beautiful, intricately detailed, and unique. Alongside these are woven tapestries—made for European tourists—depicting the Last Supper, Napoleon on his horse, and Kate and Leo on the prow of the *Titanic*.

Chaotic as it seems, Tehran does hold pockets of tranquility. Darakeh, in the foothills of the northern part of the city, is a pastoral area. ▶

The restaurant
Hammam-e Vakil, in a
former bathhouse in
Shiraz. Opposite: Si-o-Seh
Bridge on Zayandeh River
in Esfahan, Iran.

211

AFRICA
+ THE
MIDDLE
EAST

Iran

An Iranian woman in a manteau and head scarf, at the ruins of Persepolis, above. Left: The lobby of the Abbasi Hotel in Esfahan. Opposite: The interior of a café beneath the Si-o-Seh Bridge in Esfahan.

A rushing brook, clear as a Colorado stream, cuts through a ravine crisscrossed by hiking trails where you can stop at a trailside *chaykhuneh* (teahouse) for wood oven–baked eggs and lavash. The area has become a bit of a lovers' lane, with dozens of young couples holding hands—up here there are no authorities to keep watch, and some women even remove their government-mandated head scarves.

Three hundred miles south of Tehran is Esfahan, by far the loveliest city in the country; old-world charm radiates from its gardens, mosques, and bridges, not to mention the graceful vernacular architecture of its everyday buildings. The 17th-century wooden palace of Chehel Sotun features accomplished frescoes, richly detailed tableaux of the Safavid kings' epic battles. The vast Imam Square, at the center of town—with the dazzling, aquamarine-tiled Imam Mosque—is said to be the second-largest urban plaza in the world, after Tiananmen Square. Crossing the Zayandeh River are five historic bridges (and six newer ones), where you'll find numerous waterside teahouses.

Farther south, Shiraz is Iran's most soulful city and its intellectual center, with several top-rated universities. It's also the avowed ▶

T+L Tip

CUTTING THROUGH THE RED TAPE

Americans are allowed to travel independently in Iran, but getting a visa can be a headache—you need a sponsor, the process takes months, and rejections are common. The easiest option is to book your trip through an American tour operator, which will handle all paperwork, as well as trip details. Even if you book with an operator, it is wise to check the latest travel advisory from the U.S. State Department.

A Qajar painting in the hallway at Esfahan's Abassi Hotel, a former 17th-century caravansary, above. Below: Fesenjan, a stew of chicken with walnut and pomegranate at Shahrzad Restaurant.

capital of Persian literature: the poet Hafez is buried here. On moonlit evenings, crowds gather at Hafez's tomb, surrounded by rose gardens and pomegranate groves, to hear recitations of his lusty verses about wine, dancing, and nightingales. And if two of these three things are currently against the law, that hardly diminishes the mood. The audience hoots at the bawdiest double entendres and joins in unison at the most exuberant lines. As old men laugh over backgammon games, couples exchange swoon-worthy kisses. Romance continues at the restaurant Hammam-e Vakil; carved out of a historic *hammam* (bathhouse), with vaulted ceilings and a gurgling fountain, this is the most seductive setting in town.

The ruins of Persepolis lie just 40 minutes by car from Shiraz. The palace complex was conceived by Darius the Great in 518 B.C. and is renowned not just for its grandeur—sweeping staircases, towering sculptures of winged lions—but also for its graceful synthesis of foreign elements. The Achaemenids of ancient Persia were a remarkably catholic people, noted for their tolerance of other cultures. An endless stream of foreign guests was received at Persepolis, including Egyptians, Syrians, and Babylonians. These and other peoples were respectfully depicted in evocative bas-reliefs—clad in their native dress, astride camels, goats, and stallions, bearing gifts of elephant tusks, and lion skins from their homelands. The tableau is a stirring reminder of an age when Iran was literally at the center of the world. ✚

For The Guide, see page 277.

jordan's lost city

A PILGRIMAGE TO **PETRA**

YOU KNOW AN ANCIENT PLACE is something special when it is featured in both the Bible and the canon of Steven Spielberg. The Jordanian "rose-red city half as old as time" is Biblically referenced as the land of the ancient Edomites and is believed to be the area where Moses' brother Aaron is buried. It is also often referred to as the eighth wonder of the world. As for Spielberg, he used Petra as the setting for the climax of *Indiana Jones and the Last Crusade*.

The soaring soapstone canyons, painted salmon pink and rust, look like something from the planet ▶

Taxis outside the Abu Darweesh
Mosque in Amman.

214

AFRICA
+ THE
MIDDLE
EAST

Jordan

Detail of an ancient mosaic map of the Holy Land at a church in Madaba, a town near Amman, above. Below: The Roman ruins in the town of Jerash. Opposite: Al Khazneh, one of the main structures in Petra.

Mars. Walk through the *siq*, the steep gorge that serves as Petra's entrance, and take your first glance at the intricately carved buildings emerging organically from the landscape. You'll be transported to another time.

The capital of the Nabataeans in the third century B.C., Petra was forgotten for 1,000 years, only to be "discovered" in 1812 by Europeans. (Bedouins had been living in the area all along.) The Assyrians, Egyptians, Greeks, and Romans all built settlements in the region over time, and their architectural styles are also represented. It's the Nabataean influence, though, that makes Petra unlike anyplace else in the world. If you can find a spot away from the crowds and watch as the sun and shadow tint the tawny canyon walls from pink-orange to a purplish blue, you will almost feel how enchanting this thriving city was—more than 2,000 years ago. +

For *The Guide, see page 277.*

T+L Tip

HISTORY BEYOND PETRA

The metropolis of **Amman** has its share of mosques, the most distinctive of which is the black-and-white Abu Darweesh Mosque, set atop the city's highest point. A 20-minute drive takes you to the town of **Jerash**, considered to be one of the best-preserved Ancient Roman settlements in the Middle East. **Medaba**, a half-hour southwest, is renowned for its Byzantine mosaics, especially the 6th century Madaba Map; more than two million stones are elaborately composed to depict the Holy Land.

In the dining room at Bhutan's Amankora resort.

Asia

cultural
immersion

LANNA INFLUENCES IN **CHIANG MAI**

Thai ceramics at La Luna Gallery, along the Ping River, above. Left: Cocktail seating at The House, in Chiang Mai. Opposite: Dancers perform at the Mandarin Oriental Dhara Dhevi.

A SPIRIT OF INTENSE REGIONAL pride reigns in the northern city of Chiang Mai. The local dialect has made a pronounced return over the past few decades, as has the custom of wearing traditional clothing on Fridays (Culture Day). Classical dances and folk songs are performed in schools, while architects and interior designers are using northern motifs in new buildings.

It wasn't always so: during the 20th century, as Thailand modernized, its northern customs, language, and art fell by the wayside. The recent state-endorsed reclamation of northern culture, however, is so energized that observers now speak of a "Lanna revival." To travel to Chiang Mai now is to experience a broader understanding of its Lanna history.

In its heyday between the 13th and the 16th centuries, the Lanna kingdom encompassed all of northern Thailand and parts of present-day Laos and Burma (Myanmar). Lanna—the name means "one million rice fields"—was really an amalgam of disparate cultures, its ethnic base ranging from Chinese to Indian to tribal Burmese. The Lanna alphabet differs from modern Thai, just as Lanna cuisine, with its sticky rice and pork sausages, remains distinct from southern Thai cooking. The Chiang Mai staple *khao sawy*, a blend of Indian-style curry broth and crisp Chinese noodles, testifies to the culture's hybrid origins.

Yet it was in art and architecture— particularly temple design—that Lanna made its greatest mark. Though more modest than those in Bankgok, many Chiang Mai temples feature carved fretwork and mirror-glass mosaics. Wood is the dominant material; gold is less common here than in the wealthier south. A hallmark of Lanna construction is the *cho fa*, the V-shaped finial that crowns the apex of a roof. Builders often left ceiling beams exposed to highlight a temple's "honest architecture." ▶

Chiang Mai

Al fresco dining at Baan Suan Sri, outside Chiang Mai. Opposite, clockwise from top left: Sandals made of dried water hyacinth, outside a guest suite; a porter at the resort; Thai style at Living Space; at the Wat Chedi Luang temple.

One of the new hotels in the area bearing this out is the Mandarin Oriental Dhara Dhevi, a 164-room resort that mimics a northern village. Traditional Lanna culture provides much of the inspiration; in fact, the hotel hopes to play a role in preserving Lanna traditions. Many of the buildings on the property are representative of Lanna style, as are incidental details such as the terra-cotta pots of "drinking water" placed as offerings outside villa gates. Guests in search of inventive takes on Lanna cuisine need only meander through the hotel's rice terraces to Le Grand Lanna, Chiang Mai's poshest restaurant. Instructional programs abound as well. Honeymooners can plant rice alongside farmers in the fields, executives on retreats can prepare duck curry at the cooking school, and kids can learn to play *takraw* (the Thai version of volleyball).

The Dhara Dhevi also brings the neighboring countryside to its guests. Three weather-beaten stilt houses were carted in and resurrected near the tennis courts; they now function as a working crafts center, where wizened ladies from nearby villages are invited to drop by to practice basketry, weaving, and woodcarving in public view. And on any given day, a guest could arrive to find a musician ping-panging on the xylophone-esque *ranak lek* in the lobby. ✚

For The Guide, see page 278.

T+L Tip

CHIANG MAI MODERN

Experience the city's contemporary culture at:

The House Danish designer Hans Christensen runs Chiang Mai's most fashionable gathering spot, in an impeccable Indochine setting. Make sure to have drinks and tapas at the wine bar.

La Luna Gallery Painters and photographers from Thailand, Vietnam, Burma, Malaysia, and the Philippines are exhibited in this eclectic space.

fashion nation

A SHOPPING TOUR OF **VIETNAM**

Minh Hanh's collection of *ao dais*, in her Ho Chi Minh City shop. Opposite: An outfit from Hanoi's Ipa-Nima boutique.

THANKS TO A NEW POPULATION of entrepreneurs, restaurateurs, designers, and artists—many born after the war—Vietnam is having a moment in the spotlight. This is no longer the hermetic country of a generation ago: two-thirds of the population is younger than 30 and eager to engage in the world at large. Nowhere is this more evident than in the fashion and design realms. The two major cities—moody, reflective Hanoi and brash younger sibling Ho Chi Minh City (Saigon)—provide shoppers with two perfect antipodes, and antidotes, to each other, teetering giddily between the traditional (silk *ao dai* tunics) and the cutting-edge (fur and vinyl *ao dai* tunics).

While Ho Chi Minh City has always had the most forward-looking clothing designers, once-conservative Hanoi now claims a growing number of edgy boutiques. Beloved by fashionable foreigners and chic young Vietnamese women are a number of shops proffering classic floral dresses, Capri pants in crisp twills and cottons, summery tops, and prim A-line skirts that conjure Audrey Hepburn. Handbag guru Christina Yu chose the capital as the headquarters for her playfully flamboyant Ipa-Nima label, now shown from Hong Kong to London; her shop sells the famous bags for substantially less than the overseas price. ▶

In the city's Cathedral District, 25-year-old Nguyen Hoang Ngan owns Nymph, housed in a closet-sized storefront, where her flirty camisoles, taffeta sleeveless tops, and miniskirts recall Catherine Malandrino—at H&M prices. Working out of Ho Chi Minh City, Minh Hanh is the leading light of Vietnamese couture. Her theatrical designs are on view at several showrooms, the most outrageous of which is the Ao Dai boutique, where the famous tunic-and-trousers outfit of Vietnamese women gets a Björk-worthy reworking in fur, velvet, suede, denim, and other unorthodox materials. Minh Khoa is another progressive designer, whose beautifully textured creations—blouses, jackets, and dresses—employ intricate beadwork and ruching to great effect. The street-smart styles of Le Thanh Phuong range from casual tops to formal dresses. Tha Ca is a two-story upmarket shop selling sophisticated, East-meets-West clothing, sandals, and handbags.

The tranquil and pretty village Hoi An, on the eastern shore just 20 miles away from the metropolis of Da Nang, is the country's capital of bespoke, with dozens of tailors offering quick turnaround and low prices. Chief among Hoi An's workshops is A-Dong Silk, where the young head seamstress is familiar with the latest looks. In Hanoi and Ho Chi Minh City, the selection of fabrics is better and the workmanship more refined, though the tailors require more money and more time (up to a week for a dress or a suit). Most can create cheongsams and mandarin-collar jackets from scratch, but if you're looking for Western-style designs, bring a specific piece to copy: photos from magazines won't get the same results. The tailoring shops on Hanoi's Hang Gai Street are good places to start—especially Tan My, which sells embroidered linens, pillow covers, and cotton lingerie bags.

A bowl of *pho* at Mai Anh, above. Right: La Fenêtre Soleil in Ho Chi Minh City. Opposite, from left: A silk top from designer Nguyen Hoang Ngan at Nymph in Hanoi; handbags and shoes at Ipa-Nima.

Vietnam is also one of the top places in Asia to purchase housewares, furnishings, and antiques. In Hanoi, Mosaïque sells lotus-shaped lanterns with taffeta panels; lamps made to look like opium pipes; and tobacco-finished lacquerware. Nearby La Casa has a broad selection of high-end housewares, including wooden trays, hand mirrors, photo frames, pillow covers, joss-stick holders, and silver candlesticks. Classic Chinese furniture and fine art, such as oil portraits of young Mandarins, fills the Vanloi Oriental Style shop. For contemporary paintings, sculpture, woodblock prints, and etchings, all by native Vietnamese artists, American Suzanne Lecht's store Art Vietnam is a must. The evidence of her keen eye for emerging talent unfolds over three floors of a traditional house in Hanoi's Old Quarter. Lecht is also a good source for advice on what to do and see throughout the country. In Ho Chi Minh City, essential stops are Precious Qui, which sells accessories and jewelry, and Celadon Green, specializing in minimalist ceramic and lacquer tableware. For furniture and collectibles in the colonial mode, drop by Monsoon. A recent discovery: four rosewood Deco chairs, salvaged from an old villa and beautifully restored. +

For The Guide, see page 278.

T+L Tip

SHOPPING BREAKS

For the national dish, *pho ga*, a spicy consommé spiked with herbs, fish sauce, and meat, check out **Mai Anh** in Hanoi. Ho Chi Minh City's **La Fenêtre Soleil** serves cappuccino and sandwiches in a sweet little tearoom.

haute himalayas

EXPLORING THE REMOTE
KINGDOM OF **BHUTAN**

IN 1910 ONE BRITISH EXPLORER called Bhutan "the last great piece of true exploration." It's an observation that remains valid a century later.

For years the hereditary monarchs of Bhutan deliberately kept the country shuttered against the outside. The result is that travelers who fly halfway around the world will be rewarded with one of the least sullied landscapes on earth. Go 10 miles in any given direction in Bhutan, and the trappings of the modern age give way with astonishing alacrity to pastoral scenes largely unaltered for hundreds of years. It is not just the absence of telephone lines and satellite dishes; it is the absence of any giveaway that we live in a postindustrial time. Connoisseurs of anachronism would have trouble finding another nation more to their liking than this one.

In remote Bhutan, all is wild abundance and subtle beauty. Steep trails of scrub pine and scree give way suddenly to mountain meadows, where herders graze yaks. Gunmetal streams flow through rice terraces skirted with willows that pale to a melancholy flickering gold come late autumn. The stillness that is also a feature of this landscape creeps up on you slowly, the absence of media static alerting you to the ►

At the Cheli La Pass.
Opposite: The Taktshang
Goemba Monastery
in the Paro Valley.

movement of wind, the turning of the planet in the sky.

A day trip over the Cheli La Pass, one of the highest drivable points in Bhutan, allows visitors to explore the Haa Valley, first opened to tourists in 2001. Hundreds of prayer flags flutter at the pass, with an elevation of more than 12,000 feet. Below, the diamond-clear Haa Chhu river cuts through the lush valley, and the sun shines with the flat openness of light in places at the outer limits of the earth's curve. The adventurous should head east to the Phobjikha Valley to see the winter nesting place of the black-necked crane.

Great, fortresslike Buddhist *dzongs* (monasteries) beckon as well. Their massive walls are whitewashed and ornamented with Tantric paintings hectically populated with fanged demons, ethereal goddesses, and a thousand kinds of hell. Inside, young monks pray with rigorous devotion.

In the main town of Paro, the monastery complex includes a great collection of Buddha statuary and ceremonial paintings. A pilgrimage to the nearby Tiger's Nest monastery is as necessary a part of a nonbeliever's itinerary as it is for the most pious

A street in Paro City, above. Opposite, clockwise from top left: A guest bathroom at Amankora; young monks in Bhutan's Haa Valley; a traditional house in Haa Valley; dried fruit compote for breakfast at Uma Paro.

Buddhist seeking a road map for his lives down the line. It's never open according to a set plan, however, and the structure is reachable only by hiking up 9,000 feet and then following a trail of 800 stone stairs overhanging a gorge. Perched above the monastery is Uma Paro, a facsimile of a traditional Bhutanese farmhouse—and a prototype of the new type of high-end resort being cultivated in Bhutan. The 29 rooms blend indigenous pieces with modern amenities. Bhutanese carvings and wood-burning stoves share space with DVD players and Internet hookups—which were introduced to the country just six years ago. Down the road at Balakha Village is Amankora, from the luxe hotel group Amanresorts. A cluster of rammed-earth villas are fitted out with authentic Bhutanese details: bed clothes of refined patterns are rendered in burlap, and bottle holders are woven of bamboo.

Northwest of Paro is the Punakha Dzong, the country's most elaborate and baroque monastery, which sits at the confluence of the Mo Chhu and Pho Chhu rivers. Visitors should be aware that it's not rare for the *dzongs* to be closed in observance of religious ceremonies or even on account of a lama's caprice. +

For The Guide, see page 278.

T+L Tip

WHAT TO DO IN THIMPHU

Bhutan's capital, Thimphu, can be experienced in a day. It is home to the **National Textile Museum**, with good exhibits on traditional crafts. Despite its name, the **Sunday market** is held here on Fridays, Saturdays, *and* Sundays; among other products, you'll find a selection of spices and Tibetan relics.

An arbored path in one of Pondicherry's parks, above. Below: Small statues outside a room in L'Hotel de l'Orient. Opposite: A house in the Indian district of Ville Noire.

spiritual oasis

PILGRIMAGE TO THE INDIAN TOWN OF **PONDICHERRY**

IT'S BEST TO COME to Pondicherry with an open mind. This former stronghold of French India, in the southern coastal state of Tamil Nadu, is now most famous as a spiritual site. The ashram there, founded in 1926, developed around the yogi Sri Aurobindo and his French counterpart, Mirra Alfassa, known to her followers as the Mother.

If you truly want to experience the ashram, you should rent a room. At the Park Guest House, one of several of the ashram's places to stay, the view is over the Bay of Bengal; at about six dollars a night, it's one of the best bargains anywhere. Though not on the ashram, L'Hôtel de l'Orient, located in a colonial building in Pondy's French district, offers more luxurious accommodations.

Travelers who go to Pondy should also take the bumpy, 20-minute ride to Auroville. Philosophically, the town is distinct from the ashram, dedicated not to Aurobindo's Integral Yoga but to the Mother's vision of international "human unity." The 95-foot-high Matrimandir, an enormous sphere covered with gold-plated discs, marks the center of the community. Inside, guests sit on white cushions around the Mother's globe—a flawless crystal sphere, illuminated by a single beam of light from a skylight directly overhead. **+**

For The Guide, see page 278.

A *Shirodhara* treatment
at the Taj Malabar on
Willingdon Island in Kochi.

indian healing

THE AYURVEDIC SPAS OF **KOCHI**

THE RESIDENTS OF the southern coastal city of Kochi, a sybaritic retreat in the Indian state of Kerala, are dedicated to their twice-daily baths, their cream-colored raiments, and their use of ayurvedic medicine, an ancient system of herbal treatments designed to tune their bodies much like mechanics realign Porsches.

Keralites pride themselves on these rituals, which, together with their beautiful surroundings, they believe make them superior to the barbarians up north. Indeed, this sliver of land along the Lakshadweep Sea has been branded as God's Own Country. What draws visitors is not only the promise of rejuvenation, but the pungent tag of Old India nostalgia: the Fort Cochin district has a canopy of tamarind and rain trees that surround a bastion of the European fort. And the cozy Dutch Palace in nearby Mattancheri has just the right number of paintings of wicked-looking rajahs.

The biggest draw of the region lately, however, are "medical tours," the latest form of Western fascination with Indian gurus who claim to understand what the rest of us have long forgotten. Foreign visitors will find them in the form of ayurveda—Sanskrit for "knowledge for prolonging life"—a practice based on the belief that nature is the remedy for all ailments: cinnamon oil ▶

Coconuts drying in the sun at a coconut-oil mill, Bannamali
Kochi, above. Below: Banana leaves at Ernakulam Market. Opposite,
from left: A bamboo boat on the backwaters; an antique bed in one of
the rooms at the Brunton Boatyard in Fort Cochin.

alleviates mumps and, when applied to the soles of your feet, "wintertime quakes"; king-coconut oil restores "falling hair"; the powdered seeds of bastard teak, eaten daily with gooseberry juice, make the old young again.

Kochi, a 600,000-strong city that's an aqueous braid of canals and lagoons, is utterly unlike what everyone thinks of India: all quietude and clarity. Religious and philosophic enthusiasm is everywhere. Here, travelers can try all kinds and levels of ayurveda. *Dinacharya*, for instance, is a "daily health-maintenance therapy." It sounds benign but can require a steely will. Such a treatment at the Taj Malabar, a five-star hotel in Kochi, might involve a numbing gum cleaning, with fluids like oil, honey, and milk being held in the mouth for three to eight minutes, and a bracing eye wash with a few drops of tender coconut oil and rose water. It's followed by a massage on a long wooden table that consists of soothing body swoops and wrist snaps. All the while, your ears are stopped up with camphorated drops and your nose filled with medicated goat's-milk snuff. Other exotic features of ayurveda include a steam cabinet—a box that only your head sticks out of—in which the steam is "medicated" with turmeric leaves, neem leaves, lemongrass, and ginger, all for sweating off the unguents afterward; and a tablespoon of cow ghee every morning on an empty stomach as the key to better health.

Another therapy is *shirodhara*, an ayurvedic treatment in which medicated coconut oil is drizzled on the forehead, which supposedly

addresses virtues deficient in the soul that lead to bodily ailments. The procedure is reputed not only to sharpen wits and rejuvenate memory but also to cure both Alzheimer's disease and schizophrenia. *Shirodhara*, however, isn't easy to come by in Kochi unless you have the time and commitment: some *vaids*, or ayurvedic doctors, require up to three weeks of a visitor's time, during which guests must forgo meat, alcohol, and sex. And the *vaids* are insistent that *they* decide what treatments patients need; don't even think of asking for a simple, quick drizzle.

Travelers with fewer days and less discipline can try the Brunton Boatyard spa, housed in a reconstruction of an 1849 boatyard. The *vaidya* will likely concoct a milk-and-herb mixture to be poured down a cotton rope and onto your forehead. Potential benefits include looking years younger—and being newly aligned with the world.

Good health can also be found in the correct preparation of various foods. When the weather is hot, a bath of boiled vetiver root is thought to cool the system. When it's cold, a cup of coffee with jaggery—a sweetener made from date palm—and crushed ginger, pepper, and coriander seeds is considered to warm and clear the respiratory system. For foods of all kinds, go to the Ernakulam market, where travelers will find vendors stretched out on gunnysacks piled beside—or, often, atop—their produce, a bedding of manioc and string beans and snake gourds, and of jack-fruit and orange cucumbers and pale-red pumpkins shaped like pattypan squash. ✦

For The Guide, see page 278.

T+L Tip

KOCHI'S CRAFTERS

Only seven local houses are inhabited in Jew Town, home to over-400-years-old Paradesi Synagogue; the rest have become antiques stores. **Crafters**, a complex of five antiques shops, all within a few minutes' walk of one another, is owned by the Malayil brothers, former spice traders who decided to turn 33,000 square feet of warehouse space into storage for a beguiling hodgepodge of Shiva statues, cedar chests, and old-fashioned rice measures.

an epic culinary tour

THE FOOD IN **CHINA**

The cuisine at Yu Qi Ling, in Hangzhou. Opposite: Designer Han Feng at the Guo family Garden, a park in Hangzhou, where she grew up.

IN THE PAST SEVERAL YEARS, the art of cooking in China has risen from the ashes. There is now a level of efficiency and sophistication that rivals any major culinary city. And while the changes are most easily found in Beijing and Shanghai's smartest restaurants, they can also be seen in country inns and at street dumpling stands.

Shanghai's superb Yong Foo Élite is the brainchild of a local decorator; it's furnished with antiques, and has the aura of Old Shanghai: decadent, elegant, and sophisticated. The menu is equally interesting, featuring such specialties as sweet shrimp and fish fried with pine nuts.

Less flashy places boast excellent food as well. Crystal Jade is in a nondescript Shanghai mall, but the Cantonese dim sum there is delightful—fried potato dumplings that melt in your mouth; roasted skin of baby pig, duck, and chicken; shredded daikon with dried shrimp, layered in phyllo pastry. There's always a line for one of the plastic stools on the sidewalk in front of Jia-Jia Juicy Dumplings. You can get a huge plate of

dumplings filled with soup and pork, shrimp, or hairy crab (a regional delicacy) for about a dollar. Nearby, Jade Garden sits on top of a nightclub, but no music can drown out their dishes.

Southwest of Shanghai is Hangzhou, childhood home of internationally acclaimed fashion designer Han Feng and cuisine that is equally as celebrated. There is a saying in this country that when you die there is heaven, but when you live there is Hangzhou. The city lies beside the West Lake, where boats travel from island to island, and the sun glints off the urban skyline on one shore, with tall, elegant pagodas on another. A typical dinner includes *chou doufu*, or "stinky tofu," an acquired taste. Rare delicacies, like a broth of locusts and aged ducks, can be found at Longjing, a tiny ▶

establishment with just eight tables arranged in private pavilions around a lush garden in the middle of a tea plantation.

While Longjing serves food that is exotic to a Westerner's mind, Zhiweiguan is accessible, with dishes such as whole chicken stuffed with garlic and encased in salt before baking. A decidedly less-touristy Zhejiang province, Shaoxing, is ribboned with romantic canals and lined with Ch'ing dynasty houses that are built right down to the water. At Xianheng, visitors can find a fermented specialty, Shaoxing rice wine, as

well as sweetly rich caramelized-pork buns.

For the Chinese, there are two great cuisines: Sichuan and Cantonese. Travelers have long experienced Cantonese at its source, because it is what's most commonly found in Hong Kong, but the Sichuan province is still off most tourist maps. Chiles are to Sichuan cooking what salt is to the sea. Indeed, Sichuan cuisine makes Mexican food seem bland. The trademark Sichuan pepper is *hua jiao*, which is in fact not a pepper at all, but the dried fruit of the prickly-ash plant. At the extravagant China Grand Plaza in Chengdu, the *kung pao* chicken is full of the freshest *hua jiao* available. At My Humble House, an unhumble restaurant in the same city, the style is upmarket modern Chinese, and the food is fusion—incorporating the influence not of Western food, but of the multiple

T+L Tip

CONSTRUCTING THE MEAL

The Chinese spend a larger proportion of their income on food than almost any other nationality does. In his seminal book, *Food in Chinese Culture*, K. C. Chang talks about "food as social language" and "food linguistics." When you're ordering a Chinese meal, conceive it as a whole. Choose hot, cold, and tepid dishes; spicy and mild tastes; fish, meat, and vegetables; heavy flavors and lighter ones. Balance is key.

Clockwise from top left: Soup at Jade Garden in Shanghai; a member of the staff at the China Grand Plaza Hotel in Chengdu, in the Sichuan province; a Sichuan offering at the restaurant there; dinnertime entertainment at Longjing in Hangzhou. Opposite: Private dining rooms at the China Grand Plaza in Chengdu.

branches of Chinese and Southeast Asian cuisines. For example, the traditional Cantonese shark's-fin soup is made with the additon of creamy pumpkin. Hot-pot restaurants abound in Chengdu. At Huang Cheng Laoma, there are two burners built into the middle of each table allowing diners to have one cauldron chockablock with chiles, the other with a mild broth of chicken and sea horse.

Beijing residents are well known for engaging in a favorite debate: Who makes the best Peking duck?

There are many details to consider: Is the preparation too refined or flashy? Is the skin too fatty or dry? Is it cooked over applewood or apricot? At no-frills Xiangmanlou, the duck is fatty, but in a sinful way, like foie gras. The duck skin is divided—the best is put on a special plate—and the so-called hard skin is served separately.

The best Beijing street food is the *jianbing*, and the place to get it is the stalls outside the Baoguo Temple complex, now a flea market. *Jianbing* is a crêpe cooked with an egg and bean-and-chile sauce, then wrapped around sweet fried bread. It's steamy and fresh and eggy and starchy and delectable—no debate necessary. ✚

For The Guide, see page 279.

up from underground

BEIJING'S NEW ARTS SCENE

Married artists Rong Rong and Inri at the site of Beijing's former East Village. Below, a portrait of Mao Tse-tung at the F2 gallery. Opposite: An installation by Guo Fengyi at Long March Space in Factory 798.

WHEN IT COMES TO ART in Beijing, the underground scene has made it into the big leagues. At home and abroad, Chinese artists are celebrated and their work sold for record prices.

Just inside the Fifth Ring Road, the tourist-friendly Dashanzi is the best place to see what Beijing artists are doing today. Dashanzi is the site of Factory 798, a cultural center of studios, galleries, shops, and cafés housed in the complex of brick workshops that was formerly Asia's largest military-electronics plant. One gallery, Long March Space, is well known for its public projects along the route of Mao's Long March, and uses its space more as a base than as a gallery. Installations have included works by Beijing-born Wang Wei, whose pieces often put the viewer in a confined or otherwise uncomfortable space. The Chinese Contemporary Art gallery, on the second floor of 798, is an airy space with an original wood-beamed ceiling. Ludovic Bois, one of its curators, has put performance artist and painter Ma Liuming's arresting self-portraits on display, as well as Beijing-born Lu Hao's architectural Plexiglas cages.

Many of Beijing's artists are forming communities. In the international group of Feijiacun, Chinese painters and sculptors work alongside visiting and expatriate foreigners. French curator Laetitia Gauden started the Imagine Gallery there in 2003. One former community, Dong Cun (East Village), is now Chaoyang, a public park.

Art lives on in its own way; today you enter the south side of the park through a futuristic red-and-yellow archway. Chaoyang is enormous—790 acres—and signs point in several directions: to the Rainbow Children's Playground, to the Boat Pier, and to an area identified as Shade of the Tree and Happy Sound of Singing. It's a fitting rebirth for a former arts hub. +

For The Guide, see page 279.

treasure hunt

SHOPPING IN **SHANGHAI**

IN CHINA'S LARGEST CITY, the Xingye Road runs through two apparent contradictions: the site of the First National Congress of the Communist Party of China, and a 560,000-square-foot retail and dining complex called Xintiandi. Together, they are a window into the history-rich city of Shanghai as it evolves into a modern metropolis. Xintiandi covers several blocks in the French Concession district, an area that was originally developed in the 1920's; since it opened in 2000, it has become a hub of fancy boutiques, expensive restaurants, and chic bars with flattering lighting and complicated cocktails. The surrounding French Concession is distinguished by tree-lined streets of gray-brick houses, many of them multiple dwellings.

The Xintiandi complex, however, is nothing like the French Concession. It's a kind of Shanghai-land; alleys run between buildings just as they did in the old days, although wider spaces have also been created to allow for open-air cafés. One store, Layefe, was founded by one of China's best-known contemporary artists, Chen Yifei. Layefe is opulent and filled with objects of desire, like woven-fur scarves, made from a choice of rabbit or mink. Around the corner from Layefe is Simply Life—a shop ▶

La Vie Boutique, in Shanghai's Xintiandi complex. Opposite: A tea house on one of the narrow streets nearby.

The Shirt Flag boutique, above. Below: Kommune café.

that could be airlifted in its entirety to SoHo without the need to change anything but the prices.

Countless shops, stores, malls, and street markets sprawl over Shanghai's nearly 2,500 square miles. If Xintiandi doesn't provide enough retail therapy, try the Bund, a grand riverfront parade of banks and merchant trade buildings that have been restored as an art-and-culture mall. Many of the top international and local designers are located at Three on the Bund, a Beaux-Arts building redesigned by Michael Graves, which also houses an art gallery, Evian spa, nightclubs, and four restaurants.

Taikeng Road in Luwen is one other former factory district turned artists' haven that's also worth a look. At Shirt Flag, graphic designer Zhong Jiji decorates T-shirts, hats, and more with cutting-edge Communist imagery. ✚

For *The Guide*, see page 279.

T+L Tip

SHOPPING BREAKS

Shanghai's restaurants are the perfect complement to its boutiques.

Ye Shanghai serves upscale Chinese food on lazy Susans and features a Shanghainese jazz band as an homage to the city's wicked past.

Karaoke bar **Cashbox** is located in nearby Fuxing Park and thronged with young Shanghainese all waiting to impersonate Frank Sinatra.

On Taikeng Road, **Kommune** is a cosmopolitan café with a communal outdoor barbecue.

At Bar 0101 in Seoul. Left: A beaded bag at Taipei's Jamei Chen.

made in taiwan

SETTING THE SCENE ON **TAIPEI**'S DA-AN ROAD

THE MOST STYLISH TAIWANESE know to go to Taipei's Da-An Road, one of the city's up-and-coming districts. The narrow lanes shooting off the road every 20 yards or so are dotted with distinctive boutiques, galleries, and happening restaurants amid 18th-century buildings. Women in search of flowing, ready-to-wear pieces go to Jamei Chen, who moved her studio and store here 10 years ago, next to old noodle shops and run-down flats. The neighbors include Isabelle Wen (the Betsey Johnson of Taipei) and Shiatzy Chen, who makes delicate, feminine women's wear. There's also Bella, one of a handful of tiny specialty shops that carry hard-to-find foreign labels such as Nude and Barbara Bui.

The area is also known for its housewares shops. Gray Area sells furniture and colorful silk-sheathed pillows. At Gallery Su, the glass shelves are chockablock with hand-painted ceramics from Europe and the Americas, much favored by the local style set.

Restaurants here take their cues from the fashion world. In the case of Fifi, the eatery's designer, Isabelle Wen, takes the same playful sensibility she used in her store, also in the neighborhood, and applied it to this Old Shanghai-inspired restaurant and lounge. The glamorous crowds that flock to the bistro's neon-green escalator often come straight from their studios, launch parties, and runway shows to pair earthy Taiwanese braises with Veuve before heading to the bar. +

For The Guide, see page 279.

korea cool

SEOUL'S HOT CAFÉ CULTURE

AFTER A HANDFUL OF galleries moved in to Seoul's Samcheong-dong neighborhood in the 1990's, a younger generation followed. The area's streets—which wend past gable-roofed houses and the east wall of the magnificent Gyeongbokgung Palace—are now the place to go for café culture. You'll find writers, brooding artists, and scholars sitting notepad to laptop in modern spaces while sipping green-tea lattes and Shiraz.

The epicenter of the scene is the Café at Kukje Gallery, frequented by artists planning their next exhibitions. Samcheong-dong restaurants also work with the arts: pocket-size Cook 'N' Heim has a gallery in the back, and Gallery Café, a wine bar lit by hanging paper lanterns, showcases rotating exhibitions of Korean painters. Meanwhile, if you can get one of the striking orange bucket seats at Bar0101, don't give it up too readily; the people-watching is among the best around. +

For The Guide, see page 279.

hot-spring heaven

JAPAN'S BATHING RESORTS

From top: A spring-fed stone pool at the Hakone Ginyu, a *ryokan* south of Tokyo; in an infinity pool at Enoshima.
Opposite: The Asaba *ryokan* in Shuzenji, known for its open-air baths of basalt rock.

THE JAPANESE BATHING RITUAL is as sacred to-day as it was thousands of years ago. Anyone who has watched Hayao Miyazaki's *Sen To Chihiro No Kamikakushi* (*Spirited Away*) needs no introduction to *onsen* (hot-spring) culture. For those who haven't seen it, the movie is an animated fantasy about a mortal girl who finds herself employed as a bathhouse attendant in the spirit realm. Before indoor plumbing became widespread, most Japanese took their daily plunge in a communal bathhouse, or *sento*, where men and women frequently shared facilities that were fed by natural hot springs. Old-fashioned bathhouses like the one depicted in *Spirited Away* have been declining in popularity, but private *onsen* bathing at a *ryokan* (tra-ditional Japanese inn) is still a part of life in the Japanese culture. *Onsen* bathing is developing a following of luminaries from around the globe, from presidents to California spa gurus. Fans include American spa authority Sylvia Sepielli—consultant on the elaborate baths at Grand Wailea on Maui and Florida's Boca Raton Resort—who was heavily influenced by her 10-year stay in Japan. Michael Stusser opened his Japanese-inspired Osmosis spa and meditation garden in Sonoma ▶

The lobby of Niki Club, a modern Terrence Conran-designed hotel and *onsen* on the edge of Nikko National Park, above. Below: A terrazzo-and-cypress *ofuro* at Murata in the spa town of Yufuin. Opposite: A shiatsu expert performing a massage inside the Meiji room at Murata.

County, California, after a stint in a Zen Buddhist monastery in Kyoto. French President Jacques Chirac favors Asaba, and chef Nobu Matsuhisa is a frequent guest at Gora Kadan—rival inns, both notable for their rigorous hospitality, two hours from downtown Tokyo in central Honshu. Indeed, there are countless *onsen* across the country, and some of the best are within easy reach of Tokyo.

About one hour's drive southwest of the city is Hakone, a resort area since the ninth century, and the gateway to Fuji-Hakone-Izu National Park. The road to Hakone rises quickly through a series of switch-backs into a group of volcanoes, where sulfurous steam puffs from vents scattered among rocky hills. Even on a misty afternoon, it's still hard to miss the 12,390-foot Mount Fuji topped with snow. Despite the swarms of hikers who lurch their way to the crater's rim, the peak's symbolism hasn't diminished since the 19th century, when it was considered so sacred that only priests were permitted to ascend to the summit. The Japanese always feel fortunate when Fuji sheds its cloudy veil. Among the resorts in the area is Hakone Ginyu, where, before bathing, you can sip sour-cherry iced tea on the wooden deck facing a deep gorge. Like most *ryokan*, Hakone Ginyu features several "public" *onsen* for in-house guests, among them two infinity pools and a hot tub on a loggia high above the Haya River. Bathing is scheduled so that everybody has a chance to sample all of the pools. Each day, the single-sex facilities are switched at least once; all it takes is a housemaid to

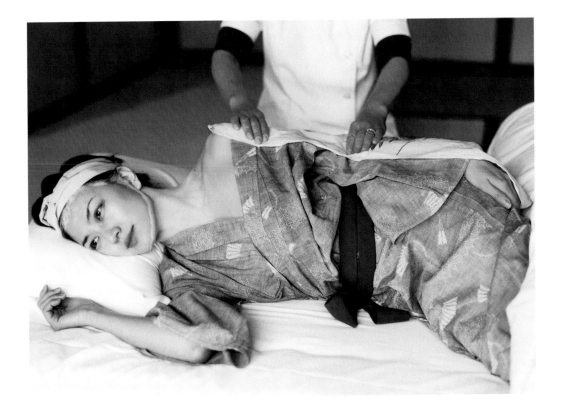

move the entrance signs around. Of course, for those who want a little more privacy, the guest room contains at least one *ofuro* (cypress tub) of its own. It's obvious why the hotel has had a recent surge in popularity among younger, Tokyo-based fans: they love its cheerful, informal feel.

Halfway down the Izu Peninsula lies the *onsen* town of Shuzenji, divided by the boulder-strewn Katsura River. Asaba—a 360-year-old *ryokan* with its own authentic-cypress Noh stage—is located past the lipstick-red bridges that span the Katsura and past the vendors selling wasabi, black rice, and bean-paste cakes near a Buddhist temple. Asaba may be ancient, but it certainly isn't outdated: Hermès desk pads and 20th-century Danish furniture dot its pebbled landscape. Basalt-rock pools offer opportunities for open-air baths.

The pastoral spa town of Yufuin, on Kyushu island, is home to Murata, a mountaintop *ryokan*. Owner Koji Fujibayashi relocated a handful of plaster-and-beam barns and thatched-roof lodges to this pine-covered slope below Mount Yufu-dake, and he also commissioned a cutting-edge designer from Tokyo to build the onsite villa Gyou, a stunning minimalist lair of concrete and steel. Le Corbusier chairs are grouped in the bar; an adjacent gallery displayed David Hockney and Wassily Kandinsky sketches. And although the main dining room uses a traditional charcoal cooking hearth, Murata also has its own Parisian-style chocolatier and Italian restaurant. ✚

For The Guide, see page 279.

T+L Tip

TOKYO RELAXATION

If you don't have time to stay at an *onsen*, relax at one of these top hotel spas:

Four Seasons Tokyo at Marunouchi The spa has two treatment rooms, stunning *onsen*-style baths, and not-to-be-missed shiatsu massages with Kyoko Nakamura.

Park Hyatt Tokyo You'll find facials and jet-lag therapies, plus a sky-high pool with view of Mount Fuji.

the wild east

POST-SOVIET **AZERBAIJAN**

AZERBAIJAN OFFERS more than just the usual litany of fading palaces and grilled meats. The country is a true reality tour, a vibrant portrait of how life is lived by the majority of humankind—which is to say with ingenuity, piety, and unshakable pride. Sandwiched between Russia to the north and Iran to the south, Azerbaijan has a rich history astride the tectonic plate at the conjunction of Russia, Persia, and Turkey, making it one of the most fascinating and beautiful places in the former Soviet Union. It also happens to be one of the friendliest countries you will visit.

Like most cities of the former U.S.S.R., the capital, Baku, has a solid inventory of Soviet-style museums, but the true cultural draw is its eclectic architecture. In the compact Old Town, the Maiden's Tower is perhaps the most famous of Baku's tourist sites. The ancient eight-story fortress is unduplicated: a round structure with a single buttress pillar projecting from its eastern side. The crescent of the Old Town is ringed by an assortment of *fin de siècle* mansions built during Baku's first oil boom.

A six-hour bus ride from Baku leads to the northwestern hamlet of Shaki and the most distinctive hotel in all of the former U.S.S.R. The motel-style Karvansaray Hotel, set in an 18th-century caravansary, once gave respite to the itinerant merchant and his camel. Brick-vaulted rooms, both Spartan and spacious, are built around an arched inner courtyard, beyond which distant mountain ridges form a fan shape, as if they were opening up before you. ✛

For The Guide, see page 279.

On the highway between Baku and Shaki, one of Azerbaijan's many billboards depicting deceased dictator Heydar Aliyev, above. Below: Trinkets in Linkaren. Opposite: The ancient Maiden's Tower in Baku.

Australia
+ New Zealand

Lake Wakatipu on New Zealand's South Island.

Vintage dresses line the window of the Frock Exchange in Tamarama, above. Left: The Opera House, on Circular Quay. Opposite: Custom-made shoes at Andrew McDonald Shoemakers, in Paddington.

style down under

MAKING A FASHION STATEMENT IN **SYDNEY**

SYDNEYSIDERS REVEL IN THE knowledge that they live in the cultural and style capital of the Pacific Rim. The city has spent the past several years quietly evolving into a more sophisticated, more thoughtful version of its former self, and its residents are no longer looking overseas for inspiration. Rather, they are distilling the best parts of their city's internationalism without discarding its unique cultural quirks. Exhibit A: office workers wear flip-flops to work. But that's only a glimpse of where the fashion scene is going in this sun-bleached city.

There are few better ways to witness Sydney's style transformation—or ways for a dedicated shopaholic to spend a Saturday—than to browse the neighborhood of Paddington. The long-established market area has gotten a dose of youthful vigor, now that a crop of fashion-forward boutiques has planted itself along Oxford and Glenmore on the area's once-residential

northern edge. The flagship store of Australia's hottest design team, Sass & Bide, sells flirty tanks and bohemian dresses in feminine fabrics. Scanlan & Theodore specializes in brightly printed yet sophisticated pieces for the martinis-after-work set. Filled with an international assortment of designers, Come As You Are offers boldly patterned men's pants from Italian-based Ra-Re and Michiko Koshino's tribal-inspired Yen Jeans line. Men's stovepipe pants—along with customized T-shirts—are all the rage at Roy. Andrew McDonald Shoemakers creates bespoke footwear for men in search of one-of-a-kind loafers ▶

or classic brogues. Up-and-comer Kirrily Johnston has a romantic clothing line (think Empire waists and lots of soft pleats) and equally romantic lingerie. And Sydney has found its answer to Diane von Furstenberg at Leona Edmiston, where flattering dresses, mainly in jersey and silk, fill the racks. For a Vivienne Westwood fix, the fashion-forward head to Parlour X.

Paddington's shops aren't only about clothing. Oz's answer to Sephora, Kit Cosmetics, carries hard-to-find products, all with an artisanal twist: Hei Poa body oil from Tahiti, Mudlark's goat's-milk soap. Come Saturday, the Paddington Markets roll into town. A sprawling array of jewelry and crafts takes over the grounds of the Paddington United Church; this is where you'll spot burgeoning talent in design and modern art. Many of Australia's best fashion labels—Zimmermann, Third Millennium, Lisa Ho—got their start at the market.

Across town, Tamarama, a small, sheltered bay between Bondi and Bronte beaches, is sometimes dubbed Glamarama for its disproportionate quotient of Sydney's renowned Beautiful People. Visiting fashion mavens make a beeline for the Frock Exchange, a boutique run by Belinda Seper, who has an eye for the next big thing. She also buys used pieces, much of it of

The Sydney Harbour Bridge, above. Opposite, clockwise from top left: A sign pointing to Paddington's cutting-edge William Street; handcrafted slingbacks by Andrew McDonald; Sopra, the café at Fratelli Fresh in Surry Hills; the Parlour X boutique, in Five Ways.

designer caliber, from short-attention-span shoppers unloading last season's castaways.

In the city's Central Business District, Vintage Clothing Shop stocks anything and everything that's well preserved: gowns, coats, shoes, jewelry, hats, gloves, and accessories. On a lucky day, you might even find a big-name-designer haul—Givenchy, Dior, Hermès—from a private collection.

The neighborhood of Newtown is Sydney's wild inner west, a maze of crowded streets and smoky bars populated mostly by students and tattooed artists. Don't be afraid, though—it's for show. Newtown is a great promenading neighborhood, with all the hallmarks of a college town, including an eclectic fashion boutique called Prettydog. The shop used to be the place for secondhand clothing, but it has evolved into a showcase for reworked vintage by established names like Karen Walker and Nicola Finetti, as well as young Australian designers. +

For The Guide, see page 280.

T+L Tip

SYDNEY'S RESTAURANT SCENE

Locals, priced out of ritzy Woollahra and Double Bay, have turned Surry Hills and Waterloo into a thriving urban village, and the culinary revolution here marches apace.

Red Lantern Updated versions of Vietnamese classics are served in a converted terrace house painted a provocative shade of scarlet.

Billy Kwong Celebrity chef Kylie Kwong's dishes, such as crispy duck, are inspired by her Chinese family's recipes.

Sopra Hipsters and the stroller set jostle politely for seats at this Italian café housed in the Fratelli Fresh grocery store, the Dean & DeLuca of Sydney.

Café Mint Fragrant breakfast couscous with cinnamon and honey, meze plates for two, and the best caffè lattes in town are among the top menu items at this storefront café specializing in North African–inspired dishes.

Tabou Rive Gauche ambience abounds in an old-time bistro setting, with gilded mirrors, bentwood chairs, thick steaks—and perfect *pommes frites*.

Movida's bartender in action, above.
Left: Breakfast special at Switchboard.

mod oz cuisine

THE CULINARY MOVEMENT IN **MELBOURNE**

AUSTRALIA'S SECOND CITY is first-rate when it comes to food. Unlike in many metropolitan areas, some of the best restaurants in Melbourne happen to be in the business district. Piadina Slowfood, hidden on a pedestrian-only street, is a neighborhood favorite. By 9 a.m., the office workers have cleared out, and you can take advantage of the calm by lingering over one of the grilled flat-bread sandwiches (don't miss the scrambled egg–Parmesan–spinach). Nearby, two twentysomething friends (Jade's a barista; Kate's a graphic designer) have transformed a former DVD-rental kiosk in a landmark building into Switchboard, the grooviest coffee spot in town. The only acceptable drink to order is Australia's most popular caffeinated concoction, the "Flat White": a latte with no foam, served in a teacup.

On a graffitied laneway across from Federation Square, Movida could just as well be in Barcelona, with its *tarifa de consumición*. The room is dominated by a massive Tasmanian-blackwood bar; waiters with matinee-idol looks deliver bottles of wine to execs indulging in three-Tempranillo lunches. Try the anchovies with smoked-tomato sorbet, the roasted lamb cutlet (swathed in Catalan pork pâté), or the piquillo peppers stuffed with *bacalao* (dried salt cod). The cavernous new Thai restaurant Longrain, an outpost of the legendary Sydney hot spot, has more than 50 novel (and tasty) cocktails. Pick a perch at the spotlit bar, order the My Thai martini (chile, cucumber, lemongrass, vodka, mint, and ginger), and sit back to watch fish swimming in the giant aquarium and people swanning by outside. +

For The Guide, see page 280.

beaching it aussie-style

SUNNY WEEKENDS IN **NOOSA**

WHEN IN-THE-KNOW Australians want a quiet beach getaway, perfectly temperate water, and a relaxed vibe (sarongs and flip-flops), they head to Noosa, a small seaside town in Queensland on what's known as the Sunshine Coast. In this secluded spot just an hour and a half north of Brisbane, coastal paths wind through rain forests, surfers ride impressive waves off uncrowded shores, and naturalists scope out kookaburras, koalas, and wallabies.

Thirty years ago, surfers camped at the end of Hastings Street. Now, instead of tents, there's a cluster of boutique hotels, among them Noosa Blue Resort, where the penthouse has a private rooftop barbecue.

A perfect morning in Noosa starts with berry pancakes at Café Le Monde. Noosa Holiday Hire rents necessities, including boogie boards and towels. While surfboards cost about $15 a day, insider tips on where to get the best milk shake are given out free.

Noosa National Park is a lovely place to take a break from all the sand. The park has walking trails through one of the most beautiful forests in Australia, with eucalyptus and cypress pines and fields of wildflowers, which sprout up most stunningly in spring. **+**

For The Guide, see page 280.

Noosa National Park, north of Brisbane, above. Below: The view from the penthouse at Noosa Blue Resort.

Wine casks at Fromm Winery, above. Left:
Allan Scott winery. Opposite: Cycling along
Rapaura Road.

new zealand's napa

BIKING THROUGH THE **SOUTH ISLAND**'S VINEYARDS

IN THE NORTHEAST CORNER of the South Island,
Marlborough's gentle landscape, seasonable weather,
and ample vineyards make it one of the most beautiful
places in the country to take a long bike ride.

It's easy enough to arrange your own itinerary. The
Marlborough Winegrowers Association distributes free
maps of the region. A good starting point is Antares
Homestay, west of Blenheim. Owned by English
expats Jane and Ray Adams, Antares is a small bed-
and-breakfast on four acres of gardens, ponds, and
orchards. Unlimited use of a hybrid bike is included in
the cost of an overnight stay.

The area around Antares and Blenheim is home to
dozens of wineries, including Fromm Winery, known
for its Pinot Noir. On a hill above State Highway 6,
Highfield Estate, established in 1989, is more than a
winery: it's also a restaurant and a Tuscan-style one-
room B&B. The narrow farm road is flanked by vine
tresses; in the distance you can see windmills, which
are used to warm plants on frosty nights.

Riding on Highway 6 toward Renwick, you'll pass
towering pines, eucalyptus trees, and a few other
vineyards before reaching Te Whare Ra, the region's

oldest boutique winery. Jason and
Anna Flowerday unveil their latest
vintages as if they are introducing their children. Gewürztraminer
is the specialty here, but the
Sauvignon Blanc is also excellent.

If a guided trip is more your speed,
Pacific Cycle Tours offers a five-day
excursion of the area called Wine
Trail Magic, which begins and ends
in Blenheim. Averaging 14 miles a
day, the tour takes in the Allan Scott
winery, among others. Across the
road is Cloudy Bay, one of the first
wineries in Marlborough to export
Sauvignon Blanc. The narrow farm
road to Highfield Estate, nearby, is all
uphill. But amateur riders needn't
worry—this is about as strenuous as
it gets—and the payoff, a glass of one
of their Rieslings or Elstree Cuvée, is
well worth the exertion. +

For The Guide, see page 280.

kiwi bounty

FARM FRESH ON THE **NORTH ISLAND**

THE NORTH ISLAND OF New Zealand has been known to inspire feeding frenzies. Almost anything could come from the land, and almost everything does: house-roasted coffees, varietal olive oils, grass-fed beef, and heirloom gooseberries. Over the past five years, the restaurant scene has caught up with the supply of home-grown comestibles, thanks in part to increased immigration from the Pacific Rim. The best way to experience the full range of food outlets—from fresh farmers' markets to *haute* restaurants—is to take a drive.

As it turns out, the capital city of Wellington has more bars, restaurants, and cafés per capita than New York. Maria Pia's Trattoria, near the Parliament district, radiates the kind of *Big Night* energy of a small-restaurant owner's dreams. A fire glows in the freestanding fireplace whose chimney seems to have witnessed a half-century's worth of buzzing Friday nights. Chef Maria Pia De Razza-Klein impresses Kiwis with her rustic Italian food; her fresh pasta with wild-boar sausage and *ciabatta* is a favorite. De Razza-Klein, an expert on Maori customs and cuisine, is a supporter of Slow Food, the international organization dedicated to saving and celebrating regional cooking.

Indigenous ingredients are also celebrated on the menu at Logan Brown, in a renovated 1920's bank on the corner of Cuba and Vivian streets. The signature ravioli dish contains *paua*, New Zealand's version of abalone, which is rare and absolutely worth trying. Off Tory Street, the eclectic produce store Moore Wilson Fresh is a regular stop for chefs looking for seasonal fruits grown exclusively for the market. ►

Prime restaurant in Auckland, above. Below: Local radicchio. Opposite: Herds of New Zealand's prized cattle and sheep graze on the North Island.

2002 *Mate's Vineyard Chardonna*

2002 *Kumeu River Chardonna*

2000 *Kumeu River Pinot Noir*

1999 *Kumeu River "Melba"*

2000 *Kumeu River Merlot*

2002 *Kumeu River Pinot Gris*

2002 *Brajkovich Chardonn*

2000 *Brajkovich Merlot*

Route 2 runs over alluvial plains on the east side of the island. On one side you'll see spinal mountain ranges; on the other, windy roads lead to wild beaches. From Wellington, take Route 2 about 200 miles to the sleepy town of Napier. The temperate climate is ideal for agriculture, and the farmers' market, in a field outside Hastings, south of Napier, has a bounty of heirloom potatoes, goat cheeses, and organic meats.

When it comes to fresh food, Kumeu and Waimauku are two of the best-served towns off State Highway 16. In Waimauku, BeesOnline creatively incorporates honey into almost every one of its organic dishes; even the salads are dressed in Honeygar, a naturally fermented wine vinaigrette. And Kumeu River, a family-run vineyard, specializes in Chardonnay, Pinot Gris, and Pinot Noir.

In Auckland, the farm-fresh theme continues even amid the high-rises. The French Café was voted Best Restaurant of 2006 by local *Cuisine* magazine, and at Hilton Auckland's Bellini Bar, bartenders bring a creative touch to the cocktail menu with their lychee-and-rhubarb Capi Capi, made with rice wine and fresh cranberry juice. Prime, a sun-splashed lunch-only bistro in the PricewaterhouseCoopers tower, is another excellent place to experience Auckland's cosmopolitan food scene.

On a Sunday, it's worth taking a quick side trip from Auckland to the suburb of Avondale to track down another legendary New Zealand produce market. Crowds from all over gather in the parking lot of Avondale racetrack, where the smells of damp gingerroot, mint, and lemon thyme hang in the air, while women in saris and burkas compete for raw peanuts, long melons, bok choy, and the last watercress of the season. **+**

For The Guide, see page 280.

T+L Tip

THE FOOD SCENE

The up-and-coming wine region of **Hawke's Bay** is also the setting of a Sunday-morning market. "We massage and pat our cows," says one producer of grass-fed beef. The region also sponsors a **Food Trail**. A map is available from Hawke's Bay visitor information center or online at hawkesbaynz.com.

Kalamata olives at one of the many small groves on the North Island. Opposite, from left: Bellini Bar at the Hilton Auckland; the wine choices at the Kumeu River vineyard, near Auckland.

the guide

United States
+Canada

Maine

WHERE TO STAY

Portland Harbor Hotel On the Old Port. 468 Fore St., Portland; 888/795-9090; www.portlandharborhotel.com;

WHERE TO EAT

555 Local ingredients. 555 Congress St., Portland; 207/761-0555; **$$$**; **Barnacle Billy's** Classic lobster rolls. 50 Perkins Cove Rd., Ogunquit; 207/646-5575; **$$**; **Bayview Market & Takeout** Crab rolls. Bayview Rd. (Rte. 175), Penobscot; 207/326-4882; **$**; **Browne Trading Co.** New England's finest seafood market. 262 Commercial St., Portland; 207/775-7560; **Chase's Daily Farmstand** Vegetarian. 96 Main St., Belfast; 207/338-0555; **$$**; **Clam Shack** Fried clams. 2 Western Ave., Kennebunkport; 207/967-2560; lobster rolls for two: **$$**; **Duckfat** The city's best sandwiches. 43 Middle St., Portland; 207/774-8080; lunch for two: **$$**; **Fore Street** Famous for roasted mussels. 288 Fore St., Portland; 207/775-2717; **$$**; **Francine Bistro** Earthy

flavors in a charming setting. 55 Chestnut St., Camden; 207/230-0083; **$$$**; **Hugo's** Run by a Thomas Keller protégé. 88 Middle St., Portland, 207/774-8538; **$$$**; **Joshua's** Farm-fresh food. 1637 Post Rd., Wells; 207/646-3355; **$$**; **MC Perkins Cove** Classic coastal fare. 111 Perkins Cove Rd., Ogunquit; 207/646-6263; **$$$**; **Morse's Sauerkraut** A Maine tradition. 3856 Washington Rd. (Rte. 220), N. Waldoboro; 866/832-5569; **$**; **Primo** Garden-based menu. 2 S. Main St. (Rte. 73), Rockland; 207/596-0770; **$$$**; **Red's Eats** Juicy lobster rolls. 41 Water St., Wiscasset; 207/882-6128; **$$**; **Sewall's Orchard** Wild blueberries. Masalin Rd., Lincolnville; 207/763-3956; **Smiling Hill Farm** 150-plus home-made ice cream flavors. 781 County Rd. (Rte. 22), Westbrook; 207/775-4818; **Standard Baking Co.** Tasty ginger cake. 75 Commercial St., Portland; 207/773-2112; **White Barn Inn** Converted barn. 37 Beach Ave., Kennebunkport; 207/967-2321; **$$$**

Quechee Lakes, VT

WHERE TO STAY

Woodstock Inn 142 sophisticated rooms with stunning views. 14 The Green, Woodstock; 800/448-7900; www.woodstockinn.com;

WHAT TO DO

Quechee Lakes Ski Area 802/295-9356; www.quecheeclub.com

The Berkshires

WHERE TO STAY

Stonover Farm Suites in 1890 Berkshires cottage with fireplaces. 169 Under Mountain Rd., Lenox; 413/637-9100; www.stonoverfarm.com; breakfast included;

WHAT TO DO

Hancock Shaker Village 20 restored Shaker buildings. 800/817-1137; www.hancockshakervillage.org; guided tours available year-round

Litchfield Hills, CT

WHERE TO STAY

Mayflower Inn English country-style hotel and spa. 118 Woodbury Rd. (Rte. 47), Washington Depot; 860/868-9466; www.mayflowerinn.com;

WHERE TO EAT

The Pantry Gourmet specialty foods. Titus Rd., Washington Depot; 860/868-0258; lunch for two: **$**

WHERE TO SHOP

Adeptus Arts Art-glass studio. 38 Bee Brook Rd. (Rte. 47), Washington Depot; 860/868-2326; **Dawn Hill Antiques** 18th- and 19th-century Swedish and French furniture. 11 Main St., New Preston; 860/868-0066; **Finial Home & Garden** Floral arrangements and country furniture. 13 River Rd., Washington Depot; 860/868-2577; **Grape in the Shade** Vintage clothes. 13 River Rd., Washington Depot; 860/868-9119; **Judy Hornby Decora-**

tive **Antiques** Vast emporium of European art and furniture. 725 Bantam Rd. (Rte. 202), Bantam; 860/567-3162; **Michael Trapp** Global antiques. 7 River Rd., West Cornwall; 860/672-6098; **New Preston Kitchen Goods** Specialty cookware and accessories. 11 E. Shore Rd. (Rte. 45), New Preston; 860/868-1264; **Personal Best Monogram Shoppe** Linens and gifts. 2 Green Hill Rd., Washington Depot; 860/868-9966; **Ragamont House Antiques** Louis XVI armchairs, hunting trophies, and oil portraits. 8 Main St. (Rte. 44), Salisbury; 860/435-8895; **Richard J. Lindsey Bookseller** Rare and used books. 15 N. Main St. (Rte. 7), Kent; 860/927-3025; **R. T. Facts** Home and garden. 22 S. Main St. (Rte. 7), Kent; 860/927-1700; **Washington Connecticut Antiques Show** Early fall. 860/868-7586; www.gunnlibrary.org/antiques.html

New York City

WHERE TO STAY

Hotel QT Hip on a budget. 125 W. 45th St.; 212/354-2323; www.hotelqt.com; **Mandarin Oriental New York** Asian-inspired. 80 Columbus Circle; 212/805-8000; www.mandarinoriental.com;

WHERE TO EAT

Aurora Rustic Italian. 70 Grand St., Brooklyn; 718/388-5100; **$$**; **Café Henri** Light Bistro fare. 10-10 50th Ave., Queens; 718/383-9315; **$**; **Cookshop** High-end, down-home American. 156 Tenth Ave.; 212/924-4440; **$$**; **Del Posto** Mario Batali's opulent Italian restaurant. 85 Tenth Ave.; 212/497-8090; **$$$$**; **Diner** Gourmet comfort food. 85 Broadway, Brooklyn; 718/486-3077; **$$**; **Lounge 47** Casual pub menu. 47-10 Vernon Blvd., Queens; 718/937-2044; **$**; **Marlow & Sons** Small general store and restaurant. 81 Broadway, Brooklyn; 718/384-1441; $$; **Tia Pol** Bite-sized tapas bar. 205 Tenth Ave.; 212/675-8805; $$$; **Tournesol** Late-night French cuisine. 50-12 Vernon Blvd., Queens; 718/472-4355; $

WHAT TO DO

Clementine 623 W. 27th St.; 212/243-5937; www. clementine-gallery.com; **Dorsky Gallery** 11-03 45th Ave., Queens; 718/937-6317; **Gagosian** 555 W. 24th St.; 212/741-1111; www. gagosian.com; **Jack the Pelican Presents** 487 Driggs Ave., Brooklyn; 646/644-6756; **John Connelly Presents** 625 W. 27th St.; 212/337-9563; **Marian Goodman** 24 West 57th St.; 212/977-7160; www.mariangoodman. com; **Matthew Marks** 523 W. 24th St.; 212/243-0200; www.matthewmarks.com; **Noguchi Museum** 9-01 33rd Rd., Queens; 718/204-7088; www.noguchi.org; **Outrageous Look** 103 Broadway, Brooklyn; 718/218-7656; www.outrageouslook.com; **Participant Inc.** 95 Rivington St.; 212/254-4334; www. participantinc.org; **Paula Cooper** 534 W. 21st St.; 212/255-1105; **Pierogi** 177 N. 9th St., Brooklyn; 718/599-2144; www.pierogi 2000.com; **The Project** 37 West 57th St.; 212/688-1585; www.elproyecto.com; **PS1 Contemporary Art Center** 22-25 Jackson Ave., Queens; 718/784-2084; www.ps1.org; **Reena Spaulings Fine Art** 371 Grand St.; 212/477-5006; www.reena spaulings.com; **Sarah Bowen** 210 N. 6th St., Brooklyn; 718/302-4517; www.sarah bowengallery.com; **SculptureCenter** 44-19 Purves St., Queens; 718/361-1750; www.sculpture-center.org; **Sean Kelly** 528 W. 29th St.; 212/239-1181; www.skny. com; **Socrates Sculpture Park** 32-01 Vernon Blvd., Queens; 718/956-1819; www. socratessculpturepark.org

Long Island

WHERE TO STAY

Greenporter Hotel & Spa Refurbished 1950's-era motor inn. 326 Front St.; 631/477-0066; www. thegreenporter.com; ⌐

WHERE TO EAT

Fifth Season Island produce and local wines. 45 Front St.; 631/477-8500; $$$; **La Cuvée Wine Bar & Bistro** Hip food. 326 Front St.; 631/477-0066; $$$

WHAT TO DO

Castello di Borghese Tastings in wood-paneled room. Rte. 48 (Sound Ave.) and Alvah's Lane, Cutchogue; 631/734-5111; **The Old Field Vineyard** Family-run winery. 59600 Main Rd., Southold; 631/765-0004; **Palmer Vineyards** Classically structured vinifera wines. Aquebogue; 631/722-9463; **Shinn Estate Vineyards** Weekend walking tours and tastings. 2000 Oregon Rd., Mattituck; 631/804/0367

Asheville, NC

WHERE TO STAY

Inn on Biltmore Estate 213-room limestone manor-style house overlooks the famous Vanderbilt winery. 1 Antler Hill Rd.; 800/858-4130; www.biltmore.com; ⌐⌐

WHERE TO EAT

Early Girl Eatery Southern classics with a mountain spin. 8 Wall St; 828/259-9292; $$

WHERE TO SHOP

Ariel Gallery Contemporary craft cooperative. 46 Haywood St.; 828/236-2660; **Blue Spiral 1** Southeastern painters and sculptors. 38 Biltmore Ave.; 828/251-0202; **Longstreet Antiquarian Maps & Prints** Maps and prints. 8 Biltmore Ave.; 828/254-0081; **New Morning Gallery** Artisan-made fountains, pottery, and wrought iron items. 7 Boston Way; 828/274-2831; **Penland School of Crafts**

Esteemed center for pottery, glassblowing, metalworking, with an on-site gallery. 67 Doras Trail, Penland; 828/765-2359; www.penland.org

Charleston, SC

WHERE TO STAY

Battery Carriage House Inn Historic inn. 20 S. Battery; 800/775-5575; www.battery carriagehouse.com; ⌐; **Charleston Place Hotel** 442 traditionally appointed rooms in the historic district. 205 Meeting St.; 800/611-5545; www.charlstonplace.com; ⌐⌐⌐⌐; **Wentworth Mansion** Ornate Second Empire–style. 149 Wentworth St.; 888/466-1886; www.wentworth mansion.com; ⌐⌐⌐

WHERE TO EAT

Circa 1886 Seasonal menus and a 280-bottle wine list. 149 Wentworth St.; 843/853-7828; $$$; **Hominy Grill** Southern regional dishes. 207 Rutledge Ave.; 843/937-0930; lunch for two: $$; **Peninsula Grill** Sophisticated atmosphere and food to match. 112 N. Market St.; 843/723-0700; $$$; **Slightly North of Broad** Shrimp and grits. 192 E. Bay St.; 843/723-3424; $$$

WHERE TO SHOP

B'zar Edgy clothes. 541 King St.; 843/579-2889; **ESD-Elizabeth Stuart Design** Handmade jewelry, vintage lighting fixtures, and regional cookbooks. 314 King St.; 843/577-6272; **Magar Hatworks** Couture millinery. 557½ King St.; 843/577-7740; **Moo Roo** Locally designed scarves, brooches, and handbags. 316 King St.; 843/724-1081; **Reuben's Mens & Boys Wear** Stylish men's clothes. 480 King St.; 843/723-5421; **What-cha-Like-Gospel** CD's and tapes. 499 King St.; 843/577-9786

WHAT TO DO

Edmondston-Alston House Furniture, silver, treasures. 21 E. Battery; 843/722-7171;

www.middletonplace.org; **Middleton Place** 1741 plantation. 4300 Ashley River Rd.; 843/556-6020; www. middletonplace.org; **Old Slave Mart Museum** Former slave-trade salesroom turned museum. 6 Chalmers St.; 843/958-6467; **Preservation Society of Charleston** Tours of historic properties and private houses. 147 King St.; 843/722-4630; www. preservationsociety.org

Miami

WHERE TO STAY

Biltmore Hotel National landmark property. 1200 Anastasia Ave., Coral Gables; 800/727-1926 or 305/445-1926; www.biltmorehotel. com; ⌐⌐; **Delano** Celebrity favorite. 1685 Collins Ave., Miami Beach; 305/672-2000; www.delano-hotel. com; ⌐⌐⌐⌐; **The Raleigh** Redone South Beach original. 1775 Collins Ave., Miami Beach; 800/848-1775; www. raleighhotel.com; ⌐⌐; **Sagamore** All suites, with contemporary art. 1671 Collins Ave., Miami Beach; 305/535-8088; sagamore hotel.com; ⌐⌐⌐⌐; **The Setai** Asian-accented gem. 2001 Collins Ave., Miami; 305/520-6000; www.setai. com; ⌐⌐⌐⌐⌐; **The Shore Club** Hopping hotel lobby. 1901 Collins Ave., Miami Beach; 305/695-3100; www. shoreclub.com; ⌐⌐⌐

WHERE TO EAT

Bahamian Pot Specializing in chowder. 1413 N.W. 54th St., Miami; 305/693-5053; lunch for two: $; **Chef Creole Seafood Takeout** Fritters and salads. 200 N.W. 54th St., Miami; 305/754-2223; $$; **El Rey De Las Fritas** Meat and shoestring potatoes. 1177 S.W. Eighth St., Miami; 305/858-4223; $; **Jimbo's Shrimp** Virginia Key Beach, Miami; 305/361-7026; $; **King's Ice Cream** Soda floats. 1831 S.W. Eighth St., Miami; 305/643-1842; $

key

lodging:
⌐ under $150
⌐⌐ $150-299
⌐⌐⌐ $300-699
⌐⌐⌐⌐ $700-999
⌐⌐⌐⌐⌐ $1000+up
⌐⌐⌐⌐⌐⌐ $10,000/week
Prices listed are doubles for two.

dining:
$ under $25
$$ $25-74
$$$ $75-149
$$$$ $150-299
$$$$$ $300 + up
Prices listed are dinner for two.

WHERE TO SHOP

Books & Books Literary epicenter. 265 Aragon Ave., Coral Gables; 305/442-4408; **Botanica Nena** One-stop shopping for the occult. 902 N.W. 27th Ave., Miami; 305/649-8078; **Genius Jones** Design store for children and adults. 1661 Michigan Ave., Miami Beach; 305/534-7622

WHAT TO DO

Kampong of the National Tropical Botanical Garden Exotic plants on display. 4013 Douglas Rd., Miami; 305/442-7169; www.ntbg. org; admission: $10, open for tours and by appointment; **Venetian Pool** 1920's coral swimming pool. 2701 De Soto Blvd., Coral Gables; 305/460-5306 or 305/460-5357; www.venetianpool. com; admission: $10; **The Wolfsonian** Decorative art and propaganda. 1001 Washington Ave., Miami Beach; 305/531-1001; www. wolfsonian.org

Chicago

WHERE TO STAY

Four Seasons Hotel Chicago Complimentary access to Grant Park and Lincoln Park Zoo. 120 E. Delaware Place; 800/332-3442; family suites:

WHERE TO EAT

Greek Islands Famous for *saganaki*. 200 S. Halsted St.; 312/782-9855; dinner for four: **$$**; **Original Pancake House** Country look. 22 E. Bellevue Place; 312/642-7917; lunch for four: **$$**; **Wiener's Circle** Hot dogs and cheese fries. 2622 N. Clark St.; 773/477-7444; **$**

WHAT TO DO

Adler Planetarium & Astronomy Museum Tour the solar system. 1300 S. Lake Shore Dr.; 312/922-7827; www.adlerplanetarium.org; **Art Institute of Chicago** Massive armor collection; miniature period rooms. 111 S. Michigan Ave.; 312/443-3600; www.artic.edu; **Blue Chicago Store** Saturday-night all-ages shows. 534 N. Clark St.; 312/661-1003; **Chicago Children's Museum** Interactive exhibits. 700 E. Grand Ave.; 312/527-1000; www.chichildrensmuseum. org; **Chicago History Museum** Lincoln's hat, death-bed, and original draft of the Emancipation Proclamation. 1601 N. Clark St.; 312/642-4600; **Chicago Shakespeare Theater** From Shakespeare to Sondheim. Navy Pier; 312/595-5656; www. chicagoshakes.com; **Field Museum** Home to one of the largest T. Rex skeletons. 1400 S. Lake Shore Dr.; 312/922-9410; **The Hancock Observatory** 80-mile-wide views of four states. 875 N. Michigan Ave.; 888/875-8439; **Lincoln Park Zoo** Booming gorilla population. 2200 N. Cannon Dr.; 312/742-2000; free; **Navy Pier** Mile-long stretch of entertainment. 600 E. Grand Ave.; 800/595-7437; **Notebaert Nature Museum** A butterfly haven. 2430 N. Cannon Dr.; 773/755-5100; **Sears Tower Skydeck** 1,353 feet high. 233 S. Wacker Dr.; 312/875-9696; **Shedd Aquarium** World's largest indoor aquarium. 1200 S. Lake Shore Dr.; 312/939-2438; **Smith Museum of Stained Glass Windows** Works from 1870. 600 E. Grand Ave.; 312/ 595-5024; **Water Tower Place** 100-plus stores on eight levels. 806 N. Michigan Ave; **Wrigley Field** Home of the Cubs. 1060 W. Addison St.; 773/404-2827

Iowa

WHERE TO STAY

Hotel Winneshiek Built in 1904. 104 E. Water St., Decorah; 563/382-4164;

WHERE TO EAT

Breitbach's One of the state's oldest restaurants. 563 Balltown Rd., Balltown; 563/552-2220; **$**; **David's Milwaukee Diner** Hearty diner food. 515/465-7370; breakfast for two: **$**; **Suzie Q Café** 1940's diner. 14 Second St. N.W., Mason City; 641/423-502; lunch for two: **$**; **Taylor's Maid-Rite** Iowa-born chain. 106 S. Third Ave., Marshalltown; 641/753-9684; lunch for two: **$**

WHERE TO SHOP

Granary Antique Mall Cavernous barn with rustic handicrafts. 602 Pearl St., Walnut; 712/784-3331; **Main Street Antique Mall** Dozens of dealers. 105 W. Main St., Marshalltown, 641/752-3077

WHAT TO DO

Bily Clock Museum Intricate, antique musical clocks. 323 S. Main St., Spillville; 563/562-3569; www.bilyclocks.org

Minneapolis

WHERE TO STAY

Graves 601 21 stories of cool design. 601 First Ave. N.; 612/677-1100; www.graves601hotel.com;

WHERE TO EAT

Chino Latino Fusion food. 2916 Hennepin Ave.; 612/824-7878; **$**

WHERE TO SHOP

Bill's Imported Foods An assortment of Mediterranean and exotic specialties. 721 W. Lake St.; 612/827-2891

WHAT TO DO

Bakken Library and Museum Thousands of rare books and scientific instruments. 3537 Zenith Ave. S.; 612/926-3878; **Guthrie Theater** Vanguard drama company in Jean Nouvel–designed space. 818 S. 2nd St.; 612/377-2224; www.guthrietheater. org; **Mill City Museum** The history of the flour-milling industry. 704 S. Second St.; 612/341-7555; www.millcitymuseum.org; **Walker Art Center** Contemporary art and a famous sculpture garden. 1750 Hennepin Ave.; 612/375-7622; www. walkerart.org

Door County, WI

WHERE TO STAY

White Gull Inn Victorian lodge. 4225 Main St., Fish Creek; 888/364-9542; www. whitegullinn.com; cottages for four:

WHAT TO DO

American Folklore Theatre Midwestern humor. 9462 Shore Rd., Fish Creek; 920/854-6117; www.folklore theatre.com; **Lautenbach's Orchard Country** Family-run winery and market. 9197 Hwy. 42, Fish Creek; 920/868-3479; **Peninsula State Park** Bike the trails and swim at Nicolet Bay Beach. 608/266-2621; www. dnr.state.wi.us; **Red Putter** Mini-golf in nearby Ephraim. 10404 Hwy. 42; 920/854-5114; **Skyway Drive-in Theater** Classic 1950's big screen. 3475 Hwy 42, Fish Creek; 920/854-9938

Marfa, TX

WHERE TO STAY

Thunderbird Motel Contemporary design with Western flourishes. 601 W. San Antonio St.; 432/729-1984; www.thunderbirdmarfa.com;

WHAT TO DO

Chinati Foundation Guided visits: Wednesday–Sunday. 1 Cavalry Row; 432/729-4362; www.chinati.org

Texas Hill Country

WHERE TO STAY

Kindred Spirits Guesthouse with grand view, two minutes from the river. South Fork, Hunt; 866/427-8374; www. fbglodging.com;

Yellowstone, MT

WHERE TO STAY

Big EZ Lodge Privately owned lodge far from the crowds. 7000 Beaver Creek Road, Big Sky, Mont.; 406/995-7000; www.big ezlodge.com; from

Salt Lake City

WHERE TO STAY
Grand America Hotel Carrara marble, Italian silk comforters. 555 S. Main St.; 800/621-4505; www.grandamerica.com; ↵↵

WHERE TO EAT
Cup of Joe Mellow hangout. 353 W. 200 South; 801/363-8322; **Metropolitan** Award-winning restaurant. 173 W. Broadway; 801/364-3472; **$$$**; **Squatter's Pub Brewery** Homemade beer, classic pub fare. 147 W. 300 South; 801/363-2739; lunch for two: **$$**

WHERE TO SHOP
King's English Bookshop Independent bookstore. 1511 S. 1500 East; 801/484-9100

WHAT TO DO
Clark Planetarium IMAX films, light shows. 110 S. 400 West; 801/456-7827; www.clarkplanetarium.org; **Salt Lake City Public Library** Books, shops, and reading galleries. 210 E. 400 South; 801/524-8200; www.slcpl.lib.ut.us; **Utah Museum of Fine Arts** 17,000-plus works. 410 Campus Center Dr.; 801/581-7332; www.umfa.utah.edu; **Utah State Historical Society** In the 1910-built Rio Grande Depot. 300 South Rio Grande St.; 801/533-3500; www.history.utah.gov

San Francisco

WHERE TO STAY
Hotel Vitale Waterfront property with complimentary yoga instruction. 8 Mission St.; 888/890-8688; www.hotelvitale.com; ↵↵

WHERE TO EAT
A16 Wood-fired pizzas. 2355 Chestnut St.; 415/771-2216; **$$$**; **Blue Bottle Coffee Co.** Hip spot. 315 Linden St.; 415/252-7535; **Boulette's Larder** Artisanal French food. 1 Ferry Building; 415/399-1155; **$$$$** based on 10-person table; **Canteen**

Unfussy food. 817 Sutter St.; 415/928- 8870; **$$**; **Emmy's Spaghetti Shack** Comfort food, weekend DJ's. 18 Virginia St.; 415/206-2086; **$$**; **Foreign Cinema** California-Mediterranean menu, films in courtyard. 2534 Mission St.; 415/648-7600; **$$$**; **Michael Mina** San Francisco marquee chef. 335 Powell St.; 415/397-9222; **$$$$**; **Myth** Cushy dining room. 470 Pacific Ave.; 415/677-8986; **$$$**; **Quince** Elegant and rustic. 1701 Octavia St.; 415/775-8500; **$$$**; **Slanted Door** Organic Vietnamese. 1 Ferry Building; 415/861-8032; **$$$**

Bend, OR

WHERE TO STAY
McMenamins Old St. Francis Hotel Converted school with 19 rooms and four cottages. N.W. Bond St.; 877/661-4228; www.mcmenamins.com; ↵; **Sunriver Resort** Stately lodge, tennis courts, pools, and three golf courses. 800/547-3922; www.sunriver-resort.com; ↵↵

WHAT TO DO
Mount Bachelor One of the finest peaks for skiing. 800/829-2442; www.mtbachelor.com; full-day lift ticket: $15/summer, $49/winter; **Patient Angler** 90-minute fly-fishing course. 822 SE Third St.; 541/389-6208; $50

Seattle

WHERE TO STAY
Inn at the Market Peaceful retreat in heart of the shopping district. 86 Pine St.; 800/446-4484; ↵↵

WHERE TO EAT
The Hi-Life Updated regional dishes. 5425 Russell Ave. N.W.; 206/784-7272; **$$**; **La Carta de Oaxaca** Mexican specialties. 5431 Ballard Ave. N.W.; 206/782-8722; **$$**; **La Isla Seattle** Washington's first Puerto Rican restaurant. 2320 N.W. Market St.; 206/

789-0516; **$**; **Volterra** Contemporary Tuscan food. 5411 Ballard Ave. N.W.; 206/789-5100; **$$**

NIGHTLIFE
Portalis Huge wine list. 5205 Ballard Ave. N.W.; 206/783-2007; **Sambar** Inventive cocktails. 425 N.W. Market St.; 206/781-4883; **Thaiku** Exotic drinks. 5410 Ballard Ave. N.W.; 206/706-7807

North Shore, Oahu

WHERE TO STAY
Turtle Bay Resort Access to horse trails, golf courses, tennis courts, restaurants, and spa. 57–091 Kamehameha Hwy., Kahuku; 800/203-3650; www.turtlebayresort.com; ↵

WHAT TO DO
Hans Hedemann Surf School Private lessons. 57-091 Kamehameha Hwy., Kahuku; 808/447-6755; **Waimea Valley Audubon Center** A fecund wonderland. 59-864 Kamehameha Hwy., Haleiwa; 808/638-9199

Alaska

WHERE TO STAY
Alyeska Resort Postmodern take on a traditional Alpine property. 1000 Arlberg Ave., Girdwood; 800/880-3880; www.alyeskaresort.com; ↵↵; **Van Gilder Hotel** Registered historic landmark. 308 Adams St., Seward; 800/204-6835; www.vangilderhotel.com; ↵

WHERE TO EAT
Café Cups Tropical-themed restaurant. 162 W. Pioneer Ave., Homer; 907/235-8330; lunch for two: **$**

Whistler, B.C.

WHERE TO STAY
Four Seasons Resort Whistler Year-round luxury resort. 4591 Blackcomb Way; 888/935-2460; www.fourseasons.com; ↵↵↵↵

Vancouver

WHERE TO STAY
Four Seasons Hotel Vancouver Centrally located. 791 West Georgia St.; 604/689-9333; from ↵↵↵; **Opus Hotel** Boutique property with a minimalist aesthetic; 322 Davie St.; 800/332-3442; www.opushotel.com; ↵↵↵

WHERE TO EAT
Shiru-Bay Chopstick Café Japanese street food in hip space. 1193 Hamilton St.; 604/408-9315; **$$**; **Vij's** Unique Indian. 1480 W. 11th Ave.; 604/736-6664; **$$$**

WHERE TO SHOP
Eugene Choo Beautifully tailored clothing. 3683 Main St.; 604/873-8874; **Peridot** Jean-Harlow-goes-to-Paris loungewear and furnishings. 1512 W. 14th Ave.; 604/736-4499; **Pleasant Girl** Clothing and accessories. 2541 Main St.; 604/677-4024; **Motherland** Sophisticated punk sportswear. 2539 Main St.; 604/876-3426; **Richard Kidd** Fashion atelier in a glass row house. 65 Water St.; 604/677-1880

WHAT TO DO
Aquabus Ferry to Granville Island and Yaletown. 1617 Foreshore Walk; 604-1689-5858; **Grouse Mountain SkyRide** Largest sky tram in North America. 6400 Nancy Greene Way; 604-184-0661

Montreal

WHERE TO STAY
Hôtel Gault Design aficionados' choice. 449 Rue Ste.-Hélène; 866/904-1616 or 514/904-1616; www.hotelgault.com; breakfast included; ↵↵; **Hôtel St.-Paul** Creatively outfitted rooms. 355 Rue McGill; 866/380-2202; www.hotelstpaul.com; breakfast included; ↵↵

WHERE TO EAT
Cluny Artbar Old foundry turned bar and gallery; 257 Rue Prince; 514/866-1213; drinks for two: **$**

270

BERMUDA+
THE
CARIBBEAN
+THE
BAHAMAS

Bermuda+
the Caribbean
+the Bahamas

Bermuda

WHERE TO STAY

9 Beaches 84 overwater bungalows with simple décor. 441/232-6655; www.9beaches.com;

WHERE TO EAT

The Reefs Al-fresco meals and 180-degree panoramic ocean vistas at Ocean Echo Terrace. 56 South Shore Rd., Southampton; 800/742-2008; $$$$$

Anguilla

WHERE TO STAY

Cap Juluca Like a Moorish fantasy. Domed exterior; marble bathrooms; spa, massage, yoga, Pilates. 888/858-5822 or 264/497-6666; www.capjuluca.com; breakfast, water sports, and afternoon tea included; **Malliouhana Hotel & Spa** Glamorous beach resort with alluring art-filled rooms; on-site restaurant features French cuisine. 800/835-0796 or 264/497-6111; www.malliouhana. com; **St. Regis Temenos, Anguilla** Villa resort with personal butlers; private infinity pool with beach views. Long Bay; 264/222-9000; www.temenosvillas. com;

WHERE TO EAT

Blanchard's Chef's signature dishes are creamless corn chowder and tuna filet mignon. Meads Bay; 264/497-6100; $$$; **CuisinArt Resort & Spa** Guests can cook with fresh, local ingredients and eat their own dishes. Rendezvous Bay; 800/943-3210; $$$$

Turks and Caicos

WHERE TO STAY

Amanyara Luxurious South Asian–style resort set on a rugged coastline. Northwest Point, Providenciales; 65/6887-3337; www.aman-resorts.com; **Parrot Cay** Sheer style on a private island. 877/754-0726; www.parrotcay.como. bz.

British Virgin Islands

WHERE TO RENT A BOAT

Prices are for a seven-day rental that sleeps six. **Moorings** Bareboat and crewed sailboats. 800/521-1126; www.moorings. com; from $4,480; **Sunsail** Multi-day sailing courses and sailboat rentals. 888/350-3568; www.sunsail.com; from $2,860

St. Bart's

WHERE TO STAY

Hotel Guanahani & Spa Nestled between two beaches; colorful bungalows; tennis, fitness center, water sports, and scuba; on-site restaurants and lounges; hair, beauty, massages and spa. Grand Cul de Sac; 590-590/276-660; www. leguanahani.com;

WHERE TO EAT

Le Gaïac Four-course meals ranging from classic to island-spicy at the exquisite Hôtel Le Toiny. Anse de Toiny; 590-590/ 278-888; $$$; **Le Ti St-Barth** The epicenter of island cool: live music, daily barbecue specials, fashion shows, and theme parties. Pointe Milou; 590-590/ 279-771; $$; **Nikki Beach** International following. Plage de St.-Jean; 590-590/276-464; $$$

WHERE TO SHOP

Blue Coast Men's linen shorts and shirts; fresh colors and classic styles. 5 Rue du Bord de Mer; 590-590/296-018; **Calypso** World-renowned upscale boho-chic clothing and accessories. Le Carré d'Or; 590-590/276-974; **Lolita Jaca** Selection of young European designers; baroque interior with wrought iron furniture. Les Hauts du Carré d'Or; 590-590/275-998; **Metis** Slingbacks, sandals, and espadrilles are just some of the choices. Les Hauts du Carré d'Or; 590-590/298-108; **Mia Zia** Sporty Moroccan-inspired knits and accessories. Zia 8 Villa Creole; 590-590/275-548; **Syysuna by Free Mousse** Knickknacks and imported housewares from Latvian tablecloths to Laguiole corkscrews. Le Carré d'Or; 590-590/277-504; **Terra** Located between Nikki Beach and Eden Rock, eclectic shop sells rough-cut gems, pareus, and beaded bags. Pelican Plage; 590-590/275-750

Jamaica

WHERE TO STAY

Jake's Surfside shacks on stilts. Treasure Beach, St. Elizabeth; 800/688-7678; **Rockhouse Hotel** Lush, secluded hotel with thatched-roof stone villas. Negril, Westmoreland; 876/957-4373; www.rockhousehotel. com; **Round Hill Hotel & Villas** One of the island's older resorts; on an amphitheater-like hill; breathtaking views and bamboo beds create a colonial fantasy. Montego Bay, Hanover; 800/972-2159; www.round hilljamaica.com;

WHERE TO EAT

Howie's Deluxe roadside cookshop serves delicious seafood with a distinctively peppery Jamaican flavor. Middle Quarters, St. Elizabeth; no phone; lunch for two: $; **Rockhouse Hotel Restaurant** Caribbean fusion cuisine complemented by an international wine list. Negril, Westmoreland; 876/957-4373; $$; **Scotchies** Classic roadside jerk pit; chicken, fish, and veggies. Montego Bay, St. James; 876/953-8041; lunch for two: $

WHAT TO DO

Appleton Estate Rum Tour Jamaica's oldest rum distillery. Siloah District, St. Elizabeth; 876/963-9215

Harbour Island, Bahamas

WHERE TO STAY

Oceanview Club Fashion-crowd favorite. Gaol Lane; 242/333-2276; breakfast and dinner included; **Pink Sands Resort** Balinese theme. Chapel St.; 800/688-7678 or 242/333-2030; www.islandoutpost. com; breakfast and dinner included;

WHERE TO EAT

Sip Sip Global lunch menu with diverse ingredients. Court St.; 242/333-3316; $$

Mexico+ Central +South America

Riviera Maya, Mexico

WHERE TO STAY

Amansala Beachfront yoga retreat. Km 7.7, Carr., Tulum–Boca Paila; 52-984/100-0805; www.aman sala.com; ; **Casa Magna** Pablo Escobar's former estate. 9.5 Km. Boca Paila; casamagna@amansala.com; ; **Fairmont Mayakoba** Expansive jungle-and-beach development. Carr. Federal Cancún, Playa del Carmen; 800/441-1414; www.fair mont.com; ; **Ikal del Mar** Eco-conscious hideaway. Frac 7, Playa Xcalacoco; 888/230-7330 or 52-984/877-3000; www. ikaldelmar.com;

Puebla and Querétaro, Mexico

WHERE TO STAY

La Casa de la Marquesa 18th-century palace. 41 Madero, Centro Histórico, Querétaro; 52-442/212-0092; www.lacasadelamar quesa.com;

WHERE TO EAT

Compañía European and Asian imports. 6 Sur 304 Callejón de los Sapos, Puebla; 52-222/242-3554; $$

Mexico City

WHERE TO STAY

Condesa DF Small, stylish hotel. 102 Avda. Veracruz; 52-55/5241-2600; www. condesadf.com;

WHERE TO SHOP

Artefacto Chic homewares. 94 Calle Amatlán, Condesa; 52-55/5286-7729; **Carmen Rion** Breezy linens. 30A Avda. Michoacán, Condesa; 52-55/5264-6179; **Chic by Accident** Antique furnishings and home accessories. 180 Calle Colima, Roma; 52-55/5514-5723; **Galería OMR** Contemporary artwork. 54 Plaza Río de Janeiro, Roma; 52-55/5511-1179; **Kulte** Trendy sneakers. 118 Calle Atlixco, Condesa; 52-55/5211-7389; **Local** Avant-garde women's fashions. 248 Avda. Amsterdam, Condesa; 52-55/5564-9148

Argentina

WHERE TO STAY

Park Hyatt Mendoza Colonial-style. 1124 Chile; 54-261/441-1234; www. parkhyatt.com; ; **Posada San Eduardo** 19th-century adobe farmhouse. Calle San Martín and Los Enamorados, Barreal; 54-26/4844-1046;

Costa Rica

WHERE TO STAY

Caribbean Conservation Corporation Basic beachside accommodations. 800/678-7853; www.ccuturtle.org; all-inclusive; nine-day packages from $2,798 for two; **Hotel Punta Islita** Thatched-roof villas. 011-506/231-6122; www.hotelpuntaislita. com; ; **Inn at Coyote Mountain** Hacienda-style inn. 011-506/383-0544; www.cerrocoyote.com; $1,500, three nights, classes included

TOUR OPERATOR

Costa Rica Expeditions Adventure-oriented tours. 011-506/257-0766; www. costaricaexpeditions.com. 10-day packages from $3,616 for two

Panama

WHERE TO STAY

Azueros Villa Camilla Tropical setting. Pedasí, Los Santos; 011-507/232-6721; www.azueros.com; ; **Panamonte Inn & Spa** Mountain lodge. Avda. 11 de Abril, Boquete; 011-507/720-1324; www.pana monteinnandspa.com;

Brazil's Beaches

WHERE TO STAY

Mosquito Blue Hotel Simply furnished rooms. Rua Ismael. Jericoacoara, Ceará; 55-88/3669-2203; www.mosquitoblue.com. br; ; **Pousada Maravilha** Minimalist bungalows. BR 363, Sueste, Fernando de Noronha, Pernambuco; 55-81/3619-0028; www. pousadamaravilha.com.br; ; **Sombra e Água Fresca** Small inn. 1000 Rua Praia do Amor, Praia da Pipa, Rio Grande Do Norte; 55-84/3246-2144; www. sombraeaguafresca.com. br;

Manaus, Brazil

WHERE TO STAY

Tropical Manaus On the banks of the Rio Negro. 1320 Avda. Coronel Teixeira, Ponta Negra; 55-92/2123-5000; www.tropicalhotel. com.br;

WHERE TO EAT

Bar do Armando Open-air restaurant. 593 Rua 10 de Julho; 55-92/3232-1195; $$

WHAT TO DO

Teatro Amazonas Praça São Sebatião; 55-92/3622-2420

Lima

WHERE TO STAY

Miraflores Park Hotel Lima's most luxurious option. 1035 Avda. Malecón de la Reserva, Miraflores; 800/237-1236; www. mirapark.com;

WHERE TO SHOP

Claudia Stern Unusual jewelry. By appointment only; 103 Calle Saenz Peña, Barranco; 51-1/477-0921; **Dédalo** Contemporary crafts. 295 Saenz Peña, Barranco; 51-2/477-5131; **Ester Ventura** Natural baubles. 1157 Avda. Malecón Almirante Grau, Chorrillos; 51-1/467-1180; **Helena Chocolatier** Specializes in *tejas*. 897 Calle Chiclayo, Miraflores; 51-1/242-8899; **Las Pallas** Folk art and traditional weavings. 212 Calle Cajamarca, Barranco; 51-1/477-4629; **Mercado Indio** Local artisans' works. 5245 Auda Petit Thouars, Miraflores

Santiago

WHERE TO STAY

Ritz-Carlton Santiago South America's first Ritz. 15 Calle el Alcalde; 800/241-3333 www.ritzcarlton.com;

WHERE TO EAT

Confitería Torres Restored landmark building. 1570 Alameda; 56-2/688-0751; $$

WHERE TO SHOP

Chantal Bernsau Semiprecious gems. 5211 Monseñor Escrivá de Balaguer; 56-2/418-5991; **Galería Animal** Local artists. 3105 Avda. Alonso de Córdova; 56-2/371-9090; **Galería de Arte Trece** The city's most venerable gallery. 3980 Avda. Nueva Costanera, Vitacura; 56-2/378-1981; **GAM** Fashion cooperative. 138 Calle La Pastora; 56-2/474-5109

WINERIES

Bar Liguria Chilean wines and comfy bar stools. 019 Luis Thayer Ojeda; 56-2/231-1393; www.liguria.cl

WHAT TO DO

Ruta del Vino de Colchagua Best area winery, 85 miles south of Santiago. www.colchaguavalley.cl; **Wine Travel Chile** Private tours. 1860 Avenida II de Septiembre, Santiago; 56-2/334-8842; www.winetravelchile.com

Buenos Aires

WHERE TO STAY

Alvear Palace Hotel Recently renovated landmark hotel in a 1932 palace; gilded Lobby Bar. 1891 Avda. Alvear; 800/223-6800; www.alvearpalace.com; ✂✂✂; **Faena Hotel + Universe** Modern hotel in a converted grain depository. 445 Martha Salotti; 54-11/4010-9000; www.faenahotelanduniverse.com; ✂✂✂; **Hotel Home Buenos Aires** Funky boutique hotel in Palermo Soho. 5860 Honduras; 54-11/4778-1008; www.homebuenosaires.com; ✂

WHERE TO EAT

Dora Sophisticated, top-notch international and regional dishes, meats, and seafood. 1016 L.N. Alem; 54-11/4311-2891. Lunch for two: $; **Restaurant Sucre** Warehouse-style space; menu emphasizes local ingredients. 676 Sucre; 54-11/4782-9082; dinner for two: $$

NIGHTLIFE

Bar Sur DJ's spin in this modernized tango bar; audience participation is encouraged. 299 Estados Unidos; 54-11/4362-6086; dinner and show: $$$; **El Taller** Hip café in the Palermo Soho neighborhood. 1595 Serrano, Palermo Viejo; 54-11/4831-5501

WHERE TO SHOP

Cora Groppo Argentinean fashionista's namesake shop sells flirty cocktail dresses and elegant wedding and evening attire. 4696 El Salvador; 54-11/ 4832-5877; **Malu y Carla Ricciardi** Eccentric boutique features these two independent designers. 2212 Malabia; 54-11/4833-5965

WHAT TO DO

Museo de Arte Latinoamericano de Buenos Aires Contemporary Latin American art; gift shop showcases local Argentinean talent. 3415 Avda. Figueroa Alcorta; 54-11/4808-6500; www.malba.org.ar

Punta del Este, Uruguay

WHERE TO STAY

Club Hotel Casapueblo Moorish structure on a hill outside town. Punta Ballena; 598-42/578-611; www.clubhotel.com.ar; ✂✂; **Conrad Punta del Este Resort & Casino** Glamorous Vegas-style mega-resort with over 300 luxurious rooms; a year-round scene. Avda. Barritz and Artigas, Parada 4; 598-42/491-111; www.conradhotels.com; ✂✂✂; **Hotel Serena** Boutique hotel on the beach; incredible views from the pool. Rambla Williman; Parada 24; 598-42/233-441; www.serenahotel.com.uy; ✂✂

Western Europe

Devon, England

WHERE TO STAY

Bovey Castle Restored British grandeur in Dartmoor National Park. North Bovey, Dartmoor National Park; 44-1647/445-016; www.boveycastle.com; ✂✂✂; **Hotel Endsleigh** Renovated stone manor surrounded by 108 acres of lush parkland. Milton Abbot, Tavistock, Devon; 44-1822/870-000; www.hotelendsleigh.com; ✂✂

WHERE TO SHOP

James Bowden & Son Family-owned department store. 54 The Square, Chagford; 44-1647/433-271; **Wood & Rush** Sustainable artisans' cooperative. 1A The Square, Chagford; 44-1647/231-330

London

WHERE TO STAY

The Berkeley Posh rooms in Knightsbridge, overlooks Hyde Park. Wilton Place; 44-20/7235-6000; ✂✂✂✂; **Knightsbridge Hotel** A boutique favorite with 44 individually designed guest rooms and suites. 10 Beaufort Gardens, Knightsbridge; 44-20/7584-6300; www.firmdale.com; ✂✂

WHERE TO SHOP

Alexander McQueen Dramatic leathers, silks, and fashions. 4–5 Old Bond St.; 44-20/7355-0088; **Bracher Emden** Ultra-cool rocker-chick handbags. Factory 6G, 784–788, The High Rd.; 44-20/8801-4967; **Dunhill** Men's classics. 48 Jermyn Street; 44-84/5458-0779; **Fiona Knapp** Sleek jewels. 178a Westbourne Grove; 44-20/7313-5941; **Georgina Goodman** Couture shoes. 12–14 Shepherd St.; 44-20/7499-8599; **Kilgour** Sophisticated flat-front trousers. 8 Savile Row; Kilgour 44-20/7734-6905; **Pamela Blundell** Bespoke tailored suits. 35 Sackville Street; 44-7/8810-0836; **Philip Treacy** London's mad hatter. 69 Elizabeth St.; 44-20/7730-3992; **Pringle** Argyle heaven. 141/142 Sloane St.; 44-20/7881-3060; **Solange Azagury-Partridge** Inventive baubles, perfect for souvenirs. 187 Westbourne Grove; 44-20/7792-0197; **Tanner Krolle** High-style leather bags and purses. 5 Sloane St.; 44-20/7823-1688; **Virginia** Vintage clothing. 98 Portland Rd.; 44-20/7727-9908; **Vivienne Westwood** Renegade classics. 44 Conduit St.; 44-20/7439-1109

Hay-on-Wye, Wales

WHERE TO STAY
Rest for the Tired B&B in 17th-century town house. 6 Broad St.; 44-1497/820-550; ⌐ʼ

WHERE TO SHOP
B & K Books Over 500 tomes. Riverside, Newport St.; 44-1497/820-386; **Mark Westwood Books** Scientific texts and antiquarian books. High Town; 44-1497/820-068; **Murder and Mayhem** Detective fiction. 5 Lion St.; 44-1497/821-613; **Poetry Bookshop** First editions, anthologies, poetry books. Ice House, Brook St.; 44-1497/821-812; **Richard Booth's Bookshop** Second-hand books. 44 Lion St.; 44-1497/820-322

Amsterdam

WHERE TO STAY
Ambassade Hotel A 17th-century canal-side house. 341 Herengracht, 31-20/555-0222; www.ambassade-hotel.nl; ⌐ʼ⌐ʼ⌐ʼ; **Lloyd Hotel** Small, modern rooms. 34 Oostelijke Handelskade; 31-20/561-3636; www.lloydhotel.com; ⌐ʼ

WHERE TO SHOP
BLGK Postmodern jewelry. 28 Hartenstraat; 31-20/624-8154; **Droog Design** Whimsical designs. 7a Staatstraat; 31-20/523-5050; **Frozen Fountain** Contemporary furnishings. 645 Prinsengracht; 31-20/622-9375; **Hester Van Eeghen** Colorful handbags. 37 Hartenstraat; 31-20/622-9212; **Klamboe Unlimited** Decorative canopies. 232 Prinsengracht; 31-20/622-9492; **Shoebaloo** Designer shoes. 80 P.C. Hooftstraat; 31-20/671-2210; **Trunk** Odds and ends, from bracelets to tablecloths. 12 Rosmarijnsteeg; 31-20/638-7095; **Van Ravenstein** Fashion-forward designs for the home. 359 Keizersgracht; 31-20/639-0067

Zurich

WHERE TO STAY
Hotel Baur au Lac Grand, family-owned hotel. 1 Talstrasse; 41-44/220-5020; www.bauraulac.ch; ⌐ʼ⌐ʼ⌐ʼ⌐ʼ

WHERE TO EAT
Café/Bar Odeon Frequented by artists, intellectuals, and eccentrics. 2 Limmatquai; 41-44/251-16-50; $$; **Restaurant Kronenhalle** Culinary classics. 4 Rämistrasse; 41-44/251-6669; $$$

NIGHTLIFE
Acapulco Party spot. 56 Neugasse; 41-44/272-6608

WHERE TO SHOP
Brunos Italian men's wear. 44 Bahnhofstrasse; 41-44/211-0290; **Confiserie Sprüngli** Miniature macaroons. 21 Bahnhofstrasse; 41-44/224-4711; **Orell Füssli** Books on art and architecture. 70 Bahnhofstrasse; 41-44/211-0444

Germany

WHERE TO STAY
Dornröschenschloss Sababurg Castle turned hotel. Sababurg; 49-5671/8080; www.sababurg.de; ⌐ʼ⌐ʼ; **Hotel Burg Trendelburg** 13th-century tower. 1 Steinweg, Trendelburg; 49-5675/9090; www.burg-hotel-trendelburg.com; ⌐ʼ⌐ʼ

WHAT TO DO
Brothers Grimm House Storytellers' home on the Fairy Tale Route. 80 Bruder-Grimm-Strase, Steinau an der Strase; 49-6663/7605; www.steinau.de

Zürs and Lech, Austria

WHERE TO STAY
Hotel Almhof Schneider Lech Fireplaces and handmade quilts. 43-5583/3500; www.almhof.at; ⌐ʼ⌐ʼ⌐ʼ⌐ʼ; no credit cards; **Hotel Gasthof Post** Alpine luxury in a former post house; Lech; 43-5583/22060; www.postlech.com; ⌐ʼ⌐ʼ⌐ʼ⌐ʼ; **Hotel Zürserhof** Farmhouse chic. 43-5583/25130; www.zuserhof.at; ⌐ʼ⌐ʼ⌐ʼ⌐ʼ; includes all meals

WHERE TO SHOP
Strolz Sporthouse Sports emporium; Lech 116; 43-5583/2361

WHAT TO DO
Lech Ski School 43-5583/2355; www.skischule-lech.at; **Skihütte Schneggarei** Ultra-hip hangout. Lech; 43-5583/39888; **Zürs Ski School** 43-5583/2611; www.skischule-zuers.at

Brittany

WHERE TO STAY
Les Maisons de Bricourt Grand 1920's villa. Château Richeux, St.-Méloir-des-Ondes, three miles from Cancale; 33-2/99-89-64-76; www.maisons-de-bricourt.com; ⌐ʼ⌐ʼ

WHERE TO EAT
L'Étrave Classic Breton lobster dinners on Brittany's westernmost point. Rte. Pointe du Van, Cléden-Cap-Sizun; 33-2/98-70-66-87; $$$; **Relais Gourmand Olivier Roellinger** *Haute* cuisine from Brittany's star chef. 1 Rue Duguesclin, Cancale; 33-2/99-89-64-76; $$$$$

WHERE TO SHOP
Épices Roellinger Freshly roasted spices and oils. Rue Duguesclin, Cancale; 33-2/23-15-13-91; **Grain de Vanille** Salted butter caramels, homemade ice cream, sorbets, and pastries. 12 Place de la Victoire, Cancale; 33-2/23-15-12-70

Paris

WHERE TO STAY
Hotel Meurice Louis XVIII–style décor. 228 Rue de Rivoli, First Arr.; 33-1/44-58-10-10; www.hotelmeurice.com; ⌐ʼ⌐ʼ⌐ʼ⌐ʼ

WHERE TO EAT
Aux Noctambules One of the city's oldest cabaret bars. 24 Boulevard de Clichy, 18th Arr.; 33-1/46-06-16-38; **Café Burq** Live jazz. 6 Rue Burq, 18th Arr.; 33-1/42-52-81-27; $$; **La Mascotte** Views of the Seine. 6 Ave. du Président Wilson, 18th Arr.; 33-1/47-20-83-47; $$

WHERE TO SHOP
20 Sur 20 Vintage Bakelite. 3 Rue des Lavandières, St.-Opportune, First Arr.; 33-1/45-08-44-94; **Adelline** Understated necklaces, bracelets, and earrings. 54 Rue Jacob, Sixth Arr.; 33-1/47-03-07-18; **Atelier du Bracelet Parisien** Accessories in ostrich, crocodile, and shagreen. 7 Rue St.-Hyacinthe; First Arr.; 33-1/42-86-13-70; **Calesta Kidstore** Baby clothes and accessories. 23 Rue Debelleyme, Third Arr.; 33-1/42-72-15-59; **Colette** Hip women's boutique. 213 Rue St.-Honoré, Eighth Arr.; 33-1/55-35-33-90; **E. B. Meyrowitz Opticiens** Designer eyewear. 5 Rue Castiglione, First Arr., 33-1/42-60-63-64; **Editions de Parfums** Sultry scents. 21 Rue du Mont-Thabor, First Arr.; 33-1/42-22-77-22; **Emmanuel Perrotin** Renowned art gallery. 76 Rue de Turenne; 33-1/42-16-79-79; **Fifi Chachnil** Pinup–style lingerie. 231 Rue St.-Honoré, First Arr.; 33-1/42-61-21-83; **Galerie du Passage** 20th-century French furniture and contemporary art. 20-22 Galerie Véro-Dodat, First Arr.; 33-1/42-36-01-13; **Guerlain** More than 70 scents. 68 Ave. des Champs-Élysées, Eighth Arr.; 33-1/45-62-52-57; **L'Habilleur** Last season's designer clothes. 44 Rue de Poitou, Third Arr.; 33-1/48-87-77-12; **Librairie 7L** Karl Lagerfeld's photography bookshop. 7 Rue de Lille, Seventh Arr.; 33-1/42-92-03-58; **L'Oeil du Silence** Books, DVD's, graphic novels, hard-to-find magazines.

91 Rue des Martyrs, 18th Arr., 33-1/42-64-45-40; **Lydia Courteille** Estate jewelry. 231 Rue St.- Honoré, First Arr.; 33-1/42-61-11-71; **Madame André** The Gilles Dufour collection, plus a mix of inexpensive items. 34 Rue du Mont-Thabor, First Arr.; 33-1/42-96-27-24; **Mona** The latest collections. 17 Rue Bonaparte, Sixth Arr.; 33-1/44-07-07-27; **Palais de Tokyo** Contemporary art exhibits in a soaring space. 13 Ave. du Président Wilson, 16th Arr.; 33-1/47-23-38-86; **Roger Vivier** Status-symbol shoes in an airy boutique. 29 Rue du Faubourg St.-Honoré, Eighth Arr.; 33-1/53-43-00-85

Nice

WHERE TO STAY

Hi Designed by Philippe Starck protégée; unique hotel bar inspired by ship's interior. 3 Ave. des Fleurs; 33-4/97-07-26-26; www.hi-hotel.net; ⌐⌐⌐⌐; **Hôtel Beau Rivage** The town's only beach club. 24 Rue Saint-François-de-Paule; 33-4/92-47-82-82; www.nicebeaurivage.com; ⌐⌐⌐⌐; **Hôtel Negresco** Belle Époque luxury hotel. 37 Promenade des Anglais; 33-4/93-16-64-00; www.hotel-negresco-nice.com; ⌐⌐⌐⌐; **Palais de la Méditerranée** Renovated 1930's Art Deco landmark hotel and casino. 13–15 Promenade des Anglais; 33-4/92-14-77-00; www.lepalaisdelamediterranee.com; ⌐⌐⌐⌐

WHERE TO EAT

Chez Simon Pizza restaurant. 275 Rte. de St.-Antoine-de-Ginestiére; 33-4/93-86-51-62; $$; **Le Café de Turin** Bistro-style seafood. 5 Place Garibaldi; 33-4/93-62-29-52; $$$; **Le Grand Balcon** Steps from the opera. 10 Rue Saint-François-de-Paule; 33-4/93-62-60-74; $$$

WHERE TO SHOP

Harter Antiquités 18th- and 19th-century paintings, furniture, and furnishings. 34 Rue Catherine Ségurane; 33-4/93-55-17-39; **Jacqueline Morabito** Visionary decorator's gallery; furniture and jewelry. 42/65 Rue Yves-Klein, La Colle sur Loup; 33-4/93-32-64-92; **Maison Auer** Fifth-generation sweet shop, specializes in *fruits confits.* 7 Rue St.-François-de-Paule; 33-4/93-85-77-98

WHAT TO DO

Opéra de Nice 4 and 6 Rue St.-François-de-Paule; 33-4/92-17-40-00

Rome

WHERE TO STAY

Casa Howard Five individually decorated rooms. 18 Via Capo Le Case, Piazza del Popolo; 39-06/6992-4555; www.casahoward.com; ⌐⌐⌐; **Hotel Hassler** Former 1885 palace. 6 Piazza Trinità Dei Monti; 800/223-6800; www.hotelhassler.com; ⌐⌐⌐⌐

WHERE TO EAT

Café de Paris Site of famous scene from *La Dolce Vita.* 90 Via Vittorio Veneto; 39-06/4201-2257; $$$$; **Cesarina** Emilia-Romagna specialties. 109 Via Piemonte; 39-06/4201-3432; $$$

NIGHTLIFE

Caffè Della Pace Artist and literati hangout. 3–7 Via della Pace; 39-06/686-1216; **Harry's Bar** Legendary piano bar. 150 Via Vittorio Veneto; 39-06/484-643

WHAT TO DO

Cinecittà Fellini's celebrated movie studios. 1055 Via Tuscolana; 39-06/722-931; **Pino's Barbershop** Get a shave and a haircut from Fellini's former barber. 121 Via Piemonte; 39-06/488-4236; **Scooters for Rent** 84 Via della Purificazione; 39-06/488-5485

Bologna

WHERE TO STAY

Grand Hotel Baglioni Gilded mirrors, crystal chandeliers, 16th-century paintings. 8 Via Indipendenza; 39-051/225-445; www.baglionihotels.com; ⌐⌐⌐⌐

WHERE TO EAT

Gelatauro Internationally famous homemade organic gelato. 98 Via San Vitale; 39-051/230-049; **La Sorbetteria Castiglione** Flavors named after family members. 44 via Castiglione; 39-051/233-257; **Pappagallo** Tortellini in *brodo.* 3 Piazza Mercanzia, 39-051/232-807; $$$$; **Ristorante Diana** Old-fashioned Bolognese style food. 24 Via Indipendenza; 39-051/231-302; **Roccati** Family-owned open-air chocolate laboratory. 17A Via Clavature; 39-051/261-964; **Trattoria ai Butteri** Thickly cut *fiorentina* steak. 20 Via Muri; 39-051/347-718; $$$

WHERE TO SHOP

37 San Felice Designer Giovanna Guglielmi's two clothing labels. 37 Via San Felice; 39-051/864-204; **Branchini Calzoleria** Dress shoes. 19 Strada Maggiore; 39-051/648-6642; **Cappelleria Trentini** Up-and-coming designers. 33 Via Indipendenza; 39-051/224-276; **L'Inde Le Palais** High-concept creations. 6 Via de' Musei; 39-051/648-6587; **Spazio Minghetti** Fendi furniture store. 3 Piazza Minghetti; 39-051/265-670

Florence

WHERE TO STAY

Hotel Cellai One of Florence's last family-run hotels. 14 Via 27 Aprile; 39-055/489-291; www.hotelcellai.it; ⌐⌐; **J.K. Place** Chic 20-room boutique hotel. 7 Piazza Santa Maria Novella; 800/525-4800; www.jkplace.com; ⌐⌐⌐

WHAT TO DO

Charles H. Cecil Studios Florence's oldest operating fine art studio offers intensive life drawing and painting classes. 68 Borgo San Frediano; 39-055/285-102; from $2,541 for July session; **Florence Academy of Art** Month-long course taught in English in July. 21R Via delle Casine; 39-055/245-444

Barcelona

WHERE TO STAY

Neri Hotel 18th-century palace. 5 Carrer Sant Sever; 34/93-304-0655; www.hotelneri.com; ⌐⌐⌐

WHERE TO EAT

Arola Hip tapas restaurant. Hotel Arts Barcelona, 19–21 Carrer de la Marina; 34/93-483-8090; $$$; **Caelis** Chef Romain Fornell's vibrant Spanish *nueva cocina.* Hotel Palace, 668 Gran Vía de les Corts Catalanes; 34/93-510-1205; lunch for two: $$$$; **Can Fabes/Espai Coch** Traditional Catalan cuisine in two different metropolitan settings. 6 Sant Joan, Sant Celoni; 34/93-848-4384; $$$$$ at Can Fabes; $$$$ at Espai Coch; **Cinc Sentits** Canadian chef with Catalan origins. 58 Carrer Aribau; 34/93-323-9490; $$$; **Drolma** Hotel Majestic, 70 Passeig de Gràcia; 34/93-496-7710; $$$$$; **Moo** Creative food and wine pairings. Hotel Omm, 265 Carrer Rosselló; 34/93-445-4000; tasting menu for two: $$$$; **Restaurant Gaig** Retro cooking with traditional ingredients like salt cod and suckling pig. Hotel Cram, 214 Carrer Aragó; 34/93-429-1017; $$$$; **Sant Pau** Contemporary Catalan cuisine by chef Carme Ruscalleda; three-star restaurant in a seaside village, 45 minutes from Barcelona by train. 1 Carrer Nou, Sant Pol De Mar; 34/93-760-0662; $$$$

Madrid

WHERE TO STAY
HH Campomanes Like upscale dorms. 4 Calle Campomanes; 34/91-548-8548; www.room-matehotels.com; ⌐⌐; **Hotel Urban** Mod 96-room oasis steps from the Prado. 34 Carrera de San Jerónimo; 34/91-787-7770; www.derbyhotels.es; ⌐⌐⌐⌐

WHAT TO DO
Museo Nacional Centro de Arte Reina Sofía Jean Nouvel–designed building. 52 Calle Santa Isabel; 34/91-467-5062; museoreina sofia.es; **Museo Nacional del Prado** The Met of Madrid, open until 8 p.m. Tuesday through Sunday. Paseo del Prado; 34/91-330-2800; www.museoprado.es; **Museo Thyssen-Bornemisza** Old Masters share wall space with major 19th- and 20th-century works. Open until 11 p.m. all summer. 8 Paseo del Prado; 34/91-369-0151; www.museothyssen.org

Majorca

WHERE TO STAY
La Residencia Luxurious 16th- and 17th-century manor houses. Son Canals, Deya; 800/223-1236; www.hotel-laresidencia.com; ⌐⌐⌐; **Puro** Casbah-chic design hotel. 12 Monte Negro, Palma; 800/337-4685; www.purohotel.com; ⌐⌐⌐⌐; **Son Brull Hotel & Spa** Renovated minimalist monastery. Km. 49.8, Carretera Palma-Pollença, Pollença; 800/735-2478; www.sonbrull.com; ⌐⌐⌐

Valencia

WHERE TO STAY
Hospes Palau de la Mar Two remodeled 19th-century buildings; gilded age meets sleek contemporary. 14 Navarro Reverter; 34/96-316-2884; www.hospes.es; ⌐⌐⌐; **Hotel Neptuno** Miami in Spain. 2 Passeig de Neptuno; 34/96-356-7777; www.hotelneptunovalencia.com; ⌐⌐

WHERE TO EAT
Budeos in Love Favorite of locals and tourists. 4 Calle del Mar; 34/96-391-4350; $$$; **Ca'Sento** Forward-thinking cuisine. 17 Carrer Méndez Núñez; 34/96-330-1775; $$$

WHAT TO DO
Ciutat de les Arts i de les Ciències Santiago Calatrava's collection of arts buildings. 1–7 Avda. Autopista del Saler; 34/90-210-0031; www.cac.es

Alentejo, Portugal

WHERE TO STAY
Hotel Convento de São Paulo Excellent restaurant. Aldeia da Serra, Redondo; 351-226/989-160; www.hotelconventospaulo.com; ⌐⌐

WINERIES
Herdade do Esporão One of the area's best-known wineries; also produces artisanal olive oils and vinegars; restaurant on premises. 31 Apartado, Reguengos de Monsaraz; 351-266/509-280; lunch for two: $$$; www.esporao.com; **Herdade do Mouchão** Traditional winemaking methods; try the Mouchão Tinto. 351-268/539-228; www.mouchaowine.pt; **Quinta do Carmo** Known for its red wines, this venerable, well-tended winery dates back to the 17th century. Herdade das Carvalhas, Estremoz; 351-268/337-320; www.lafite.com

Lisbon

WHERE TO STAY
Bairro Alto Hotel 55 rooms in an art-filled 18th-century structure. 2 Praça Luis de Camões; 351-21/340-8288; www.bairroaltohotel.com; ⌐⌐⌐; **Four Seasons Hotel Ritz Lisbon** Modernist temple. 88 Rua Rodrigo da Fonseca; 800/819-5053; www.fourseasons.com; ⌐⌐⌐⌐; **Hotel Avenida Liberdade** 41-room boutique hotel. 28 Avda. da Liberdade; 351-21/240-4040; www.heritage.pt; ⌐⌐⌐⌐; **Palácio Belmonte** Antique-filled, 11-room hotel in a restored 15th-century house. 14 Páteo Dom Fradique; 888/222-8859 or 351-21/881-6600; ⌐⌐⌐⌐; **Solar do Castelo** Former mansion inside castle walls. 2 Rua das Cozinhas; 866/376-7831; www.heritage.pt; ⌐⌐⌐⌐

WHERE TO EAT
A Travessa A local favorite with a hearty Belgian menu. 12 Travessa do Convento das Bernardas; 351-21/390-2034; $$$; **Bica do Sapato** Chic restaurant, co-owned by John Malkovich. Armazém B, Avda. Infante Dom Henrique; 351-21/881-0320; $$$; **Luca** Portuguese-inspired Italian food. 35 Rua Santa Marta; 351-21/346-4811; lunch for two: $$; **Pastelaria-Padaria São Roque** The city's best vanilla *pastéis de nata*. 57 Rua Dom Pedro V; no phone; dessert for two: $; **Pap'Açorda** Minimalist décor; first-rate Portuguese fare. 57 Rua da Altalia, Bairro Alto; 351-21/346-4811; $$$; **Restaurante Eleven** Lisbon's only Michelin-starred restaurant features modern Mediterranean cuisine. Rua Marquês da Fronteira, Parque Eduardo VII; 351-21/386-2211; $$$$; **Santo Antonio da Alfama** Portuguese comfort food. 7 Beco de São Miguel; 351-21/888-1328; $$

NIGHTLIFE
Frágil Fixture nightclub attracts artists, eccentrics, and party-goers. 128 Rua da Atalaia; Bairro Alto; 351-21/346-9578; **Lux** Lisboans' club of choice. Armazém A, Avda. Infante Dom Henrique, Santa Apolónia; 351-21/882-0890; **Sr. Vinho** Authentic *fado* club in the Lapa neighborhood. 18 Rua do Meio a Lapa; 351-21/397-7456; $$$

WHERE TO SHOP
Alves/Gonçalves A mainstay of Portuguese design; ready-to-wear suits and gowns. 15B Rua Serpa Pinto; 351-21/346-060; **Lojadatalaia** Mid-century-modern furniture. Armazém B, Loja 1, Avda. Infante Dom Henrique; 351-21/882-2578; **Deli Delux** Gourmet-food emporium. Armazém B, Loja, 8, Avda. Infante Dom Henrique; 351-21/886-2070

Azores

WHERE TO STAY
Convento de São Francisco Gorgeously renovated 400-year-old former convent. Vila Franca do Campo, São Miguel; 351-296/583-532; www.arteh-hotels.com; ⌐⌐; **Pousada Forte de São Sebastião** 16th-century fortress. Angra do Heroísmo, Terceira; 351-295/403-560; www.arteh-hotels.com; ⌐⌐; **Quinta das Mercês** Converted 18th-century farmhouse with an infinity pool. Angra do Heroísmo, Terceira; 351-217/803-470; www.arteh-hotels.com; ⌐⌐

WHAT TO DO
Gorreana Tea Estate Europe's only green-tea plantation. Gorreana, São Miguel; 351-296/442-349; www.gorreana.com

Mykonos

WHERE TO STAY
Hotel Belvedere The Delano of Greece; also home to the superb restaurant Matsuhisa Mykonos. School of Fine Arts District, Mykonos; 30-2289/025-122; www.belvederehotel.com; ⌐⌐⌐; **Hotel Katikies** Traditional white cave houses. Oia, Santorini. 0-22860/71401; www.katikies.com; ⌐⌐⌐

Eastern Europe

Croatia

WHERE TO STAY

Hotel Korčula Stunning sea views. 385-20/726-480; www.korcula-hotels.com; ↻↻; **Pucic Palace** 18th-century villa. 1 Ulica Od Puca, Dubrovnik; 385-20/326-200; www.the pucicpalace.com; ↻↻↻

Kraków

WHERE TO STAY

Hotel Pod Róza European elegance. 4 Ul. Flonanska; 48-12/424-3300; www.hotel podroza.com; ↻↻

WHERE TO EAT

Bunkier Sztuki Café Lively and artsy. 3A Pl. Szczepanski; 48-12/422-4021; lunch for two: $; **Café Brankowa** Centrally located. 47 Rynek Glowny; 48-12/429-5677; $

NIGHTLIFE

Bar Propaganda Kitschy nostalgia. 20 Ul. Miodowa; 48-12/292-0402; **Dym** Sultry. 13 Sw. Tomasza; 48-12/429-6661; **Pauza** Hip lounge. 18/3 Ul. Florianska; 48-60/263-7833; **Prozak** Noisy disco. 6 Pl. Dominikanski; 48-12/422-5227

St. Petersburg

WHERE TO STAY

Grand Hotel Europe Art Nouveau interiors. 1/7 Ul. Mikhailovskaya; 800/237-1236 or 7-812/329-6000; www.grandhoteleurope.com; ↻↻↻

WHERE TO EAT

Lenin's Mating Call Kitschy Soviet memorabilia. 34 Ul. Kazanskaya; 7-812/324-4014; $$; **Moscow** Hip and modern. 18 Petrogradskaya Embankment; 7-812/332-0200; $$$

WHERE TO DO

Chesme Church Neo-Gothic design. 12 Lensoveta St.; **Kazan Cathedral** 2 Kazankaya Square; **Mikhailovsky Palace and the Russian Museum** Showcases the history of Russian art. 4 Inzhernaya St.; 7-812/595-4248; www.rusmuseum.ru; **Museum of Russian Political History** Comprehensive collection. 2-4 Ul. Kuibsheva; 7-812/333-7052; **State Hermitage Museum** More than three million works of art. 34 Dvortsovaya Naberezhnaya; 7-812/710-9625

NIGHTLIFE

Dacha Foosball table. 9 Dumskaya St, Metro Nevsky Prospekt; no phone

Odessa

WHERE TO STAY

Londonskaya Hotel Neo-Renaissance design. 11 Primorskiy Blvd.; 380-487/380-110; www.londred.com; ↻↻

WHAT TO DO

Passage Hotel Soaring atrium. 34 Preobrazhenskaya; 380-442/224-849

Lapland

WHERE TO STAY

Mammut Snow Hotel Ice blocks as beds. Open January to April. Oy LumiLinna Kemi, 2 Torikatu, Kemi; 358-16/259-502; www.snowcastle.net; ↻↻↻

TOUR OPERATORS

Sampo Tours Icebreaker tours. 2 Torikato, Kemi; 358-16/256-548; www.sampo tours.com; $270 per person

King's Road

WHERE TO STAY

Hotel National Full-service, luxury hotel. 1 Mokhovaya, Moscow; 7-495/258-7000; www.national.ru; ↻↻↻

Istanbul

WHERE TO STAY

Four Seasons Istanbul Neoclassic building. 1 Tevkifhane Sokak, Sultanahmet; 800/332-3442 or 90-212/638-8200; www.fourseasons.com. ↻↻↻↻; **Yesil Ev** Former aristocrat's mansion. Kabasakal Caddesi, Sultanahmet; 90-212/517-6785; www.istanbulyesilev.com; ↻↻

WHERE TO EAT

360 Istanbul Penthouse. 32–309 Istikal Caddesi, Misisr Apt. K8, Beyoglu; 90-212/251-1042; $$; **Balikçi Sabahattin** Mezes, seafood. 1 Seyit Hasan Koyu Sokak, Cankarturan, Sultanahmet; 90-212/458-1824; $$; **Hamdi Restaurant** Kebabs. Tahmis Caddesi, 17 Kalçin Sokak, Eminönü; 90-212/526-1242; $$; **Mabeyin** Spicy Gaziantep fare. 129 Eski Kisikli Caddesi, Kisikli, Üsküdar; 90-216/422-5580; $$; **Nisantasi Brasserie** In posh Beymen. Abdi Ipekçi Caddesi, Nisantasi; 90-212/343-0443; $$$; **Reina** Open-air mall. 44 Muallim Naci Caddesi, Ortaköy; 90-212/259-5919; $$$

WHERE TO SHOP

Beymen Tony department store. 1 Abdi Ipekçi Caddesi; 90-212/343-0404

WHAT TO DO

Archaeological Museum Rich collection. Between Gülhane Park and Topkapi Palace, Sultanahmet; 90-212/520-7740; **Istanbul Modern** Modern art. 4 Antrepo, Karaköy; 90-212/334-7300; www.istanbulmodern.org; **Pera Museum** Oriental art. 141 Mesrutiyet Caddesi, Tepebasi, Beyoglu; 90-212/ 334-9900

Brno, Czech Republic

WHERE TO STAY

Hotel Slavia Central. 15/17 Solnicní; 420-5/4232-1249; www.slaviabrno.cz; ↻↻

WHAT TO DO

Nový Düm Modernist row houses. 9, 111 Bráfova; 2–10 Drnovická; 2–10 Petrvaldská; 144–148 Smejkalova; **Pavilion A** Modernist-Gothic. Brno fairgrounds, 1 Vystavisté; **Vila Tugendhat** Mies van der Rohe work. 45 Cernopolní; 420-5/4521-2118; www.tugendhat-villa.cz; tour reservations required

Slovenia

WHERE TO STAY

Hotel Mons Design hotel. 55 Pot za Brdom, Ljubljana; 386-1/470-2700; www.hotel.mons.si; ↻↻

WHERE TO EAT

Gostišče Pri Lojzetu Regional fare. Dvorec Zemono, outside Ajdovscina; 386-5/368-7007 $$$

WHAT TO DO

Lipizzian stud farm Dressage shows. Lipica; 386-5/739-1580; www.lipica.org; **Movia** Local winery. 18 Ceglo, Dobrovo; 386-5/ 395-9510; www.movia.si

Africa+
the Middle East

Essaouira, Morocco

WHERE TO STAY

Riad Gyvo Museum-like hotel. 3 Rue Mohamed Ben Messaoud; 212-24/475-102; www.riadgyvo.com; ⌐ヮ

WHAT TO DO

Atelier Le Bastion-Ouest Run by local artist Ahmed Harrouz. Rue Skala; 212-64/024-300; **Espace Othello** Paintings and sculptures. 9 Rue Mohamed Laiiachi; 212-24/475-095; **Galerie Frédéric Damgaard** Eclectic regional artwork in spacious gallery. Ave. Oqba Ibn Nafiaa; 212-24/784-446

WHERE TO EAT

Chalet de la Plage Legendary restaurant; prime beachside location with bar. Blvd. Mohamed V; 212-24/475-972; $

Tangier, Morocco

WHERE TO STAY

Dar Nour Terraced rooms with ocean views. 20 Rue Gourna, Kasbah; 212-62/112-724; www.darnour.com; breakfast included; ⌐ヮ; **Dar Sultan** Moroccan,

Italian, Turkish, and Indian *objets.* 49 Rue Touila; 212-39/336-061; www.darsultan.com; ⌐ヮ; **Dar Zuina** Straw huts and deck chairs. B.P. 244 Asilah; 212-71/273-629; www.darzuina.com; ⌐ヮ⌐ヮ; **Hotel Rif & Spa** Oceanside hotel. 152 Ave. Mohammed VI; 212-39/349-305; www.hotelsatlas.com; breakfast included; ⌐ヮ⌐ヮ

WHERE TO EAT

Relais de Paris Frequented by movers and shakers. Complexe Dawliz, 42 Rue de Hollande; 212-39/331-819; $$; **Riad Tanja** Gourmet Moroccan food. Escalier Américain; 212-39/333-538; $$$; **Villa Joséphine** Veranda; French and Moroccan food. 231 Rte. De la Vieille Montagne, Sidi Masmoudi; 212-39/334-538; $$$

Bamako, Mali

WHERE TO STAY

Kempinski El Farouk Bamako's first five-star hotel. Quartier du Fleuve; 011-223/222-3030; www.kempinski.com; ⌐ヮ; **Sofitel L'Amitié** Authentic African

feel. B.P. 1720 in the city center; 011-223/221-4321; ⌐ヮ⌐ヮ

WHERE TO SHOP

Mali Cassette Record shop. Quinzanbougou; 011-223/673-9580

NIGHTLIFE

Cheval Blanc A hard-to-find club in Torokorobougou, south of the Niger River; no phone

Tanzania

TOUR OPERATOR

Thomson Safaris Family-friendly; customized trips. 800/235-0289; www.thomsonsafaris.com; a two-week Tanzania safari starts at $5,790 per person

Namibia

WHERE TO STAY

Skeleton Coast Camp Game-viewing safari and freshwater springs. 264-61/224-248; www.skeletoncoastsafaris.com; ⌐ヮ⌐ヮ⌐ヮ; **Sossusvlei Wilderness Camp** Remote and luxurious; incredible views; each chalet has its own pool. No phone; www.wilderness-safaris.com; ⌐ヮ⌐ヮ⌐ヮ; **Wolwedans Dunes Lodge** Nine platformed chalets. 264-61/230-616; www.wolwedans.com; ⌐ヮ⌐ヮ⌐ヮ

TOUR OPERATOR

Premier Tours Custom itineraries. 800/545-1910; www.premiertours.com; seven-day trips from $4,195 per person

Mozambique

WHERE TO STAY

Matemo Island Resort 24 thatched chalets; stunning Moorish entrance. 800/524-797; www.matemoresort.com; meals included; ⌐ヮ⌐ヮ⌐ヮ; **Pemba Beach Resort Hotel** Reminiscent of an Arabian palace. 800/524-7979; www.raniresorts.com; breakfast included; ⌐ヮ⌐ヮ⌐ヮ; **Quilálea Island Resort** Air-conditioned villas on a small

island. 44-131/556-4368; www.quilalea.com; meals included; ⌐ヮ⌐ヮ⌐ヮ⌐ヮ

WHAT TO DO

Pemba Dive Shop Across the road from Caracol Hotel on Wimbe Beach. 258-82/661-1530; **World Charters** Deep-sea fishing and island charters. 258-72/20556; www.worldcharters.com; $720 for a half day of fishing, including a boat and fuel

South Africa

WHERE TO STAY

Constantia Uitsig French Country-style wine estate. Constantia; Cape Town; 27-21/794-6500; www.uitsig.co.za; ⌐ヮ⌐ヮ; **La Couronne** Formal hotel set on a hillside. Dassenberg Road; Franschhoek; 27-21/876-2770; www.lacouronnehotel.co.za; ⌐ヮ; **La Résidence** Eclectically furnished suites. Domaine des Anges, Dirkie Uys St.; 27-15/793-0150; www.laresidence.co.za; ⌐ヮ⌐ヮ⌐ヮ; **Le Quartier Français** Whitewashed buildings with an oval pool. 16 Huguenot Rd., Franschhoek; 27-21/876-2151; www.lequartier.co.za; ⌐ヮ⌐ヮ⌐ヮ; **Roggeland Country House** 17th-century, family-run hotel. Northern Paarl, Paarl; 27-21/868-2501; www.roggeland.co.za; ⌐ヮ⌐ヮ;

WINERIES

Avondale Famous for Muscat Rouge. Paarl; 27-21/863-1976; **Cabrière Estate** Home of Pierre Jourdan and Haute Cabrière labels. Pass Road, Franschhoek; 27-21/876-2630; **Dornier Wines** Award-winning wines. Blaauwklippen Rd., Stellenbosch; 27-21/880-0557; **Laibach** Famous for 2001 Pinotage. Klapmuts Rd., Stellenbosch; 27-21/884-4511; **Le Riche Wines** Cabernet Sauvignons. Jonkershoek Road, Stellenbosch; 27-21/887-0789; **Stony Brook** Powerful reds.

Excelsior Rd., Franschhoek; 27-21/876-2182; **Waterford** Tuscan-style winery. Blaauwklippen Rd. Stellenbosch; 27-21/880-0496

Iran

WHERE TO STAY
Abbasi Hotel Atmospheric hotel in a renovated 17th-century caravansary. Esfahan; 98-311/222-6010; www.abbasihotel.com; ↘

WHERE TO EAT
Hammam-e Vakil Historic Iranian *hammam*-turned-restaurant; vaulted ceilings. Taleqani St.; 98-711/222-6467; $

TOUR OPERATOR
Absolute Travel 15- to 21-day tours. 800/736-8187; www.absoluteasia.com; from $4,580 per person, double, for a 15-day, 12-stop tour; **Cyrus Travel** 16-day tour covers eight stops. 800/332-9787; www.cyrustravel.com; from $2,950 per person, double; **Geographic Expeditions** Private journeys to Persepolis, Shiraz, Esfahan, and the Blue Mosque in Tabriz. 800/777-8183; www.geoex.com; from $3,195 per person, double, for a 12-day tour; **Travcoa** Runs a 12-stop, 14-day tour. 866/591-0070; www.travcoa.com; per person: $5,995

Jordan

WHERE TO STAY
Petra Moven Pick Hotel Steps from the entrance to Petra. 800/344-6835; www.moevenpick-hotels.com. ↘; **Taybet Zeman Hotel & Resort** Refurbished buildings five miles from Petra. 962-3/215-0111; ↘↘

WHAT TO DO
Jordan Tourism Board (North America) Information includes itineraries, visitor brochures, and a list of tour operators. 877/733-5673 or 703/243-7404; www.seejordan.com

Asia

Chiang Mai, Thailand

WHERE TO STAY
Mandarin Oriental Dhara Dhevi Chiang Mai Villas, temple, and spa. 51/4 Moo 1, Chiang Mai–Sankampaeng Rd.; 800/526-6566; www.mandarinoriental.com; ↘↘↘

WHERE TO EAT
Baan Suan Sri 51/3 Chiangmai-Sankampaeng Rd.; 66-53/242-116; $$; **The House** 199 Moonmuang Rd.; 66-53/419-01; $$

WHERE TO SHOP
La Luna Gallery Paintings, ceramics. 190 Charoenraj Rd.; 66-53/306-678; **Living Space** Tabletop items and textiles. 276–278 Thaphae Rd.; 66-53/874-156

Vietnam

WHERE TO STAY
Sofitel Metropole A 1901 Landmark. 15 Ngo Quyen St., Hanoi; 800/763-4835; www.sofitel.com; ↘↘

WHERE TO EAT
La Fenêtre Soleil Café French tearoom. 135 Le Thanh Ton St., Second Floor, Ho Chi Minh City; 84-8/822-5209; lunch for two: $; **Mai**

Anh *Pho ga*, the national dish. 32 Le Van Huu St., Hanoi; 84-4/943-8492; lunch for two: $

WHERE TO SHOP
A-Dong Silk Expert tailoring. 40 Le Loi St., Hoi An; 84-510/863-170; **Art Vietnam Gallery** Contemporary artists. 30 Hang Than St., Hanoi; 84-4/927-2349; **Celadon Green** High-gloss housewares. 51 Ton That Thiep St., HCMC; 84-8/914-4697; **Ipa-Nima** Handbags, shoes. 34 Han Thuyen, Hanoi; 84-4/942-1872; **La Casa** Housewares. 12 Nha Tho St., Hanoi; 84-4/828-9616; **Le Thanh Phuong** Hip styles. 40D Ly Tu Trong St., HCMC; 84-90/385-9266; **Minh Hanh** Unorthodox couture. 1288 Hai Ba Trung St., HCMC; 84-8/829-5714; **Minh Khoa** Blouses, jackets, dresses. 48 Nguyen Hué St., HCMC; 84-8/829-8934; **Monsoon** Colonial collectibles. 49 Ton That Thiep St., HCMC; 84-8/914-2149; **Mosaïque** Lanterns, lacquerware. 22 Nha Tho St., Hanoi; 84-4/971-3797; **Nymph** Silk shirts, short skirts. 10 Au Trieu St., Hanoi; 84-4/928-6347; **Precious Qui** Gifts and accessories. 29A Dong

Khoi St., HCMC; 84-8/825-6817; **Tan My** Tailoring and linens. 66 Hang Gai St., Hanoi; 84-4/825-1579; **Tha Ca** East-meets-West. 106 Nam Ky Khoi Nghia St., HCMC; 84-8/823-4465; **Vanloi Oriental Style** Classic Chinese furniture and fine art. 87 Hang Gai St., Hanoi; 84-4/828-6758

Bhutan

WHERE TO STAY
Amankora Serene, ultra-luxurious. 800/477-9180; www.amanresorts.com; ↘↘↘↘↘; **Uma Paro** Nine villas overlooking the Paro Dzong monastery. 011-975/827-1597; www.uma.como.bz; ↘↘

Pondicherry, India

WHERE TO STAY
L'Hôtel de L'Orient Luxurious. 17 Rue Romain Rolland; 91-413/234-3067; ↘; **Park Guest House** Bay of Bengal views. 3 Rangapillai St.; www.sriaurobindoashram.org; ↘

WHAT TO DO
Healing Center Ayurvedic treatments. Auroville; 91-413/262-2329; www.auroville.org/health/quiet.htm; **Sri Aurobindo Ashram** Bookshop, dining facilities, and collective meditation. 3 Rangapillai St.; 91-413/339-648; www.sriaurobindoashram.org

Kochi, India

WHERE TO STAY
Brunton Boatyard Antique beds, treatment rooms. Calvetty Rd., Fort Cochin; 91-484/221-5461; www.cghearth.com; ↘↘↘; **Taj Malabar** Historic. Willingdon Island; 800/448-8355; www.tajhotels.com; ↘↘

WHERE TO SHOP
Crafters Complex of five antique shops. V1/141, Jew Town; 91-484/222-3346

Chengdu, China

WHERE TO EAT

China Grand Plaza Private rooms, and massages as aperitif. 8 Huo Che Nan Zhan Xi Rd.; 86-28/8518-0041; $$$; **Huang Cheng Laoma** Chinese hot pots. 20 Nan Shan Duan Second Ring Rd.; 86-28/8513-9999; $$; **My Humble House** Chinese fusion. 18 Song Xian Qiao Jing Hua Rd.; 86-28/8736-1111; $$$

Shaoxing, China

WHERE TO EAT

Xianheng Rice wine, pork buns, and *chou doufu* (stinky tofu). 149 Lu Xun Zhong Rd.; 86-575/522-7279; $$

Hangzhou, China

WHERE TO EAT

Longjing Refined, with rare delicacies. 10 Wai Ji Long Shan, Longjing Rd.; 86-571/8796-9230; $$$; **Zhiweiguan** Implausibly juicy meat. 83 Renhe Rd.; 86-571/8701-8638; $$$

Beijing, China

WHERE TO STAY

Bamboo Garden Hotel Charming hotel near the Jiugulou subway stop. 24 Xiao Shiqiao Jiugulou Street, Xicheng; 86-10/6403-2229; www.bbgh.com.cn; ⌐; **Grand Hyatt** Modern, elegant retreat. 1 E. Chang An Ave.; 800/233-1234 or 86-10/8518-1234; www.grand.hyatt.com; ⌐⌐

WHERE TO EAT

Silk Road Restaurant Traditional food in modern space. 3rd Ring Rd./Changan Ave.; 86-10-8580-4286; $; **Xiangmanlou** Perfect Peking duck. Xin Yuan Xi Li, Beijing; 86-10/6460-6711; $$

WHAT TO DO

Factory 798 In a former plant; galleries include F-2,

Chinese Contemporary, Long March Space, and Red Gate. 4 Jiuxiangqiao Rd.; 86-10/8456-2421; www.chinesecontemporary.com; www.longmarchspace.com; **Imagine Gallery** Global artists. Feijiacun Yish Gong-zuoshi, Feijiacun Donglu, Laiguangying Donglu, Chaoyang; 86-10/6438-5747; www.imagine-gallery.com

Shanghai, China

WHERE TO STAY

Grand Hyatt Shanghai Floor-to-ceiling windows in world's highest hotel. 88 Century Blvd., Pudong; 800/233-1234 or 86-21/5049-1234; www.shanghai.grand.hyatt.com; ⌐⌐

WHERE TO EAT

Jade Garden Mellow. 1121 Yan An Zhong Rd.; 86-21/6248-5161; $; **Jia-Jia Juicy Dumplings** Outdoor stand. 638 S. Henan Rd., Shanghai; 86-21/6366-3570; dumplings for two: $; **Kommune Café** Lattes, focaccia sandwiches. No. 190 Huangpi Bei Road; 86-21/6372-1088; $; **Shanghai Crystal Jade** Meat and dumplings. Units 12A & 12B, House 6–7, Xintiandi S. Block, Lane 123, Xingye Rd., Shanghai; 86-21/6385-8752; $$; **Ye Shanghai** Red lanterns and dark woods. 338 Huang Pi Nan Rd., North Block, Xintiandi; 86-21/6311-2323; $$; **YongFoo Élite** Lavish décor. 200 Yong Foo Rd., Shanghai; 86-21/5466-2727; $$$

WHERE TO SHOP

La Vie Boutique Traditional women's wear. Taikang Rd., Ln. 210, Courtyard 7; 86-21/6445-3585; **Layefe** Edgy wear. 12 North Block, 181 Lane, Tai Cang Rd.; 86-21/6226-0716; **Shirt Flag** T-shirts and bags with Communist icons. Taikang Rd., Ln. 210, No. 7; 86-21/6466-7009; **Simply Life** Household items. 123 Xingye Rd.; 86-21/6387-5100

WHAT TO DO

Cashbox Karaoke palace. 208 Chongqing Nan Rd., Fuxing Park; 86-21/5306-3888

Taipei

WHERE TO STAY

Shangri-La's Far Eastern Plaza Hotel Gleaming silver towers. 201 Tun Hwa South Road, Sec. 2; 886-2/2378-8888; ⌐

WHERE TO SHOP

Bella Hard-to-find labels. 85 Da-An Rd., Section 1; 886-2/2751-0117; **Gallery Su** Hand-painted ceramics. 19-21 Tun-Hua South Rd., Section 1; 886-2/8773-1108; **Gray Area** Furniture and colorful silk-sheathed pillows. 3 Lane 116, Da-An Rd., Section 1; 886-2/2711-8891; **Isabelle Wen** Taipei's Betsey Johnson. 118 Da-An Rd., Section 1; 886-2/2771-9021; **Jamei Chen** Flowing ready-to-wear. 132 Da-An Rd., Section 1; 886-2/2776-4235; **Shiatzy Chen** Delicate, feminine women's wear. 140 Da-An Rd., Section 1; 886-2/8773-1729

WHERE TO EAT

Fifi Glamorous Old Shanghai–inspired restaurant. 15 Ren-Ai Rd., Section 4, second floor; 886-2/2721-1970; $$

Seoul

WHERE TO STAY

W Seoul-Walkerhill High-tech Zen meets Las Vegas theatrics. 21 Gwangjang-Dong, Gwangjin-Gu; 877/946-8357 or 82-2/465-2222; www.whotels.com; ⌐⌐

WHERE TO EAT

Bar0101 Simple Italian pastas and cappuccinos. 124-2 Samcheong-dong; 82-2/723-1259; lunch for two: $$; **Café at Kukje Gallery** Blond wood oasis. 59-1 Sokyuk-dong; 82-2/735-8449; $$; **Cook'N'Heim** Small café in a

garden. 63-28 Samcheong-dong; 82-2/733-1109; $$; **Gallery Café** Intimate wine bar. 110-220 Palpan-dong; 82-2/734-9466; lunch for two: $$

Japan

WHERE TO STAY

Ryokan rates include daily full breakfast (Western on request) and dinner. **Asaba** 360-year-old *ryokan*. 3450-1 Syuzenji, Izu-Shi, Shizuoka; 81-3/5368-0790; www.luxuryryokan.com; ⌐⌐; **Enospa** Island-based *ryokan*. 2-1-6 Enoshima, Fujisawa City, Kanagawa; 81-466/290-688; www.enospa.jp; **Four Seasons Tokyo at Marunouchi** Great shiatsu massages. 1-11-1 Marunouchi, Chiyoda-Ku; 800/332-3442; www.fourseasons.com; ⌐⌐⌐; **Gora Kadan** Celebrity chef Nobu Matsuhisa is a patron. 1300 Gora, Hakone, Kanagawa; 81-460/23331; www.gorakadan.co.jp; ⌐⌐⌐⌐; **Hakone Ginyu** Cheerful. 100-1 Miyashita, Hakone, Kanagawa; 81-3/5368-0790; www.luxuryryokan.com; ⌐⌐⌐⌐; **Murata** Rustic-chic wooden bathing houses. 1264-2 Kawakami-Torigoe, Yufuin, Oita; 81-3/5368-0790; www.luxuryryokan.com; ⌐⌐⌐⌐⌐; **Niki Club** Design-forward *onsen*. 2301 Takakuotsu Michishita; 800/337-4685; ⌐⌐⌐; **Park Hyatt Tokyo** Pool with views of Mt. Fuji. 3-7-1-2 Nishi-Shinjuku, Shinjuku-ku; 800/233-1234; www.parkhyatt.com; ⌐⌐⌐

Azerbaijan

WHERE TO STAY

Karvansaray Hotel Spare, spacious brick-vaulted rooms. Mf Axundov St., Shaki; 994-177/44814; ⌐; **Park Hyatt Baku** Luxury hotel. 1033 Izmir St., Baku; 800/233-1234; ⌐⌐

key

lodging:
⌐ under $150
⌐⌐ $150-299
⌐⌐⌐ $300-699
⌐⌐⌐⌐ $700-999
⌐⌐⌐⌐⌐ $1000+up
⌐⌐⌐⌐⌐⌐ $10,000/week
Prices listed are doubles for two.

dining:
$ under $25
$$ $25-74
$$$ $75-149
$$$$ $150-299
$$$$$ $300 + up
Prices listed are dinner for two.

Australia+ New Zealand

Sydney

WHERE TO STAY

Chelsea Guest House Italian-style villa. 49 Womerah Ave.; 61-2/9380-5994; www.chelsea.citysearch.com.au; ⌐; **Establishment Hotel** Blond wood boutique hotel. 5 Bridge Lane; 61-2/9240-3100; www.establishmenthotel.com; ⌐⌐⌐⌐

WHERE TO EAT

Billy Kwong Contemporary, drop-in Chinese; expect a wait. 355 Crown St.; 61-2/9332-3300; $$$; **Café Mint** North African dishes. 579 Crown St.; 61-2/9319-0848; $; **Red Lantern** Authentic Vietnamese. 545 Crown St.; 61-2/9698-4355; $$; **Sopra** Simple sandwiches and salads. 7 Danks St.; 61-2/9699-3174; $$; **Tabou** Classic French. 527 Crown St.; 61-2/9319-5682; $$$

WHERE TO SHOP

Andrew McDonald Shoemakers Bespoke shoes. 58 William St.; 61-2/9358-6793; **Come As You Are** Designer men's pants. 126 Oxford St., Paddington; 61-4/9331-3350; **Frock Exchange** Vintage dresses. 221 Clovelly Rd.; 61-2/9664-9188; **Kirrily Johnston** Modern women's wear. 6 Glenmore Rd.; 61-2/9380-7775; **Kit Cosmetics** International skin-, hair-, and body-care products. 140 Oxford St.; 61-2/9360-7711; **Leona Edmiston** Dresses, heels, and purses. 88 William St.; 61-2/9331-7033; **Paddington Markets** Clothing, jewelry, and crafts. Saturdays 10 to 5; 395 Oxford St.; 61-2/9331-2923; **Parlour X** International designers. 213 Glenmore Rd.; 61-2/9331-0999; **Prettydog** 70's-style clothing. 1A Brown St.; 61-2/9519-7839; **Roy** Contemporary men's sportswear. 2 Glenmore Rd.; 61-2/9331-3144; **Sass & Bide** Flirty women's wear. 132 Oxford St., Paddington; No. 4; 61-2/9360-3900; **Scanlan & Theodore** Sophisticated dresses and slacks. 122 Oxford St., Paddington; 61-2/9380-9388; **Vintage Clothing Shop** Classic finds. 147-49 Castlereagh St.; 61-2/9267-7155

Melbourne

WHERE TO STAY

The Prince Boutique hotel. 2 Acland St.; 61-3/9536-1111; www.theprince.com.au; ⌐⌐

WHERE TO EAT

Longrain Modern Thai. 44 Little Bourke St.; 61-3/9671-3151; drinks for two: $; **Movida** Traditional Spanish food. 1 Hosier Lane; 61-3/9663-3038; lunch for two: $$; **Piadina SlowFood** Grilled flatbread sandwiches. Rear 57 Lonsdale St.; 61-3/9662-2277; breakfast for two: $; **Switchboard** Hip café. Shop 11/12, Manchester Unity Arcade, 220 Collins St.; no phone; coffee for two; $

Noosa, Australia

WHERE TO STAY

Noosa Blue Resort Stunning views; penthouses have private rooftop barbecues. 16 Noosa Dr.; 61-7/5447-5699; www.noosablue.com.au; ⌐⌐

WHERE TO EAT

Café Le Monde Casual sidewalk café. 52 Hastings St.; 61-7/5449-2366; breakfast for two: $

WHAT TO DO

Noosa Holiday Rentals of towels, boogie boards, and other beach necessities. 4-4 Venture Dr.; 61-7/5440-5111; **Noosa National Park** Walking trails, native forests, secluded rocky beaches. Park Rd.; 61-7/5447-3243

Marlborough, New Zealand

WHERE TO STAY

Antares Homestay Two-room modern B&B. 106 Jeffries Rd.; 64-3/572-9951; www.antareshomestay.co.nz; ⌐

TOUR OPERATOR

Pacific Cycle Tours Accessible for beginners and intermediates; 800/732-0921; www.bike-nz.com; $1,045, includes accommodations for four nights and bicycle

WINERIES

Allan Scott Wines + Estates Ltd On-site restaurant serves seasonal fare. Jackson's Rd., Marlborough; 64-3/572-9054; **Cloudy Bay** Sparkling Pelorus wine. Jackson's Rd.; Blenheim; 64-3/520-9140; **Highfield Estate Winery** Stainless-steel-fermentation; restaurant matches local produce to wines. Brookby Rd., RD2, Blenheim; 64-3/ 572-9244; **Marlborough Winegrowers Associations** Information on wineries and wine-related events. 64-3/577-9299; www.wine-marlborough.co.nz; **Te Whare Ra** Marlborough's oldest boutique winery. 56 Anglesea St., Renwick; 64-3/572-8581

North Island, New Zealand

WHERE TO STAY

Hilton Auckland Feels like a docked ship. 147 Quay St.; 64-9/978-2000; www.hilton.com; ⌐⌐

WHERE TO EAT

Avondale Sunday Market Legendary produce market in Avondale racecourse. Ash St., Avondale, Auckland; 64-9/818-4931; **BeesOnline** Honey in every dish. 791 State Hwy. 16, Waimauku; 64-4/411-7953; brunch for two: $$; **French Café** French-Asian fusion. 210 Symonds St., Auckland; 64-9/377-1911; $$$; **Logan Brown Restaurant & Bar** Locally caught seafood. 192 Cuba St., Wellington; 64-4/801-9776; $$$; **Maria Pia's Trattoria** Rustic meat dishes. 55 Mulgrave St., Wellington; 64-4/499-5590; lunch for two: $$; **Moore Wilson** Fresh take-out foods. Corner of Tory and College Streets, Wellington; 64-4/384-9906; **Prime** Tapas with a view. PricewaterhouseCoopers Tower, 188 Quay St., Auckland; 64-9/357-0188; lunch for two: $$

WHAT TO DO

Hawke's Bay Farmers' Market Fresh vegetables and grass-fed beef. Sunday mornings; Tomoana Showgrounds, Kenilworth Rd., Hastings; www.savourhawkesbay.co.nz; **Kumeu River vineyards** Award-winning Chardonnays. 550 State Hwy.; Kumeu; 64-9/412-8415

Lake Wakatipu, on New
Zealand's South Island.

index

trip directory

Laying low in the town of Ephraim,
in Door County, Wisconsin.

contributors

Paul Alexander p. 49, from "Art Oasis," September 2005

Henry Alford p. 46, from "Feeling Minnesota," April 2005

Richard Alleman p. 69, from "Anguilla Heats Up," February 2005; p. 188, from "Morocco's Secret Sands," October 2004; p. 191, from "Morocco's St.-Tropez," August 2006

Tom Austin p. 32, from "Rights of Passage," February 2006; p. 35, from "Mondo Miami," November 2003; p. 57, from "World on a Wave," July 2006

Rich Beattie p. 90, from "Five Ways: Costa Rica," April 2006

Thomas Beller p. 126, from "Cinematic Rome," October 2004

Carly Berwick p. 24, original content

Jane Bills p. 138, from "Full of Bologna," May 2005

Malia Boyd p. 182, "The Best of the British Islands," December 2000

Alan Brown p. 61, from "Mountain Magic," January 2006

Chip Brown p. 52, from "Born Again," November 20

Tyler Brûlé p. 120, from "A Zurich Affair," September 2005

Josh Dean p. 88, from "Andean Highs," April 2006; p.177, from "Border Crossing," April 2005

Gabriella De Ferrari p. 98, from "Lima Evolving," February 2006

Julie Earle-Levine p. 259, from "The Down Low Down Under," September 2005

Andrew Ferren p. 148, from "Madrid's Capital Gains," May 2005

Gayle Forman p. 213, original content

Natasha Fraser-Cavassoni p. 128, from "Best of Paris," November 2005

Nell Freudenberger p. 230, from "Passage to Pondy," June 2005; p. 240, from "Made in China," April 2006

Tad Friend p. 232, from "Jewel of India," November 2005

Julia Gardner p. 56, from "Seattle Goes Global," September 2005

Adam Goodheart p. 174, from "City of Dreams," May 2005

Alice Gordon p. 50, from "Take Me to The River," August 2005

Michael Gross p. 68, from "Stay in an Overwater Bungalow," September 2006; p. 80, original content; p. 84, from "The Next Riviera: Resort Phenomenon," January 2006

Peter S. Green p. 166, from "Kraków's New Gilded Age," April 2005

John Heminway p. 51, from "American Splendor," June 2004

James Patrick Herman p. 160, from "Temptation Islands," August 2004

David Hochman p. 156, from "Isles Apart," April 2005

Kristin Hohenadel p. 128, from "Unsung Paris," November 2005

Karrie Jacobs p. 65, from "The Next Design City: Bilbao Effect," January 2006; p. 182, from "Form and Function," November 2005

Mark Jacobson p. 96, from "The River's Edge," April 2006

Xander Kaplan p. 176, from "Snapshot: Gulf of Bothnia," March 2006; p. 197, from "Snapshot: Namibia," April 2006

Ted Katauskas p. 56, from "On a Bender," April 2006

David A. Keeps p. 62, from "Vancouver Rising," July 2006

Walter Kirn p. 43, from "American Pie," March 2006

Elizabeth Larsen p. 48, from "The Heartland on Half Speed: Fish Creek, WI," June 2005 (T+L Family)

Matt Lee and Ted Lee p. 30, from "Carolina on My Mind," August 2005; p. 77, from "Real Jamaica Flavor," March 2005; p. 126, from "Tastes of Brittany," April 2006; p.262, from "Bounty Hunters," November 2003

Peter Jon Lindberg p. 14, from "Maine Course," August 2006; p. 72, from "Fantasy Island," April 2006; p. 164, from "Croat d'Azure," August 2005; p. 208, from "Iran," July 2005; p. 218, from "Chiang Mai Pleasure Palace," April 2005; p. 222, from "The Best of Vietnam Now," September 2003

Nathan Lump p. 204, from "Vintage South Africa," June 2004

Charles Maclean p. 142, from "Master Class," March 2006

Alexandra Marshall p. 152, from "Lisbon Lights Up," February 2006

Connie McCabe p. 101, from "Santiago Cleans Up," April 2005

Rob McKeown p. 245, from "Asia Major," November 2005

Rebecca Mead p. 242, from "Shanghai Surprises," July 2004

Clark Mitchell p. 122, from "Take a Storybook Drive," June 2005

Shane Mitchell p. 74, from "Isle of Style," October 2001; p. 246, from "Spirited Away," June 2005

Susan Morgan p. 86, from "The Soul of Mexico," December 2005

Bob Morris p. 158, from "Beyond the Sea," May 2005

Niloufar Motamed p. 258, from "Dishing Up Melbourne," March 2006

Meg Lukens Noonan p. 19, from "Mom 'n' Pop Mountains," October 2005

Mitchell Owens p. 21, from "Country Chic," March 2005; p. 104, from "Buenos Aires Steps it Up," July 2005

Barbara Peck p. 196, from "Choose Your Adventure," June 2005 (T+L Family)

Kevin Raub p. 94, from "Brazil's Hidden Beaches," January 2006

Douglas Rogers p. 200, from "Under African Skies," October 2005

Gary Shteyngart p. 170, from "A St. Petersburg Christmas," December 2005; p. 250, from "Frontierland," September 2005

Daniel Shumate p. 260, from "Vintage New Zealand," February 2006

Alex Shoumatoff p. 194, from "Blues Traveler," December 2004

Horatio Silva p.108, from "The Party Picks Up," March 2006

Emma Sloley p. 254, from "Sydney Steps Out," February 2005

Raymond Sokolov p. 151, from "Uncorking Portugal," June 2005

Andrew Solomon p. 236, from "All The Food in China," October 2005

Andrea Strong p. 29, from "Long Island's Grape Expectations," July 2005

Rima Suqi p. 87, from "One Cool Capital," October 2004

Elizabeth Taylor p. 39, from "Chicago's Greatest Hits," Spring/Summer 2002 (T+L Family)

Guy Trebay p. 123, from "Twin Peaks," January 2004; p. 178, from "Istanbul," October 2005; p. 226, from "A World Away," February 2005

Rachel Urquhart p. 20, from "Shakes Alive!" March 2006

Tom Vanderbilt p. 150, from "Valencia Rising," December 2005

Anya Von Bremzen p. 144, from "Dishing Up Barcelona," June 2005

Hannah Wallace p. 184, from "Slovenian Rhapsody," September 2005

Valerie Waterhouse p. 117, from "Shelf Life," May 2005

Amy Wilentz p. 92, from "Continental Divide," November 2005

Jeff Wise p. 59, from "Into the Wild," November 2005

Lynn Yaeger p. 54, from "New Heights," September 2005; p. 114, from "Best of London Shopping," October 2004; p. 118, from "Dutch, by Design," November 2004

Lucie Young p. 114, from "London Tailor Made," April 2005; p. 242, from "On the Map: Shanghai," April 2006

Most of these stories originally appeared in *Travel + Leisure* magazine, and have been updated and adapted for this book. To read the original stories or for more information about the destinations in this book, go to travelandleisure.com.

photographers

For 35 years, *Travel + Leisure* magazine
has been the authority for the
discerning traveler, offering the most
comprehensive service information
of any travel magazine, and reporting
on the places and the trends that are
defining modern global culture. With
award-winning writing, photography,
and design, *T+L* delivers practical
insights and crucial commentary
on everything from hotels and
restaurants, shopping and the arts, to
politics, security, health, and the latest
innovations, so readers are informed
and inspired to take their next trip.
Visit us at travelandleisure.com.